RESEARCHING LESSER-EXPLORED ISSUES IN COUNSELLING AND PSYCHOTHERAPY

RESEARCHING LESSER-EXPLORED ISSUES IN COUNSELLING AND PSYCHOTHERAPY

edited by

Peter Madsen Gubi and Valda Swinton

KARNAC

First published in 2016 by
Karnac Books Ltd
118 Finchley Road, London NW3 5HT

Copyright © 2016 to Peter Madsen Gubi and Valda Swinton for the edited collection and to the individual authors for their contributions.

The rights of the contributors to be identified as the authors of this work have been asserted in accordance with §§77 and 78 of the Copyright Design and Patents Act 1988.

All rights reserved. No part of this publication may be reproduced, stored in a retrieval system, or transmitted, in any form or by any means, electronic, mechanical, photocopying, recording, or otherwise, without the prior written permission of the publisher.

British Library Cataloguing in Publication Data

A C.I.P. for this book is available from the British Library

ISBN 978 1 78220 404 6

Edited, designed and produced by The Studio Publishing Services Ltd
www.publishingservicesuk.co.uk
email: studio@publishingservicesuk.co.uk

Printed in Great Britain

www.karnacbooks.com

CONTENTS

ABOUT THE EDITORS AND CONTRIBUTORS — vii

INTRODUCTION — ix
   Peter Madsen Gubi and Valda Swinton

CHAPTER ONE
Sexuality after breast cancer: voices of young, — 1
single women
   Susan Shortt

CHAPTER TWO
"I am losing my last chance at motherhood": — 33
an exploration of delayed childbirth, pregnancy loss,
and involuntary childlessness
   Amanda Sives

CHAPTER THREE
If only: adult reflections on being an only child — 61
   Caroline Fletcher

CHAPTER FOUR
Processing perceived parental rejection through personal development 93
Tracey Clare

CHAPTER FIVE
The impact of emotional labour on secondary school teachers 129
Eileen Doyle

CHAPTER SIX
The impact of inappropriately referred clients on the counselling trainee in placement 157
Mair Elinor Sides

CHAPTER SEVEN
Is talking enough? School-based counselling in Wales 187
Gary Tebble

INDEX 225

ABOUT THE EDITORS AND CONTRIBUTORS

Tracey Clare, BA (Hons), MSc, MA, MBACP, currently practises as a counsellor for the NHS and in the third sector, and is a student on the Doctor of Professional Studies in Counselling and Psychotherapy Studies, at the University of Chester.

Eileen Doyle, MA, MBACP, is a person-centred counsellor working in private practice. She was a secondary school teacher for over twenty years.

Caroline Fletcher, BA, MA, MA, MBACP, is a counsellor in the voluntary sector.

Peter Madsen Gubi, BEd, MA, MA, MA, MTh, PhD, MBACP (Reg. Snr. Accred.), FRSA, FHEA, is Professor of Counselling and Spiritual Accompaniment at the University of Chester. He is Programme Leader for the Doctor of Professional Studies in Counselling and Psychotherapy Studies and for PhD research in counselling and psychotherapy. He is the author of *Prayer in Counselling and Psychotherapy: Exploring a Hidden Meaningful Dimension* (2008); *Spiritual Accompaniment and Counselling: Journeying with Psyche and Soul* (2015);

Listening to Less-heard Voices (2015). He is also Minister of Dukinfield Moravian Church, Manchester.

Susan Shortt, BSc (Hons), MA, MBACP, is a person-centred counsellor with experience of primary care work, currently counselling bereaved clients in a hospice setting.

Mair Elinor Sides, BSc (Hons), PGCE, MA, MBPsS, MBACP, is a former programme co-ordinator and further education lecturer in psychology. She works as an associate counsellor in a medical practice and university setting, and volunteers on a Mental Health Helpline for Wales. She is also a visiting lecturer at the University of Chester.

Amanda Sives, BA (Hons), MA, MPA, MA, PhD, MBACP, spent twenty years as a social science researcher and lecturer in higher education working in the UK and abroad. She is working as a counsellor in a higher education setting and in the NHS.

Valda Swinton, BSc (Hons), MA, DCouns, MBACP (Reg. Snr. Accred.) is Senior Lecturer in Counselling at the University of Chester. She is Programme Leader for the MA in Clinical Counselling.

Gary Tebble, BA (Hons), MA, MBACP, is a child psychotherapist who works in an educational setting. He is currently a student on the Doctor of Professional Studies in Counselling and Psychotherapy Studies at the University of Chester.

Introduction

Peter Madsen Gubi and Valda Swinton

This book disseminates some interesting research into lesser-explored issues in counselling and psychotherapy. Each chapter is motivated by the personal experience of the chapter authors, and comes from a place of passion within the researchers. It is aimed at informing counsellors and psychotherapists about aspects of human experiencing that are not written about much (if at all) in the counselling and psychotherapy related literature. Each of the chapters comes from research that has been undertaken for a Masters degree in Clinical Counselling at the University of Chester. They are all qualitative pieces of distinction standard. They were undertaken to satisfy the deeply held questions and curiosities that arose from the researchers' experiencing. It is from this place of questioning and curiosity that the best research is motivated and formulated. Each chapter is written by those whom some might consider to be "unseasoned researchers", who are, first and foremost, practitioners, and who, because of that, bring a fresh perspective to the topic that each has studied. Theirs are voices that have something very worthwhile to contribute to professional dialogue. The format of this book, rather than that of the academic journals, allows a fuller expression of their voices, and those of their participants, to be heard, and it is a privilege to host such a range of voices and experiences in this book.

Counselling and psychotherapy training has not always contained elements of research training, or the need to engage significantly with empirical research. Since the development of graduate and postgraduate level training programmes, there is now a requirement to undertake research. In addition, there is now a need for evidence-based practice, and for counsellors and psychotherapists to have the skills to evaluate services to attract the necessary funding. So, students on counselling and psychotherapy training programmes have now to grapple with research methods on their training journey. However, there is often resistance, because research provokes anxiety within many. It is often seen as the domain of the academics, rather than that of practitioners. As one student remarked, "What I am interested in is what happens in the counselling room, the practice with clients, not wasting time learning research methods!" Yet, doing research does inform practice, as the researches presented in this book testify, but training in research has to engage the student's curiosity, their need to know and understand, and to discover. In so doing, their findings will become relevant to their own practice and to that of other practitioners. Research is not just about jargon and statistical calculations, written in a way that is really hard to understand (although clearly some is). As this book demonstrates, qualitative research is akin to sitting in front of a client (participant), hearing the client's (participant's) experience and then trying to make sense of what the client (participant) is saying about their experience. There are technical and academic regulations to overcome, which add validity and ethical efficacy, but the hope always is that on the journey the keenness about a research topic and the enthusiasm to find out more is enhanced by the experience of undertaking research. The researchers' journeys to find out more about their research topics can be the means of discovering more about people, and about how to better respond to the issues that are encountered in the therapeutic encounter. Ultimately, this enriches the disciplines of counselling and psychotherapy generally, as well as the researcher's own practice. The more knowledge that is available through research that can challenge accepted ways of seeing the world, the greater the impact on the "givens" of how things have always been done, and this changes professional "norms" of what is considered best practice.

As counselling and psychotherapy trainees or as established practitioners, researchers bring something of value to the endeavour of research. Their wealth of life experience and their work with their clients can form the backdrop to finding their research topic. What is it that they have experienced in their own life and development that they would like to delve into more deeply? Or, in working with clients, what has sparked their interest to find out more? This connection to the research topic can ensure that the experience is a positive one, something that they will feel able to continue to pursue, even when the going gets tough—and it does get tough. Research is not easy, but it is a creative process. In this process, having an "idea" is a place to begin the process of how the topic can be made into a researchable question. Then the process of refining begins, so that the research idea can become more concrete. There are times when the research process can be a very lonely endeavour as researchers try to meet all the demands of carrying out an ethically and academically rigorous research project with many hurdles to overcome: will the project gain ethical approval? Will any participants come forward? Then, in qualitative research, there is often interviewing, transcribing, analysing, finding themes, and generally making sense of the data. There is the pressure of doing justice to the material with which they have been entrusted.

So, within this edition is the finished product at the end of journey—minus the blood, sweat, and tears. In this book, the researchers try to do justice to the voices of their participants and contribute to the evidence base of the professions of counselling and psychotherapy.

Research choices

All of the research presented in these chapters use interpretative phenomenological analysis (IPA) as the research methodology for analysing the data. Rather than spend verbiage in each chapter explaining the methodology, a brief summary of the main points of IPA is presented here. The aim of IPA is to explore, in detail, participants' views of the topic that is under investigation (Smith et al., 2009). It is a phenomenological approach, in that it is concerned with personal perception rather than with the formation of objective statement. It is a method that seeks an insider's perspective, but which takes account of the fact that the researcher's own perceptions are needed to make sense of the other's world through a process of interpretative activity. Therefore, it is the researcher's role to comment on, and to make sense of, the participant's activity and opinion. IPA is a *bricolage* of established approach and methodology, in that it brings together a phenomenological approach and a symbolic interactionism approach, while using research instruments and methods of analysis that are commonly found in discourse analysis and thematic analysis. The philosophical paradigm on which IPA is based is that it is not necessary to go beyond the verbal statement to understand underlying cognitions or to predict the relational dimension between verbal statement and behaviour. Instead, IPA attempts to value the perception and meaning that is attributed to an object, event, or experience, while recognising that meaning can only be obtained through a process of interpretative activity. It is a dynamic process that is complicated by the researcher's own conceptions. The method of analysis is creative, not prescriptive. It relies on a method of making sense of the data through the coding of themes and subordinate themes, and the seeking of connections. It is important that the researcher's bias does not distort the selective process of the categorisation of themes. Initial themes can be governed by the prompts that are used at the interviewing stage. However, at the transcribing stage, it is important for the richness of the data to determine the emerging themes and categorisation, and for the researcher to be led by that process rather than dictate it. Once a superordinate list of themes has emerged, the researcher is then required to be selective towards the emerging subordinate themes, with the selectivity dependent on the parameters of the research and the relevance of emerging subordinate themes to the research topic. At the writing-up stage of the research, the shared themes, patterns, connections, and tensions are translated and woven into a narrative account that details the interesting and essential things about the participants' responses and the researcher's interpretative analysis of them. These data can be presented in a variety of ways (e.g., diagrammatically to detail the relationships and/or conflicts between emerging themes, or as a narrative that comprises the respondents' comments that are interpretatively analysed). However, at this stage of weaving the tapestry that is the narrative, it is important for the unique nature of each participant's experience to emerge, and, throughout, the participants' voices are heard in the rich data.

Ethical awareness

As each research project was undertaken within the Division of Counselling and Psychotherapy at the University of Chester, it was subject to the rigorous procedure of ethical approval by the university's Research Ethics Committee. Every effort was made to protect the participants from harm, to seek their consent at various stages of the research, to protect their right to withdraw without prejudice, to support them if anything emotional was stirred up within them because of the research process, to maintain the confidentiality of their identities, and to maintain the security of their data.

The structure of each chapter

Each chapter has been edited and formatted in such a way as to offer a cohesive and homogeneous presentation that enables each to set the scene for the research, to establish the research project in published literature that has been searched for, and accessed, through various academic search-engines, to introduce the participants and the questions asked of them in semi-structured interviews, to present the findings, to enable a reflexive and critical discussion of the findings in the light of the published literature, and, finally, to conclude.

Introducing each chapter

In Chapter One, Susan Shortt explores the experiences of four young, single women who were diagnosed with breast cancer, and examines the impact of this on their sexuality during and post treatment. The chapter focuses on the impact on their sexuality and includes areas such as body image, dating and relationships, and fertility. It widens awareness of the issues faced by this particular group.

In Chapter Two, Amanda Sives examines the impact of pregnancy loss and involuntary childlessness among a specific group of women who delayed childbirth, whether through choice or circumstance. The chapter highlights the devastating impact of pregnancy loss for childless women of advanced maternal age, the isolation and loneliness of their pain, and the struggle to rewrite a future that involves childlessness. Based on the lived experience of six women, the chapter concludes with recommendations for greater psychological support and a deeper understanding for this often silenced group of women.

In Chapter Three, Caroline Fletcher considers the lived experience of counsellors who grew up, and continue to live, without siblings, and looks at the significance that they attach to the experience of being an "only child". The chapter examines ideas of identity, relationships, and loss, and captures some of the complexity and richness of individual lives—something that seems to be missing from the generalisations and stereotypes associated with "only children".

In Chapter Four, Tracey Clare explores adults' experiences of parental rejection in childhood and the impact of personal development during counsellor training on processing unresolved feelings. Commonalities of experience are teased out and examined against the backdrop of the academic literature. Personal development is found to play an intrinsic role in the processing of participants' experience.

In Chapter Five, Eileen Doyle examines the notion of emotional labour and its particular impact on teachers. Because teaching involves a high degree of emotional labour, teachers are at significant risk from the adverse effects it can have on their emotional wellbeing. Recently, there has been a drive to provide counselling for pupils in UK schools, which is in contrast with the lack of similar support available to teachers.

In Chapter Six, Mair Sides considers the experiences of trainee counsellors in clinical placement working with clients perceived to be inappropriately referred to them. The impact of this work on their professional development is recognised, along with the wider implications for training.

Finally, in Chapter Seven, Gary Tebble examines the nature of school-based counselling in Wales. He investigates the assertion that talking alone is enough when engaging a young person in school-based counselling, and demonstrates the helpfulness of creative and symbolic methods and their impact on the therapeutic relationship.

Who this book is for

This book is written to disseminate research to counsellors and psychotherapists, those who are qualified and those who are in training. However, the insights that the researches provide are applicable, and will be of interest, to anyone who is interested in understanding people better, and those who are involved in people-work where the accompaniment of those in emotional difficulty is paramount (e.g., social workers, pastoral care workers, chaplains, clergy, clinical and counselling psychologists, nurses, prison wardens/warders, etc.).

*This book is dedicated to each of our mothers:
Iceline (Icy) Henry and Joyce Isabel Gubi, whom we each
greatly miss, and to whom we each owe so much.*

CHAPTER ONE

Sexuality after breast cancer: voices of young, single women

Susan Shortt

Introduction

My interest in the stories of young, single women treated for breast cancer originates in my personal experience of being a member of this group. Eight years ago, I was diagnosed, in my thirties, with breast cancer, and embarked on an intensive and lengthy treatment path. The experience has undoubtedly had an impact on my identity in many ways, some extremely positive and growth-promoting, "a wake-up call" (Gorman, 2011), but some much more painful and difficult. A breast cancer diagnosis as a young woman was described by one child-free woman as changing the entire trajectory of her life (Gould et al., 2006); this resonates.

At a counselling course residential, I found myself exploring, in front of the group, my narrative of before, during, and after treatment, in response to an invitation to consider influences on our sexuality. I had not talked through the chronology of my journey in this way before, and having this witnessed by my peers felt very powerful, affirming, and hugely emotional. It also caused me to reflect upon how this area had been one of the hardest aspects of my diagnosis, and one that is seldom talked about, both in clinical settings and among friends. The ending of a relationship during my treatment, and the subsequent search for a new partner, brought to the fore a raft of issues, both physical and psychological, for which I was completely unprepared. There was a sense of my having to rewrite the narrative of my life to accommodate this "off-time" event (Wurm et al., 2008), and I began to become interested in how major illness interrupts the predictable course of life and forces us to write a new story (Frank, 1995; Neimeyer et al., 2002).

I volunteer for Breast Cancer Care's (BCC) "Someone Like Me" service, offering support to women following diagnosis. Hearing other young women's stories and struggles in relation to their sexuality also fuelled my desire to explore this area. At young women's events, optional sessions on sexuality and intimacy are popular, and people appear relieved to have found a forum to share their concerns. However, along with much of the information literature I have come across, it is often the case that sessions such as these very much refer to "you and your partner", leaving single women isolated. So, the strands of my research topic took shape, to encompass a breast cancer diagnosis along with being younger, being single, and examining the impact on sexuality. I acknowledged that in embarking on this research, as well as wanting to bring the experiences of this group to a wider audience, it might prove to be an important part of my own personal journey.

As I began to look for existing research, I discovered little about this topic that is focused on this group. This made it feel all the more important, and I wanted in some small way to begin to redress the balance. There are distinct issues faced by young single women who have experienced breast cancer (Gluhoski et al., 1998)—for example, in the area of dating. I wanted to enable some of these women to have their voices heard, and, by doing so, broaden awareness among the counselling community of this group, and give a flavour of their experiences. I was also keen to contribute to the "pedagogy of suffering" (Frank, 1995, p. 145); this posits that someone who suffers has something to teach, and, therefore, has something to give, thus restoring agency to the ill person and giving their story parity with professional expertise. As Adams et al. (2011) note, a quarter of all cancers in adults under forty-five are breast cancers and it is the most common type of cancer for this group. It is, therefore, likely that counsellors may encounter younger women who have faced this diagnosis.

What the literature says

Each year, around 55,000 people in the UK are diagnosed with breast cancer (Breast Cancer Care, 2013). There are around 9,800 cases each year in women under fifty, and very few of these occur in women in their teens or early twenties. Breast cancer is the most common cancer in women aged under forty, and, in women aged 35–39 in the UK, around 1,300 cases of breast cancer are diagnosed each year (Cancer Research UK, 2014). These statistics position a breast cancer diagnosis in a young woman as an unexpected and relatively rare event.

Very few published studies on younger women's experiences of breast cancer conducted in the UK exist; notable exceptions are Corney and colleagues (2014), and Adams and colleagues' (2011) synthesis of the work of others. Corney's work is primarily concerned with fertility issues, although it did also consider partnership issues. Many studies have a medical slant, and aim to provide information to healthcare professionals about how they might best support patients (e.g., Ganz, 2008; Gould et al., 2006; Kissane et al., 2004; Takahashi, 2014; Thewes et al., 2004). Some research is written in medicalised language (e.g., Cardoso et al., 2012). Gould and colleagues' study was large by qualitative standards, and included sixty-five young women in ten focus groups. While its emphasis was very much on support and information needs, this did draw out some of the themes that are pertinent to younger women, including the unexpected side-effects of treatments on sexuality.

There is an abundance of quantitative studies, (e.g., Avis et al., 2004; Burwell et al., 2006; Fallbjork et al., 2013; Fobair et al., 2006; Meyerowitz et al., 1999). Avis and colleages, in their study of over 200 women, do include some open-ended questions, and note that responses to these were particularly informative, acknowledging that purely quantitative studies obscure the diversity of experiences. Far less has been written about the qualitative lived experience. Adams and co-authors (2011), in their meta-ethnography found just seventeen qualitative studies, conducted over a twenty-year period, that focused on the experiences, needs, and concerns of younger women with breast cancer. Coyne and Borbasi's (2006) study is noteworthy from a methodological perspective, with its emphasis on enabling women to tell the story of their journey without the rigidity of set questions, adopting a feminist approach to the encounter. Their aim was to give health professionals a greater understanding, and their ethos resonates with mine. This quote from a participant in a further study by Coyne and Borbasi (2009) gives a flavour of the impact of a breast cancer diagnosis at a young age:

> . . . in one fell swoop I was told everything that was feminine about me was gone, I was losing my breast, I possibly couldn't have children. . . . all of a sudden choices for the life I had planned were being taken away from me. (p. 10)

Young women can feel marginalised and isolated as they do not conform to the "normal" older profile of a woman with breast cancer (Dunn & Steginga, 2000), and, as a distinct population, they are an under-researched group in terms of specific key issues and concerns they face (Adams et al., 2011).

A recent review of twenty-eight large scale, quantitative studies conducted over a fifteen-year period among women under fifty-one or premenopausal at diagnosis found that, compared to older women diagnosed and the normal population, younger women experienced some reduction in their quality of life, with a greater impact on emotional wellbeing than physical functioning. Main anxieties were around fear of recurrence and what might happen in the future. Depressive symptoms were relatively common, and menopausal symptoms, such as hot flushes, lack of libido, and vaginal dryness were a source of concern for many, as were fertility issues (Howard-Anderson et al., 2012). While this review provides some useful pointers as to areas that might cause difficulty, it does not address the lived experience of these women and a more qualitative approach is required to uncover this.

A comprehensive review of qualitative research among younger women identified feeling "out of sync" as the issue that "permeates all others"; breast cancer is a disruption to the normal life course (Adams et al., 2011). There are clear links here with theories about "assumptive worlds" (Parkes, 2009): each person has an internal model that they assume to be true; it contains everything we take for granted, and when an event occurs to disrupt this, we become lost. Reproduction, body image, fear, and sexual activity are also identified as key issues in Adams and colleagues' review. From this, the authors construct an interesting conceptual model suggesting how women experience and respond. They propose three processes, used in varying combinations. The first is balancing: for instance, balancing the immediate priority of treatment with learning to adjust to sudden menopause, or weighing up desire for a child against future health concerns. Next comes normalising; this might be by having reconstruction to regain a sense of normality, or, for some, by normalising an "imperfect" body. Last, changing is identified as a process, often part of a wish to find a new "normal", and this can comprise both negative and positive elements. For example, infertility might force a change in plans for a family. On a more positive note, cancer might be perceived as a turning point and lead to better self-care or new activities. As with all "meta" research, the authors are distanced from the original data and findings are generalised, but this study does provide a rare and useful insight into issues specific to younger women and draw these together into a model that illustrates the complexity and fluidity of response to diagnosis. Its validity is demonstrated, for example, in the work of Kirkman and colleagues (2014), whose participants describe balancing the need to stay alive with their desire to have a child.

Until recently, research examining the impact of a breast cancer diagnosis on sexuality mainly took place within the context of a positivist–realist paradigm, and was focused on the physical aspects of women's experience and satisfaction or dysfunction in their sexual relationships (Emilee et al., 2010). However, women do not equate how often they have sex with sexual satisfaction. "Their sexuality is much more complex, involving issues of self-esteem, identity, body image, and role functioning" (Wilmoth, 2001, p. 279). Wilmoth's study asked women to define what sexuality meant to them, and the impact breast cancer had on this part of their lives. While her participants were mostly over forty-five, the resulting themes of missing parts, loss of womanhood, loss of bleeding, and loss of sexual sensation would appear pertinent to younger women, too. These combine to form an "altered sexual self". The supportiveness of partners, and the degree to which women took control of finding out information relevant to their treatment appeared important in how women adapted. Wilmoth proposed three processes: *taking in* the diagnosis and changes to the body, *taking hold* of the losses, and coming to terms with them, and those who had managed to do this moved on to *taking on* the role of breast cancer survivor and gaining some control over treatment side-effects. Her study explores menopause in some depth, which is not relevant to all participants in this study. Wilmoth's grounded theory model conveys well a sense of movement and agency for the women. It does, however, feel a little prescribed, but could be considered as a useful framework of elements and processes that could be experienced, and valuably highlights the sense of loss experienced.

Prior to Wilmoth's study, a dissertation by Turner (1999) also pioneered a more women-centred approach in inviting women to explore the impact of their diagnosis on sexuality, using their own definitions. This provided vivid quotes of their lived experiences and chimed with my aims to "get under the skin" of what a breast cancer diagnosis meant for my participants. It did not, however, focus specifically on younger women, no participants were single, and just one was childless. It does provide an early example of challenging a narrow definition of sexuality, and her model of a "reconstructed sexual self" is sociological, considering a wide range of influences. In considering sexuality in this way, it does lose its connection to individual women's stories at times.

Few studies have focused on younger women in relation to body image (Rosenberg et al., 2013), and those that do tend to look at short term rather than longer term impacts, and are quantitative (e.g., Fobair et al., 2006; Rosenberg et al., 2013). Fallbjork and colleagues (2013) did follow up women almost three years post-surgery, and illustrate the difficulties in matching such a nuanced and personal subject with a quantitative methodology. They discovered a decrease in feelings of sexual attractiveness and comfort over time, and spent much of the discussion speculating as to why this was the case; a sensitive piece of qualitative research might have revealed some answers.

Some research indicates that breast conserving surgery (lumpectomy) has less impact on body image than mastectomy, with or without reconstruction (Kissane et al., 2004; Rosenberg et al., 2013). A review by Emilee and colleagues (2010) notes that overall results are mixed as to the impact of differing types of surgery on sexuality (of which body image is a part). Varying methodologies and samples make robust comparisons difficult, and I would argue there are multiple variables that come into play: for instance, body image prior to diagnosis, and reaction of partner. It has been suggested that greater than the impact of type of surgery on sexuality is that of the chemotherapy and hormonal treatments that many women undergo (Klaeson et al., 2011). Chemotherapy is associated with increased risk of sexual difficulties (Avis et al., 2004), and for younger women the combination of sudden menopause and associated symptoms such as vaginal dryness, loss of sexual function, and loss of fertility can be particularly devastating (Ganz et al., 1998). Archibald and co-authors (2006) qualitative study, while narrow in its focus on sexual functioning following chemically induced menopause, does give some insights into the lived experience, missed by quantitative studies. For example, one single young woman is quoted wondering how any young man will handle her lack of sex drive and a body that she now perceives as old.

Chemotherapy-induced hair loss can also be extremely distressing and pose a threat to body image (Power & Condon, 2008). This is borne out by Thomas-MacLean's (2004) research on embodiment; a participant speaks of hair loss being so visible, and, as such, in some ways harder to cope with than breast loss, and a participant in Hefferon's (2008) thesis echoes this, describing her hair loss as worse than losing her breast.t helps them r

Larder (2010) notes in a BCC qualitative study on body image that for many of her respondents, while there was a degree of adjustment, the effects of breast surgery stayed with them and, as a result, they never became fully accepting of their body image. One, ten years post diagnosis, talks of learning to accept her mastectomy, but still hating it and feeling it looks ridiculous. An interesting counterpoint to studies suggesting ongoing difficulties with body image can be found in the research of Dunn and Steginga (2000), who asked participants to choose from a list of words those which best reflected their breast cancer experience. "Unattractive" was chosen by only three out of twenty-one women.

There is a paucity of research specifically examining the experiences of women who are single at some point following their breast cancer diagnosis. More commonly, brief comment is made about this group, as part of a larger sample (e.g., Archibald et al., 2006; Dunn & Steginga, 2000; Gould et al., 2006; Schover, 1991; Thewes et al., 2004), or no mention is given to singles at all (e.g., Cardoso et al., 2012; Cebeci et al., 2010; Emilee et al., 2010).

It is acknowledged that seeking new relationships after breast cancer can be a specific stressor for younger, single women (Schover,

1994). Often cited is a qualitative study by Gluhoski and colleagues (1998) among a sample of unmarried women as part of a study about pregnancy post breast cancer; all women believed they were still fertile. As such, it does not address fertility concerns, but does identify a set of unique stressors for unmarried women: pessimism about future relationships, fears about disclosing illness to partners, negative body image and impaired sexuality, pain of rejection by partners, and a sense of isolation and inadequate support. A sense of anxiety around dating, broaching the subject of cancer, fear of rejection and being found sexually undesirable, and never being able to form a new intimate relationship is echoed in the work of Holmberg and colleagues (2001). Feelings of being a liability to a future partner if the cancer recurs can be another fear (Thewes et al., 2004). An anecdote from a participant (Wilmoth, 2001) felt particularly discouraging. She told a man she was starting to date that she had breast cancer, and then went to the kitchen to pour drinks. When she came back, he had left. This caused her to completely avoid dating and male company. There is not much written about experiences when people did start to date. An early piece of research that does include this is a dissertation by Whitney (1988), from a feminist perspective; she interviewed single lesbian and heterosexual women about the impact of breast cancer on their "sexual scripts". It is notable for its qualitative approach, treating each participant as an individual case study initially, and conveying a rich sense of their varied experiences.

More recently, Corney and colleagues (2014), as part of a study concerning fertility, interviewed young, single women and similarly noted fear of rejection by potential partners, together with dilemmas around having children, and limited options for fertility treatment as some of the key issues they faced. With regard to infertility and loss of choice about having children, women believe that these concerns can sometimes be trivialised by health professionals, who feel that they should be more concerned about survival than loss of fertility (Dunn & Steginga, 2000).

Young single women with breast cancer describe an "utter silence" surrounding understanding of sexual changes in their bodies and how to feel sexual again with a new partner (Gould et al., 2006). There is not much support information specifically tailored to this group. Several years ago, I contributed quotes to a BCC publication entitled *Sexuality, Intimacy and Breast Cancer* (Breast Cancer Care, 2011) but, looking through this and other similar publications, there is generally just a paragraph about being single, with most of the information geared towards those in a relationship. A brief look at other online resources resulted in finding an informative page on the American Cancer Society (2013) website devoted to the single woman and cancer. On the Stanford Medicine website (Brandt, 2013), a doctor states that it is rare to come across anything geared to young, single women, and she blogs about dating tips. Interestingly, as far back as 1991, Schover was suggesting that being young and not in a committed relationship were "risk factors" that the healthcare team should be alert to, suggesting that this group might benefit from brief counselling, hearing about other women who have found new relationships post cancer, and help in planning how to date again and when to disclose their illness.

Of relevance to how women might make sense of their diagnosis, Neimeyer and colleagues (2002), taking a constructivist, narrative approach to their work around meaning reconstruction, write of major losses challenging our understanding of the previously adequate narratives of our life, and of the requirement to develop new ones. They call this "narrative repair" and see the goal not so much as a final truth, but as an account where things can seem meaningful once again. This seems pertinent to young women's accounts of breast cancer.

Frank's (1995) seminal work views illness as resulting in a narrative wreck: "The illness story is wrecked because its present is not what the past was supposed to lead up to, and the future is scarcely thinkable" (p. 55). He goes on to identify three types of illness narrative: restitution, which is based on a return to health, chaos, in which it is imagined life will never get better, and quest, in which the illness is accepted and the person seeks to use it positively. He discusses these in the sociological and political context of the medical profession and wider society. His comment that there is a need for clinical staff to witness the chaos rather than try to drag the patient out of it resonates with the values of person-centred counselling.

Bertero and Wilmoth (2007), in a meta-synthesis of qualitative research on breast cancer treatments affecting the Self, make reference to Frank's quest narrative. They write of a process of redefinition of the Self that includes women reflexively questioning their sense of womanhood in the aftermath of treatment. While this is a valuable concept, their methodology is several steps removed from original data and, as such, their findings are generalised.

Broyard (1992), writing eloquently of his terminal cancer, also suggests storytelling as a natural response to becoming ill; in a crisis we invent a narrative. He also speaks of developing a "style" for his illness and the importance of this in the face of the illness diminishing his sense of self. While this is clearly a very personal piece of writing based on his experiences, it does illustrate well the loss of identity in illness.

Participants

With the assistance of Breast Cancer Care (BCC), I recruited a purposive (non-probability) sample of four participants. My inclusion criteria were: diagnosed with breast cancer at least three years ago, female, under forty-five at point of diagnosis and over eighteen, single (defined as not in a partner relationship) at some point since their breast cancer diagnosis, BCC volunteer or service user, and feeling ready and able to share their story (Table 1.1). Participants' link with BCC meant a support network was in place should distressing material come up during their interview. Each participant chose a pseudonym to preserve her anonymity.

Data collection

Semi-structured interviews were used to collect my data. My aim was to witness the stories of each participant. They were invited to set the

Table 1.1. Participant details.

Pseudonym	Age at diagnosis	Time since diagnosis	Relationship status since diagnosis
Ceri	38	5.5 years	Single, partnered
Jessica	32	3 years	Partnered, single, partnered
Lizzie	23	6.5 years	Single, partnered
Sadie	34	5.5 years	Single

scene by briefly describing their breast cancer diagnosis and treatment and then, focusing on sexuality, asked to reflect on this prior to diagnosis. They were then asked to recall the impact on sexuality during treatment, and to go on to describe how they have felt about their sexuality since their initial treatment (surgery, chemotherapy, radiotherapy) has ended. The interviews took place in a quiet and private location of the participant's choice. Before the start of each digitally recorded interview, consent forms were signed by the participant.

What was discovered

The themes that emerged are set out in Table 1.2.

For context, it should be noted that none of the participants reported a sense of feeling uncomfortable with their sexuality before diagnosis. For example, Lizzie describes it as "pretty uncomplicated". Jessica, while comfortable with her body, describes having "maybe still a few issues about being gay", as she was in her first gay relationship.

Superordinate theme 1: Who am I now?

Subordinate theme 1.1: Not me any more

Three of the participants spoke of identity change or loss during their treatment. Jessica uses an arresting image in relation to surgery changing her identity. This is particularly striking, as the language of her narrative is generally quite unemotional: "On the day it happened it's almost like you're going to death row or something, obviously you are

Table 1.2. Emergent themes.

Superordinate themes	Who am I now?	Who will want me now?	The continuing themes
Subordinate themes	Not me any more	No one will want me	
		Ongoing losses	
	Taking control	Physical barriers	Fertility
	Living with my changed body	Broaching the subject	
		Being accepted	

going to wake up not the same." For Sadie, her altered body image during the treatment phase caused great distress. As she anticipates chemotherapy-induced hair loss, "I'm going to look like some freaky kind of alien". It strikes at her very core, causing her to question her identity: ". . . that [hair] is what defines you as a female, and to have some of that then taken away, are you then female?" Sadie makes many references to celebrity culture and what a woman is expected to look like; this seems important to her. Lizzie also experiences a sense of disconnection from herself as she loses her hair and puts on weight: "I do remember a sort of very distinct shift in feeling within me . . . of kind of just losing my identity . . . 'cos you sort of just don't look like yourself any more, and you look in the mirror and that person doesn't look like you." She describes her changed appearance as losing a part of her "toolkit" that she had relied on in social situations: ". . . that just wasn't even in the game . . . and so it was like I'd stepped into someone else's shoes. I didn't feel sexy any more, I didn't feel like myself any more . . ." For both Sadie and Lizzie, hair loss is, in some respects, harder to cope with than the mastectomy, as it is visible to others. Lizzie, speaking of her double mastectomy, illustrates this: ". . . at the time, it was almost less challenging than losing my hair, 'cos you could cover it up and you didn't have to be constantly conscious of it."

Subordinate theme 1.2: Taking control

For Jessica (who did not experience chemotherapy), research into reconstruction options is important in gaining some sense of control of how she will look post surgery: "I was probably quite obsessed with seeing what they looked like, and I had two people came to the office to see me, so I could have a look and feel." The oddness of this time for her is encapsulated here: ". . . upstairs, feeling someone's breast in my boss's loo, but nothing sexual!" For Sadie, taking control of the outward signs of her diagnosis is important. There is almost a defiance as she speaks of how she transforms herself from cancer patient into glamorous woman: ". . . right, put on the make-up, put on the wig, dress up, put on the killer heels, matching handbag, and go and rock that hospital room out." She has specialist hair work done. This marks the start of her return to womanhood. She says, ". . . it just made so much difference to . . . see myself in the mirror when I first got out of bed, or when I was in the bathroom, to have hair back, because then that was sort of stage one of coming back to being a woman again . . ." Lizzie, whose identity is also bound up in her hair loss, similarly takes control: "I went to that eighteen-month mark, and thought sod it, I'm just going to dye it blonde, and I dyed it blonde, and immediately it was like a shift, and . . . and I had it cut . . . into a bit more of a funky style . . . and then, that summer, I think that was the start of when I just started to feel sort of like myself again." There is a sense that Ceri blocks out any difficult feelings and takes comfort in the light-hearted directness of her nieces and nephews: ". . . initially it was like all a shock, but I just got on with it, and I didn't think about it . . . I sort of blanked it off. And having my nephews . . . he did draw a picture of me with my bandana on . . . and it had like a big bow on the back and he said, oh, that's auntie Ceri that is . . . I think having nieces and nephews around, that helped."

Subordinate theme 1.3: Living with my changed body

Jessica describes how, after her initial surgery, she feels less happy with her body: "When I had no nipple on one side, and 'cos I had an expander implant at first . . . I was really asymmetrical, so undressed I felt kind of . . . didn't like my body as much any more." After further operations, her body image improves: "so I guess after I sorted out my symmetry and stuff and had a nipple tattooing I feel much better about myself." She expresses an acceptance that this will never feel the same as a "real" breast, but there is a sense of the research she did paying off. She says, ". . . I'm very glad I went with the option I did go with, I'm kind of happy with it. I mean you know, there's certain things . . . I feel lumpy down one side, things like that, but obviously it's never going to feel like a real boob." Sadie speaks movingly of the struggles of looking at her mastectomy scar: "But I would probably say it took me about a month to six weeks before I could actually look at myself in the mirror, at my surgery scar", offering an explanation for this: "I was so worried I think that I'd just look down and I would just break down . . . I think part of it was, I've got to be strong." For Sadie, too, once her surgery is complete, her body image improves: "But then when I had the operation to sort of create the nipple, and then the tattoo . . . I don't go out flashing myself, but . . . I am more than happy to wear a bikini." There is a sense of pride in coming through the experience: "I'd say, probably if anything, I'm more likely to be strutting myself in my bra and knickers or my bikini. Because, in a way, I'm kind of wanting people to think, what's happened to her, oh my God, she's had breast cancer but hey look" [Sadie], and in having the scars to prove it: "because, yes I've got scars, but those scars are because I'm still alive, and I'm still here to tell the tale . . ." For Lizzie, there seems to be an ambivalence. Struggling to find the right words, she speaks powerfully: ". . . still sometimes I guess, if I actually bother to look at myself in the mirror, sometimes I . . . sort of shock myself. You know, obviously I see it all the time, and I'm not really bothered by it, but sometimes when you really actually look at yourself, I sort of have moments of . . . sort of horror, you know . . . 'cos it's sort of a mutilation isn't it, it's sort of a bizarre, and you know you've lost a part of your body and (pause) that's sort of an odd thing, and most of the time I just don't really think about it, but occasionally, I . . .sort of remember." There is a sense of disembodiment and disconnection for Lizzie following surgery; her implants feel separate from her. She explains, ". . . they just don't really feel part of me, you know . . . it's like I've just got two things stuck on my chest . . . and even if I run my own hands over my body, they're sort of these, they're these foreign objects." She considers having them removed, and this being kinder to her body, which would then be "all her" once more: ". . . if I just got rid of them would it give my body just a chance to just heal, and maybe it would take a long time, but it would have a shot at just healing in a new way, and then it would all be me again." She notices how her feelings have changed over the intervening years; this is an ongoing process. She continues to reflect on how it might feel to have the implants removed: ". . . me becoming more comfortable with myself, and my body, and being able to handle it I guess and being able to still feel like me, and not have them, whereas if I'd done it when I was twenty-three, I don't think I could have handled it." Ceri speaks a lot about covering up her body since her surgery, and her words suggest it is not just her outward appearance that has changed: ". . . I'd be showing . . . not showing yourself off, but, you know, wearing more revealing tops, so I was quite a bubbly and outgoing thing. But since the op now . . . I won't wear any dresses." Ceri goes on to explain, "So no, I'm just wearing all these things to . . . keep my arms covered. 'Cos you feel that you can still can see the scar, and the indentation where the lymph nodes were taken out." She describes the asymmetry of her breasts following her lumpectomy: "I suppose it's because I'm quite big, so the one side is quite big, and the other side is like half the size. So obviously . . . they don't offer reconstruction when it's a lumpectomy." There is a sadness and confusion in her voice as she goes on to wonder why she was left like this.

Superordinate theme 2: Who will want me now?

Subordinate theme 2.1: No one will want me

Following the end of her relationship during treatment, Jessica expresses fears about dating again: "I think I was really worried that no- one else would want me." Although she has had a sexual relationship since her treatment, Sadie still has concerns about not looking "normal": ". . . 'cos you're thinking, what if they see me undressed, and while I'm happy with the way I look, they think, you don't quite look like what a normal woman should look like, whatever the definition of a normal woman is, and just run to the hills screaming . . . because that's what you sort of build up in your mind." She wonders, too, whether other factors will also put men off: ". . . would he rather do that [go out with someone else] than go out with me, because I've had cancer, and perhaps because his dad had died of cancer", and ". . . a guy might think, no actually I want to have my own kid, and actually I can't help in that department" [Sadie]. For Lizzie, although she has sexual relationships during treatment, she feels unable to be proactive about this. She says, ". . . I didn't feel like I could go out and sort of look for a guy, because I just didn't feel sexy." She is also worried about the response she might get: ". . . there's always that worry that they're gonna be completely unable to deal with it." Ceri writes off her chances of ever having a relationship: "I just thought, that . . . I'd never be in a relationship ever again. Because obviously it was the low self-esteem, low self-confidence . . . and because of the treatment, you were so like up and down all the time, and the coping with all the side-effects is so draining isn't it, mentally draining, and I think it just really knocked my confidence quite a bit."

Subordinate theme 2.2: Physical barriers

Jessica and Sadie have not experienced physical changes that interfere with sex: ". . . I don't think it's particularly affected my sex drive really" [Jessica]. "... I think, so far, everything in that department seems to be absolutely fine" [Sadie]. Lizzie speaks of the shock of discovering some unwelcome side effects of treatment, and there is a sense of being kicked when she is already down: "... I hadn't really clocked all of that, and all of the ways that it interferes with the plumbing, was pretty challenging, and a bit of a shock, and not very nice. And again, to sort of be confronted with that, you know, when you're already feeling pretty vulnerable, with no hair, and with a guy you haven't seen for a long time . . ." Ceri speaks poignantly and hesitantly of feeling inadequate as she embarks on a new relationship, and of the confusion of her altered sexual response: "I just didn't feel as if I was fulfi . . . you know, fulfil . . . fulfil(ling) his needs . . . But it could have been because sometimes it was quite painful, even with the lubricants. And then I think, just because it put you off as well, and sometimes you just, you felt you were in the moment, it was just like a light switch sometimes, it was weird, bizarre isn't it."

Subordinate theme 2.3: Broaching the subject

Jessica, Sadie, and Lizzie have all experienced disclosure to new sexual partners, and when to mention it was explored by them. There is a sense of the awkwardness of broaching the subject: "probably when I got drunk with them" [Jessica]. Sadie reflects on the feeling of being between "a rock and a hard place" concerning when to disclose, but highlights her sense of owning the information and it being a case of her choosing when to share: "If you are then completely meeting someone anew, do you tell them on first date; it's probably not the conversation for a first date, but then when do you, you don't want to go so far down the line that actually you think somebody might think, well, you've hidden that from me. You think, well actually . . . but it's my, truth to hide . . . and it's up to me to tell." Lizzie adopts a kind of phased approach to disclosure, seeming to almost expect that some men might want to walk away: "... Mostly I probably tried to make them aware of the fact that I had had some sort of operation, pretty early on, before we even kind of got to that stage. I suppose I wanted to give them the opportunity to check out nice and early, and then you know, as things sort of got a bit closer to something actually happening, I probably would be pretty explicit, again probably wanting to give them, either to just give them a bit of warning . . . walk away if they wanted to." For Lizzie, who had met several men since diagnosis, there is a sense of each new relationship bringing breast cancer back to the fore: ". . . with another one, you have to tell them all about it all again, and worry about it all again, and it's a new thing, and it's sort of on your mind."

Subordinate theme 2.4: Being accepted

In contrast to their fears and expectations, all participants have experienced acceptance. For Jessica this is hugely reassuring, following her experience with her partner at diagnosis: ". . . the two girls I had a bit of a fling with before I met my current girlfriend both were very accepting of it, they said it didn't matter to them, they didn't care . . . so that was kind of a positive outcome . . . because I guess maybe my ex-girlfriend, although . . . she wasn't horrible about it or anything, because she wasn't an overly sexual person . . . she didn't want to touch my scar or anything like that." In this description of her current partner's reaction, her response goes beyond acceptance and feels something more like celebration: ". . . she's always been very complimentary about it, how, you know, it's beautiful because it you know, it saved me almost, because if I hadn't had it done would I be here still?" Sadie meets a younger man who reacts positively to her reconstruction. In her comment below, she seems to be almost making excuses for why this is the case: ". . . I think he probably thought I was going to say, actually, I was a man [laughter]. And I think to be honest, because it wasn't that, he was like, it's not a problem, and he had no issue with it whatsoever. But . . . twenty-four-year-old guys, let's face it, as long as they're getting sex, that's all they want." She sounds surprised: ". . . he didn't wince or anything, he didn't have a problem. He was actually very flattering, and you know, positive about the way I looked . . . so it was like actually, he's not run for the hills." Lizzie, too, expects things to be different: ". . . despite not having a nipple on one side, I've been probably with quite a few different guys since I was treated, and not a single one of them has been remotely fazed, not even a little bit weirded out, which I think is pretty amazing really." There is a bitter-sweetness to having a long-term partner; some difficult feelings did not surface until then: ". . . it's sort of brought up things which are difficult again, because . . . I wish I could have been with him when I still had my breasts for instance . . . it's just a real sort of shame, I suppose, and so sometimes I sort of find that a bit difficult, in a way that I didn't really find difficult when I was with guys that I didn't really care about" [Lizzie]. Ceri expresses gratitude for the patience of her new partner: "because of the way he was ... you just felt that you were comfortable ... because he didn't rush, or he wasn't pressured, I think he was a blessing, you know what I mean?" Like Sadie, she also attributes his acceptance possibly to factors other than herself: "But he's a little bit older, than myself, so whether or not, it might have been different if it was ..." [Ceri].

Superordinate theme 3: The continuing journey

Subordinate theme 3.1: Ongoing losses

Participants articulated a sense of the ongoing nature of their losses from breast cancer to varying degrees. Lizzie in particular spoke at some length. As she herself alludes to, perhaps the fact that she was diagnosed so young has contributed to some "delayed losses"' "... there's all this other stuff that I hadn't really clocked, and I'd say the last few years for me have almost been more emotionally difficult than when I went through the treatment, because there's been so much other stuff which, at the time, I just completely put in a box because there was so much going on, at such a young age, I couldn't, and also just stuff that wasn't important to me then." For example, speaking about the impact of her decision to have a double mastectomy, and how this has hit her much later on: "... although obviously I knew that I wouldn't be able to breastfeed, and that was in a way sad, as I say, that child fertility thing was so far down my list of priorities behind surviving ... not really understanding, 'cos how could I at twenty-three, never thinking about children, just what a big deal it is, and now I get it." She speaks poignantly about missing her breasts, articulating a deep sense of loss: "I often will have a sexual experience, and feel actively quite sad, and not be able to enjoy it, because I get kind of caught up in that feeling of, feeling really sad about what had to happen, and so that continues to be an issue for me." Ceri struggles to understand why she still has no sex drive, and feels there is something wrong with her: "... I could quite easily go without any ... sexual relationship, it's just not there at all, it's weird isn't it ... you think there's something wrong with you, well there is ... and like the switch, you'd think the switch would have come back on now, wouldn't you after all this time, nothing, weird isn't it" [Ceri]. To combat menopausal hot flushes, Ceri changes her wardrobe and this can add to a sense of unattractiveness: "everything's got to be 100% cotton and some of those clothes aren't particularly attractive." For her, the ups and downs of the breast cancer journey continue: ". . . people seem to think once you've had it that's that, but it's like at the back of your mind, and although you get on with life and everything, you still have, you feel like you're on a rollercoaster . . . of emotions."

Subordinate theme 3.2: Fertility

For Jessica and Lizzie, infertility is a possibility. Jessica expresses early concerns that she will be "left behind", but this seems to be less likely now: "I suppose at the time you kind of think all my friends will have had children and I won't have . . . and actually you know I'm two years into Tamoxifen now, so it's only another three years, and quite a few of my close friends haven't got kids yet . . ." Lizzie considers her options, and reflects that although fertility is a concern, other losses have possibly felt more significant: ". . . my overall stance that you know, if I can't have children it won't be the end of the world, that still is true, so you know, I am very open to adoption and I'm also very open to just not having children, if that is the path that we go down . . . some people just can't have children anyway, quite aside from anything, so I'm pretty open-minded about the whole thing in that way, but I think it's probably the double mastectomy and the breastfeeding that has kind of shook me up more I would say than the fertility." Certainly for Ceri, and probably for Sadie, loss of fertility is a reality. Sadie recalls her weighing up of options at the time: "Just, what's the point of having your eggs frozen, if you delay your treatment and it makes it worse, and then you're dead, and you still can't use them anyway." She describes an upsetting incident at work where everyone seems to be having babies, and reflects on changes since then. There is a sense of her rewriting her narrative in relation to children: ". . . it was two years down the line; it was probably still very raw, whereas now it's probably, it's sunk in and, you know, I'll be the cool auntie to everyone else's kids . . . who's the bad influence, and causes the parents problems." She rationalises, acknowledging that it is hard for her: ". . . with everything that happens in life, you have to compromise, so if my compromise for still being here is the fact that I might not be able to have children naturally, you know, it's a tough thing to deal with, and it has got me upset, and you know, I cannot watch *One Born Every Minute*." For Ceri, there is a sense of sadness at being overlooked as a single woman; she was not offered any options to preserve her fertility: ". . . at the point of diagnosis they asked if I was in a relationship, and I'd said not at that time, and then they just said because it was Grade 3, we need to get on with it." She works with children and although she now feels able to continue, her last comment hints at continuing sadness: "I thought about, wondered about giving up that job, but obviously I've managed to get through that and just, you know, but sometimes it does pull at you a little."

Bringing together the literature and the findings

Discourse around cancer might give the impression that once treatment is over, a patient no longer thinks about their illness, but emotional descriptions of memories of treatment show that this is far from the case (Thomas-MacLean, 2004). It was a striking feature of my interviews how vividly participants recalled particular points in their treatment.

Schover (1994) suggests that sexual life pre-diagnosis is a stronger predictor of sexuality issues than breast surgery. My findings would seem to indicate that a positive sexual self-image prior to diagnosis does not protect women from the impact of breast cancer on this area of their life. One can speculate that a poor adjustment prior to diagnosis would result in a more severe impact.

Two participants, Sadie and Lizzie, presented striking descriptions of the profound changes to their sense of identity during treatment. Jessica did not undergo chemotherapy, so was not affected by hair loss; the sense of change from losing a breast was powerfully evoked in her comment likening the mastectomy surgery to "going to death row".

The profound impact of chemotherapy-induced hair loss on identity emerged in Sadie and Lizzie's stories. This aspect of breast cancer is neglected in terms of studies that focus on it (Power & Cordon, 2008). Power and Cordon report that almost half of participants felt their hair loss to be more significant than loss of their breast. This might seem a surprising finding, but the participants in this study echo this, and speak of the fact that a missing breast can be covered up by clothes, but that having no hair is more visible. This supports views expressed in earlier research (e.g., Hefferon, 2008; Thomas-MacLean, 2004; Wilmoth, 2001). The links with female identity are made clear; Sadie questions whether she can even identify as female without hair, and her use of the word "alien" illustrates her sense of disconnection as she looks in the mirror. This happens for Lizzie, too, who speaks of feeling like she had "stepped into someone else's shoes", and links her hair to feeling sexy. The pervasive cultural images of beauty incorporating hair are mentioned by both, and the impact of those images is clear. Perhaps, too, there is something especially traumatic in experiencing hair loss alongside breast loss; a double assault on feminine identity.

There appears to be resonance with Wilmoth's (2001) finding that women who take control by finding out as much information as they can about treatment and side effects often adjust well, coming through breast cancer with their self largely intact. Jessica spoke extensively about the research she did, and of subsequently being satisfied with the reconstruction option she chose. Sadie and Lizzie took steps to take control of their hair loss and regrowth and articulated the positive effect of this. While it is unwise to make direct comparisons, there was less of a sense of agency throughout Ceri's narrative, and a lack of choices given to her, the impact of which she appears to continue to struggle with. Much of Sadie's narrative concerns her efforts during treatment in terms of outward appearance; hair, make-up, clothes, and this resonates with Broyard's (1992) statements about the importance of adopting a "style" during illness in order to combat the sense of his sense of self shrinking. There was a sense that Sadie had taken care of how she looked prior to her illness; this could fit with the idea that those who consider body image to be an important part of their attractiveness and self-worth struggle more to adjust to treatment (Kissane et al., 2004). The impact on this group will arguably be greater if appearance is more important to them in terms of identity.

There is a real diversity of experiences among the participants as they adjust to their altered bodies. The importance of a nipple in defining a breast comes across; for Jessica and Sadie, once this part of their surgery is complete they feel happier with their appearance. Sadie goes so far as to articulate a sense of pride about her scars and what they signify. For Lizzie, who has not had a nipple reconstruction because she does not wish to subject herself to more medical procedures, she still speaks of occasionally viewing her new body in terms of "horror" and "mutilation". This sense of the effects of surgery remaining, in spite of a degree of adjustment, echoes the findings of Larder (2010). Lizzie also describes how her implants feel like "foreign objects", and expresses how her feelings concerning the necessity of them have changed as she has become more comfortable with herself over the years since diagnosis. Adams and colleagues (2011), describe women engaging in a normalising process as they adjust to their altered body, and it seems that Lizzie's definition of what she can accept has shifted with time so that she believes now that she would "still be able to feel like me" without her implants. This suggests normalisation is an ongoing and fluid process, as definitions shift for people over time.

It is interesting to note that it is Ceri, who had breast-conserving surgery (lumpectomy), who continues to have concerns in terms of covering up her body, both in public and with her partner. Intuitively, it might be expected that this would have less impact; it is only upon hearing Ceri's story that we find out why it is so difficult for her. As she did not have a mastectomy, she was not offered any reconstruction and has been left with breasts of greatly differing sizes, making her self-conscious even when dressed, and resulting in her completely changing her style of clothes, and it seems she also mourns a deeper impact on her identity as she describes how she used to be "quite a bubbly and outgoing thing". In terms of research, the findings fit with Emilee and colleagues' (2010) review, which suggests mixed results as to the impact of type of surgery on sexuality. It seems that it is only by hearing individuals' stories that the truth for them can be revealed, and that generalisations are unwise and unhelpful.

The anxieties of the participants as they contemplate dating post treatment echo the findings of earlier studies (e.g., Gluhoski et al., 1998; Holmberg et al., 2001; Kissane et al., 2004). Apprehension was expressed by all of the participants at the possibility of ever finding an accepting partner; in Gluhoski and colleagues' research, this resulted from a mixture of women feeling they had become more selective after their illness, and of feeling men would think they were less appealing. There were many comments from this study's participants about feeling unattractive and not conforming to the normal image of womanhood. This fits with existing research (e.g., Archibald et al., 2006).

Lizzie and Ceri had both experienced physical issues with intimacy, and for Ceri this remained ongoing. The shock for Lizzie of the changes she experienced during treatment, and for Ceri the bewilderment that accompanied her altered sexual response, possibly reflect the lack of information proactively given to young women about this. This is in line with the comments of Gould and colleagues' (2006) participants that they could not find answers to their questions about the effect of treatment on their bodies and how to relate to themselves sexually again. Their experiences illustrate some of the symptoms identified by Howard-Anderson and co-authors (2012), including lack of libido and vaginal dryness. The quotes from Ceri and Lizzie bring this to life and indicate the emotional impact of these unexpected physical changes.

Disclosure of diagnosis to a potential new partner can be a "chilling prospect" (Holmberg et al., 2001). This might sound dramatic, but for the three participants who have done this, there was certainly great apprehension. Jessica, using the humour characteristic throughout her narrative, hinted at this as she described how alcohol facilitated disclosure. Lizzie tended to give hints early on in the process. Sadie's reflections on the uncertainty of when to disclose appear to be common; there are similar quotes in earlier studies (e.g., Corney et al., 2014; Gluhoski et al., 1998).

Not much in the literature details how women went about disclosing, and the results of this. The findings of this research I hope add a little to the picture. A notable exception is Whitney's (1988) detailed thesis, which illustrates the uniqueness of each woman's experience. Overall, Whitney's participants present a mixed picture in terms of positive experiences of dating post cancer, with some very encouraging stories and some less so. One of Whitney's participants expressed anger at having to explain her diagnosis again each time she met a new partner; Lizzie mentioned having to do this, but rather than anger, there was a frustration at breast cancer coming back to the fore over and over again.

The experiences of the participants present a more universally optimistic and encouraging message about the realities of dating post breast cancer than other studies. Lizzie and Jessica had both met and dated several people before embarking on their current long-term relationships. Sadie had several dates with a man, and Ceri was in a relationship with someone who had been a friend during her treatment. Without exception, each of these experiences had been good in terms of partner's acceptance. In contrast, one of the participants in Corney and colleagues' (2014) study reported that an ex-boyfriend warned her not to tell men about her diagnosis as they would not want to date someone who might get ill again. This warning was then borne out by her experiences, as the men she dated and disclosed to disappeared. Some of Gluhoski and colleagues' (1998) participants also described rejection due to fear of recurrence, but this was not mentioned by the participants in this study as an issue, apart from one comment from Sadie who wondered about one potential partner, who had been a friend many years ago, and whether his choice not to date her was related to her diagnosis, perhaps because his dad had recently died of cancer. She also wondered whether her loss of fertility might be a deterrent; this is also mentioned by Corney and colleagues (2014) as a fear that existed among their participants.

For Jessica, there is a sense of a real contrast between the reaction of her partner at the time of diagnosis and the response of her new girlfriend, who celebrates her reconstruction and her scars because this is what has saved her life. This chimes with Wilmoth's (2001) model that includes "influencing pieces"—factors that have an impact on how a woman moves through the process of having cancer. One of these is the supportiveness of partners, and Wilmoth (2001) quotes a participant speaking of her partner, telling her how beautiful she still is. Jessica speaks a lot throughout her narrative of the impact of others' responses on her. In line with their expectations, Sadie and Lizzie express some surprise and disbelief that they are accepted by partners. This again highlights how expectations of what is culturally acceptable are entrenched within a woman's sense of identity. It was interesting to hear both Sadie and Ceri speculate as to the reasons why their post treatment body is accepted by men; for Sadie it was about young men just wanting sex, and for Ceri the fact that her partner was older. It seems it is hard to believe that their partners just accept them for whom they are regardless of how they look.

There is not much qualitative research that considers the longer-term impact on relationships. One of Whitney's (1988) case studies had been diagnosed five years previously. Kissane and colleages (2004) note that research suggests, while most women adjust to their altered body, some will suffer long-term impact on sexuality; some studies that are two or three years post diagnosis indicate this. Lizzie, diagnosed 6.5 years ago, spoke poignantly of the sadness she still feels that her long-term partner did not know her when she had breasts, and links this to the depth of feeling she has for him.

Continuing exploration of the longer-term impact on sexuality, the third Superordinate theme resulted from participants' talking about the ongoing changes and losses arising from their diagnosis and treatment. Aside from a continuing apprehension around whether potential partners would accept her body as she does, menopausal hot flushes, and her not insignificant sadness at fertility loss, which is discussed later on, Sadie presented as living life to the full and being open about what she had been through, and almost defiant. Jessica seemed to feel she had been fortunate not to have experienced chemotherapy and its side effects, and seemed accepting of her new body, helped greatly by her partner's response to it. There was a sense of moving forward and it not being at the forefront of her mind on a daily basis any more.

Lizzie had the most to say about the ongoing impact, and provides a rare insight into the experience of someone diagnosed in their early twenties. The "off-time" nature of her diagnosis is extreme; she is "out of sync" with her peers (Adams et al., 2011), so it is perhaps not surprising that her feelings and priorities have shifted over time. She illustrates the concept of "balancing" (Adams et al., 2011) as she describes how immediate concerns about survival, together with her life-stage, pushed fertility and the importance of breast-feeding down the list of priorities. Lizzie's distress at her loss of the ability to breast-feed is echoed by a participant in Kirkman and colleagues' (2014) study. She articulates with poignancy the ongoing grief at her loss of breasts, speaking of often feeling *actively quite sad* during sex. This highlights the profound and enduring nature of the impact of surgery for some women: "Losing any part of the body in a mutilating operation, however necessary and however life-saving the surgery, involves grieving. This process is long and painful for some of us" (Kitzinger, 1985, p. 297). For Ceri, the "rollercoaster" of emotions continues, and there is a hint of the huge sense of loss expressed by Klaeson and colleagues' (2011) participants as to the sadness at no longer feeling any sexual desire. Her language is quite matter of fact, but her tone is not.

Young, single women can have limited options for fertility treatment and face dilemmas around having children (Corney et al., 2014);

the participants offered a range of experiences. The idea of "balancing" (Adams et al., 2011) was evident in the reflections of some participants. For instance, Sadie speaks of the futility of having her eggs frozen if it means that she later dies because her treatment to harvest them was delayed. Years later, she is still balancing the fact that she is unlikely to be able to have children against the fact that she is still alive. She rewrites her narrative (Neimeyer et al., 2002), reflecting on how the rawness she felt earlier on has now softened a little and she re-imagines her future as "the cool auntie". She invents a "consoling plot" (Kirkman et al., 2014) to make life meaningful. This is not to underestimate the continuing sadness she clearly feels.

Ceri's story echoes the experiences of some of Corney and colleagues' (2014) participants, in that, as a single woman, she was not offered any options for preserving her fertility, and she speaks of wishing there had been information readily available at the time. Like Sadie, it seems that an adjustment process has taken place, to the extent that she has been able to continue in her job with children; she felt she might not be able to. But her continuing sense of loss is evident in her words; there is something of a "preoccupying sorrow" (Kirkman et al., 2014).

Viewing each participant's story in terms of illness narratives (Frank, 1995), elements of each type—restitution, chaos, and quest—are evident throughout. The restitution narrative, in which society demands a return to being "good as new", is shown as flawed as the women progress through the confusion, and "chaos" of diagnosis and treatment to the realisation that they will have to find a new "normal"—there is no going back. Each story contains a sense of a quest narrative; all participants work with a breast cancer charity, sharing their story with others. This quote from Frank (1995) seems pertinent: "Human illness, even when lived as a quest, always returns to mourning" (p. 136). Wilmoth's (2001) model of taking in, taking hold, and taking on could be said to link with the idea of differing types of narratives, and, like participants in this study, time did not appear to be a predictor of adjustment. The "influencing pieces" of taking control of treatments and information, and the supportive relationships, did appear to be important.

A report from BCC (2014) on body image, published during the writing of this chapter, provides further evidence of the range of impacts on sexuality. While BCC (2014) is a policy report, and its main focus is on improvements to services and support, it contains a selection of often poignant quotes from women which bring the topics to life, and reflect thatm for some, treatment has resulted in ongoing difficulties and mourning of losses. Many of these reflect the mix of experiences of this study's participants, and capture the disappointment expressed, particularly by Ceri, about the lack of information to prepare and support them for what is ahead.

Conclusion

Limitations of this study include the small sample size, which could not represent a broad spread of demographic group and experience. All respondents were involved with BCC in roles that involve sharing their experiences with others, meaning they might have had less of a "freshness" to their narrative, although it could also be said they might have been more grounded and reflective about their experiences. Inevitably, analysis was conducted through my lens, and another researcher might have highlighted different aspects of the participants' experiences from those on which I chose to focus.

This study did not seek to prove or disprove, but, rather, to add some threads to the colourful tapestry of women who have been generous enough to speak with researchers like myself and share something of their experience. While there were certainly themes across participants that resonated with one another, and with existing research, the uniqueness of each woman's experience was striking and is, perhaps, the most important outcome to note. A finding that differed from some earlier studies was that of universal acceptance from prospective partners of participants' diagnosis. It is hoped that this could serve as encouragement to others.

By interviewing women who were several years post diagnosis, I hoped to convey a sense of changes over time, and each experience was very different. While each woman is moving forward in positive ways in her own life and helping others by sharing her story, there is certainly a sense of lingering sadness and long-term impacts for some participants, and these findings add to the limited qualitative research on longer-term adjustment. They demonstrate that it is not a case of getting over the losses that breast cancer has brought, but of adapting to an altered life narrative.

Many therapists are not well informed about breast cancer and its treatment (Anllo, 2000). In undertaking this study, it was my hope that the counselling community might gain some insights into the types of issues faced by younger, single women with breast cancer. Although the disease in younger women is relatively uncommon, counsellors might encounter members of this group during their careers. While each journey is unique, the themes of loss, identity change, and rewriting life's narrative to some degree seem universal. Person-centred therapy, with its emphasis on the client as expert in exploring the areas they need to, in a supportive non-judgemental environment, seems an ideal setting for the process of making sense of the experience and of exploring the challenges arising from it.

References

Adams, E., McCann, L., Armes, J., Richardson, A., Stark, D., Watson, E., & Hubbard, G. (2011). The experiences, needs and concerns of younger women with breast cancer: a meta-ethnography. *Psycho-Oncology, 20*: 851–861.

American Cancer Society (2013). *The Single Woman and Cancer*. Accessed at: www.cancer.org/treatment/treatmentsandsideeffects/physicalsideeffects/sexualsideeffectsinwomen/sexualityforthewoman/sexuality-for-women-with-cancer-single-woman.

Anllo, L. M. (2000). Sexual life after breast cancer. *Journal of Sex and Marital Therapy, 26*: 241–248.

Archibald, S., Lemieux, S., Byers, E., Tamlyn, K., & Worth, J. (2006). Chemically-induced menopause and the sexual functioning of breast cancer survivors. *Women and Therapy, 29*(1–2): 83–106.

Avis, N., Crawford, S., & Manuel, J. (2004). Psychosocial problems among women with breast cancer. *Psycho-Oncology, 13*: 295–308.

Bertero, C., & Wilmoth, M. C. (2007). Breast cancer diagnosis and its treatment affecting the self: a meta-synthesis. *Cancer Nursing, 30*(3): 194–202.

Brandt, M. (2013). Young, single, dating—and a breast cancer survivor. Accessed at: scopeblog.stanford.edu/2013/10/01/young-single-dating-and-a-breast-cancer-survivor/.

Breast Cancer Care (2011). *Sexuality, Intimacy and Breast Cancer*. London: Breast Cancer Care.

Breast Cancer Care (2013). *About Breast Cancer.* Accessed at: www.breastcancercare.org.uk/breast-cancer-information/about-breast-cancer.
Breast Cancer Care (2014). My body, myself. Altered body image, sexuality and intimacy after breast cancer. Accessed at: www.breastcancercare.org.uk/news/blog/my-body-myself-our-new-policy-report.
Broyard, A. (1992). *Intoxicated by My Illness.* New York: Ballantine Books.
Burwell, S. R., Case, L. D., Kaelin, C., & Avis, N. E. (2006). Sexual problems in younger women after breast cancer surgery. *Journal of Clinical Oncology, 20*(18): 2815–2821.
Cancer Research UK (2014). *Cancer Stats: Cancer Statistics for the UK.* Accessed at: http://www.cancerresearchuk.org.
Cardoso, F., Lobil, S., Pagani, O., Graziottin, A., Panizza, P., Martincich, L., Gentilini, O., Peccatori, F., Fourquet, A., Delaloge, S., Marotti, L., Penaut-Lorca, F., Kotti-Kitromilidou, A., Roder, A., & Harbeck, N. (2012). The European Society of Breast Cancer Specialists recommendations for the management of young women with breast cancer. *European Journal of Cancer, 48*: 3355–3377.
Cebeci, F., Yangin, H. B., & Tekeli, A. (2010). Determination of changes in the sexual lives of young women receiving breast cancer treatment: a qualitative study. *Sexuality and Disability, 28*: 255–264.
Corney, R., Puthussery, S., & Swinglehurst, J. (2014). The stressors and vulnerabilities of young single childless women with breast cancer: a qualitative study. *European Journal of Oncology Nursing, 18*: 17–22.
Coyne, B., & Borbasi, S. (2006). Holding it all together: breast cancer and its impact on life for younger women. *Contemporary Nurse: a Journal for the Australian Nursing Profession, 23*(2): 157–169.
Coyne, B., & Borbasi, S. (2009). Living the experience of breast cancer treatment: the younger women's perspective. *Australian Journal of Advanced Nursing, 26*(4): 6–13.
Dunn, J., & Steginga, S. K. (2000). Young women's experience of breast cancer: defining young and identifying concerns. *Psycho-Oncology, 9*: 137–146.
Emilee, G., Ussher, J. M., & Perz, J. (2010). Sexuality after breast cancer: a review. *Maturitas, 66*: 397–407.
Fallbjork, U., Rasmussen, B. H., Karlsson, S., & Salander, P. (2013). Aspects of body image after mastectomy due to breast cancer: a two-year follow-up study. *European Journal of Oncology Nursing, 17*: 340–345.
Fobair, P. M., Stewart, S. L., Chang, S., D'Onofrio, C., Banks, P. J., & Bloom, J. R. (2006). Body image and sexual problems in young women with breast cancer. *Psycho-Oncology, 15*: 579–594.

Frank, A. W. (1995). *The Wounded Storyteller*. Chicago, IL: University of Chicago Press.

Ganz, P. A. (2008). Psychological and social aspects of breast cancer. *Oncology*, 22(6): 42–47.

Ganz, P. A., Rowland, J. H., Meyerowitz, B. E., & Wyatt, G. E. (1998). Life after breast cancer: understanding women's health-related quality of life and sexual functioning. *Journal of Clinical Oncology*, 16(2): 501–514.

Gluhoski, V. L., Siegl, K., & Gorey, E. (1998). Unique stressors experienced by unmarried women with breast cancer. *Journal of Psychosocial Oncology*, 15(3–4): 173–183.

Gorman, E. (2011). Adaptation, resilience and growth after loss. In: D. L Harris (Ed.), *Counting Our Losses: Reflecting on Change, Loss and Transition in Everyday Life* (pp. 00–00). New York: Routledge.

Gould, J., Grassau, P., Manthorne, J., Gray, R. E., & Fitch, M. I. (2006). 'Nothing fit me': nationwide consultation with young women with breast cancer. *Health Expectations*, 9: 158–173.

Hefferon, K. (2008). Understanding the experience of posttraumatic growth following life-threatening physical illness. Unpublished doctoral thesis, Strathclyde University.

Holmberg, S. K., Scott, L. L., Alexy, W., & Fife, B. L. (2001). Relationship issues of women with breast cancer. *Cancer Nursing*, 24(1): 53–60.

Howard-Anderson, J., Ganz, P. A., Bower, J. E., & Stanton, A. L. (2012). Quality of life, fertility concerns, and behavioral health outcomes in younger breast cancer survivors: a systematic review. *Journal of the National Cancer Institute*, 104: 386–405.

Kirkman, M., Winship, I., Stern, N. C., Neil, S., Mann, G. B., & Fisher, J. R. W. (2014). Women's reflections on fertility and motherhood after breast cancer and its treatment. *European Journal of Cancer Care*, 23: 502–513.

Kissane, D., White, K., Cooper, K., & Vitetta, L. (2004). *Psychosocial Impact in the Areas of Body Image and Sexuality for Women with Breast Cancer*. Sydney, Australia: National Breast Cancer Centre.

Kitzinger, S. (1985). *Women's Experience of Sex*. London: Penguin.

Klaeson, K., Sandell, A. K., & Bertero, C. M. (2011). To feel like an outsider: focus group discussions regarding the influence on sexuality caused by breast cancer treatment. *European Journal of Cancer Care*, 20: 728–737.

Larder, M. (2010). Body image and breast cancer. An exploratory investigation to determine a policy and campaign response to identified need. Unpublished report for Breast Cancer Care.

Meyerowitz, B. E., Desmond, K. A., Rowland, J. H., Wyatt, G. E., & Ganz, P. A. (1999). Sexuality following breast cancer. *Journal of Sex and Marital Therapy*, 25(3): 237–250.

Neimeyer, R., Botella, L., Herrero, O., Pachecho, M., Figueras, S., & Werner–Wildner, L. A. (2002). The meaning of your absence. In: J. Kauffman (Ed.), *Loss of the Assumptive World: A Theory Of Traumatic Loss* (pp. 31–47). Hove: Brunner-Routledge.

Parkes, C. M. (2009). *Love and Loss: The Roots of Grief and its Complications.* Hove: Routledge.

Power, S., & Condon, C. (2008). Chemotherapy-induced alopecia: a phenomenological study. *Cancer Nursing Practice*, 7(7): 44–47.

Rosenberg, S. M., Tamimi, R. M., Gelber, S., Ruddy, K. J., Kereakoglow, S., Borges, V. F., Come, S. E., Schapira, L.,Winer, E. P., & Partridge, A. H. (2013). Body image in recently diagnosed young women with early breast cancer. *Psycho-Oncology*, 22: 1849–1855.

Schover, L. R. (1991). The impact of breast cancer on sexuality, body image and intimate relationships. *Ca-a Cancer Journal for Clinicians*, 41(2): 112–120.

Schover, L. R., (1994). Sexuality and body image in younger women with breast cancer. *Journal of the National Cancer Institute Monographs*, 16: 177–182.

Takahashi, M. (2014) Psychosocial distress among young breast cancer survivors: implications for healthcare providers. *Breast Cancer*, 21(6): 664–669.

Thewes, B., Butow, P., Girgis, A., & Pendlebury, S. (2004). The psychosocial needs of breast cancer survivors: a qualitative study of the shared and unique needs of younger versus older survivors. *Psycho-Oncology*, 13: 177–189.

Thomas-MacLean, R. (2004). Memories of treatment: the immediacy of breast cancer. *Qualitative Health Research*, 14: 628–643.

Turner, L. J. (1999). Sexuality for breast cancer survivors: reconstructing sexual self-images. Unpublished doctoral thesis, University of Alberta, Canada.

Whitney, B. B. (1988). The impact of breast cancer and breast loss from mastectomy on the sexuality of single lesbian and heterosexual women. Unpublished doctoral thesis, New York University.

Wilmoth, M. C. (2001). The aftermath of breast cancer: an altered sexual self. *Cancer Nursing*, 24(4): 278–286.

Wurm, S., Tomasik, M. J., & Tesch-Romer, C. (2008). Serious health events and their impact on changes in subjective health and life satisfaction: the role of age and a positive view on ageing. *European Journal of Ageing*, 5: 117–127.

CHAPTER TWO

"I am losing my last chance at motherhood": an exploration of delayed childbirth, pregnancy loss, and involuntary childlessness

Amanda Sives

Introduction

Pregnancy loss has long been recognised as having potentially devastating impacts on women who desire to be biological mothers (Brier, 2008). In recent years, infertility and involuntary childlessness have been investigated and have been found to have a profound effect on women's identities and sense of purpose: the repercussions have been argued to be life-long (Black & Scull, 2005; Daniluk, 1996; Wirtberg et al., 2007). In addition, the higher age at which women have their first child has led to a growing interest in the reasons behind delayed parenthood (Tough et al., 2007). Despite the existence of a number of studies in these areas, no research has been undertaken which explores the relationship between the three issues. Given that recent figures highlight that one in five women in the UK are childless at age forty-five, compared to one in nine in 1946, it is clear that research is required to explore those experiences of childlessness (Office of National Statistics, 2013). While not all of these women will be involuntarily childless, a significant number will have faced the pain of pregnancy loss, have not fulfilled their desire to be a biological mother, and a growing number will have delayed childbirth until a later stage in life. Given that no specific research has been undertaken into the multiple losses experienced by this group of women, this chapter will provide a valuable insight into the range and depth of emotional impacts of postponing pregnancy, pregnancy loss, and involuntary childlessness, thereby facilitating a deeper understanding among the counselling community.

The central focus is the impact of loss, and while it is not the aim of this work to explore grief, it is important to highlight the specific nature of grief arising from pregnancy loss and involuntary childlessness. Although earlier studies of childlessness tended to draw on traditional models of bereavement (Houghton & Houghton, 1984; Monach, 1993), later studies have focused on the particular nature of grieving as "although the loss of an adult loved one is painful and sad, the loss of a longed for pregnancy is unique and needs to be recognized as such" (Jaffe & Diamond, 2011, p. 91). For the purposes of the discussion, grief surrounding pregnancy loss and involuntary childlessness will be assumed to be disenfranchised, defined by Doka as: "the grief that persons experience when they incur a loss that is not or cannot be openly acknowledged, publicly mourned or socially supported"(Doka, 1989, p. 4).

The aim of this chapter is to explore the impact of pregnancy loss(es) among a particular cohort of women: those who are childless and who experienced the loss(es) towards the end of their fertility. It seeks to examine the extent to which these women consciously delayed their pregnancies, which the literature appears to suggest is the case, and whether there are additional emotional impacts connected to these earlier choices when grieving the loss of biological children and motherhood. A key objective of the work is to provide space for the hidden losses to be heard and to be understood by others. Pregnancy loss and involuntary childlessness continue to be taboo subjects: social embarrassment, misunderstanding, and inappropriate "trying to be helpful" comments are common responses. In shedding light on the experience, through a small-scale phenomenological project, through the voices of six women who also seek to enhance awareness, I hope that the profound destabilising impact it can have will be better understood.

What the literature says

Three interrelated groups of literature shed light on the issues under investigation: postponing childbirth, pregnancy loss, and involuntary childlessness. Studies focusing on the delay in childbirth have expanded in recent years, reflecting, no doubt, the higher age at which women in western societies give birth to their first child. According to the Office for National Statistics (ONS), the average age for first birth in the UK in 2013 was thirty (ONS, 2014). In addition, women over thirty gave birth to 46% of babies in 2006, compared to 30% in 1986 (Tromans et al., 2008). Education and employment have been identified as the most significant factors delaying childbirth in a number of quantitative studies. These assume that women make conscious choices about their fertility and they do this in the context of wider employment opportunities and changing gender roles. In this altered social environment, postponing childbearing in order to complete a higher education and forge a career has been widely acknowledged to be significant in explaining the higher age first birth rate, although there is some disagreement about which is more significant (Bhrolchain & Beaujouan, 2012; Wu & MacNeill, 2002).

Research analysing the impact of education and work on childbirth tends to operate with the assumption that women have both a sufficient level of knowledge about their fertility and control over their reproductive capacity. Recent studies in Canada and the UK, however, demonstrate that men and women lack sufficient knowledge about fertility decline and assisted reproductive technology to make informed choices (e.g., Daniluk & Koert, 2013; Maheshwari, et al., 2008; Tough et al., 2007). In addition, in terms of control over fertility, while it is the case that women have more access to contraception and fertility treatment than ever before, this does not guarantee successful childbirth. A recent qualitative study has demonstrated that "women rarely make a conscious choice to delay pregnancy", and that women felt "that timing of childbearing depended on a complex interplay of factors which were outside of their control, such as relationship, health and fertility" (Cooke et al., 2012, p. 36).

There appears to be a dearth of literature about other factors that might lead to a delay in childbirth: one area that has been identified has been finding the right partner. In a survey of childless men and women who intended to have a child in the future, partner suitability was among the top four issues identified as significant in the decision-making process (Tough et al., 2007, p. 190). In a highly significant study of high-achieving career women in the USA, Hewlett draws attention to the difficulty of finding a partner with whom to have a child when a woman works in a high pressured and competitive environment (Hewlett, 2003). More recently, a qualitative study has explored the lived experience of women who delayed childbirth, and their findings suggested that "the biggest influence on childbearing decisions was the need to have the right partner" (Cooke et al., 2012, p. 34). This is the only study that could be located that looked at the specific experience of women who had delayed childbirth in the UK.

Since a ground-breaking study by Kennell and colleagues (1970) (cited in Dick & Wimpenny, 2012, p. 161), there has been a plethora of studies undertaken into the impact of pregnancy loss. They have ranged from examining the nature and length of grief, factors explaining the incidence of depression and anxiety, and post traumatic stress disorder (Badenhorst & Hughes, 2007; Engelhard et al., 2001; Kersting & Wagner, 2012; Leff, 1987; Lok & Neugebauer, 2007; Moulder, 1998; Neugebauer & Ritsher, 2005). Other studies have focused on specific cohorts, such as African-American women (Van & Meleis, 2003), adolescents (Tonelli, 2006), and male partners (Korenromp et al., 2005; McCreight, 2004). In addition, there are studies that compare the impact of different forms of pregnancy loss (Iles & Gath, 1993; Keefe-Cooperman, 2004–2005; Kersting et al., 2005) and pregnancy following previous pregnancy loss (Franche & Bulow, 1999; Geller et al., 2004; Petersen, 1994). These studies have been primarily quantitative in nature, used large cohort groups and a number of measurement scales, including specifically designed ones such as the Perinatal Grief Scale, the Perinatal Bereavement Grief Scale and the Perinatal Grief Intensity Scale (Brier, 2008). They have tended to focus on exploring the factors that are more likely to lead to complicated grief, anxiety, depression, or traumatic symptoms. These have been complemented by a smaller number of qualitative studies that have focused on a much smaller cohort group and tended to explore the perceptions and meanings of pregnancy loss as well as the coping strategies developed to manage the level of grief. There are no studies that explore delay, pregnancy loss, and childlessness.

While none of the published material explores delay, maternal age and childlessness are mentioned in research exploring the short- and longer-term impact of pregnancy loss. When maternal age has been factored into quantitative and qualitative studies, it has generally been found to be an insignificant element when assessing the propensity to suffer long-term consequences of pregnancy loss (Neugebauer et al., 1992). Indeed, Mann and colleagues argue, based on their quantitative study, that "increasing age was protective against both depressive symptoms and grief. Perhaps greater maturity is associated with more effective coping skills" (Mann et al., 2008, p. 277). Yet research by Swanson contradicts this. She notes from her clinical observations that "although a sense of loss is not tied to age, the experiences of threat or challenge or both are greater for older women who fear that their childbearing options are diminishing" (Swanson, 2000, p. 195).

Where previous studies do show a convergence, it is in the extent to which childlessness has an adverse impact on grief and depression following a miscarriage. Schwerdtfeger and Shreffler found that "women who have the dual experience of pregnancy loss and childlessness have the most fertility-related distress" (Schwerdtfeger & Shreffler, 2009, p. 222). In a study by Stirtzinger and colleagues, which examined the levels of grief of 175 women one year after a miscarriage, "women with no living children and over thirty years of age showed the most depressive symptomatology" (Stirtzinger et al., 1999–2000, p. 242). A study by Kersting and Wagner (2001) exploring complicated grief following a perinatal loss concurred with this finding, "childless women who suffer a miscarriage have significantly higher levels of grief than women who have children" (p. 189). This finding is supported in additional studies (Franche & Bulow, 1999; Friedman & Gath, 1989; Maker & Ogden, 2003; Neugebauer et al., 1992).

There is a vast range of publications exploring the experience of involuntary childlessness. In the vast majority of cases, these studies are qualitative, as they seek to explore the meanings attributed to childlessness. While there are a number of studies which focus solely on involuntary childlessness (e.g., Anton, 1992; Black & Scull, 2005; Cooper-Hilbert, 1998; Houghton & Houghton, 1984), a second group explores infertility and involuntary childlessness and includes the reasons why it occurs, the type and nature of medical interventions, the impact of childlessness, and how to cope (Cooper & Glazer, 1994; Daniluk, 2001; Menning, 1988; Monach, 1993; Pfeffer & Woollett, 1983). Given the constraints of space, I will focus on four of the key themes that emerge in the literature: the multi-layered nature of the loss, grieving, identity and adaptation.

Experiencing involuntary childlessness is multi-layered and complex: it is not only about the loss of a specific child, but, as Black and Scull (2005) point out, "it is the loss of everything the child represents for us" (p. 179). At its heart, it represents "the loss of one of the most fundamental and taken-for-granted choices, the bearing of children" (Monach, 1993, p. 181). The loss has impacts in multiple ways. Previous studies demonstrate some of the aspects: being pregnant and giving birth to life, giving unconditional love to children and grandchildren, being a mother and the connection it gives within wider society, genetic continuance, and the support of adult children in later life (Anton, 1992; Cooper-Hilbert, 1998; Houghton & Houghton, 1984).

A central aspect of grieving childlessness is its hidden nature. This is reflected in a number of studies. Anton explains "it is silent, hidden from all but the women who experience it" (Anton, 1992, p. 2). The unseen nature of the loss can make it difficult to acknowledge, or recognise, that the associated emotions are part of a grieving process. As Menning notes, "It is a strange and puzzling kind of grief . . . There is no funeral, no wake, no burial, no grave to lay the flowers on. And friends and family may never even know" (Menning, 1988, p. 116). The normal social conventions that define bereavement are absent in the case of childlessness and yet the feelings of grief can be overwhelming. The difficulty of sharing the loss can mean that "many of these women become isolated in their grief due to the loss of their existing supports, as others are often unable to tolerate the intensity of the experiences and to understand grief from a loss that is unrecognized" (Harris, 2011, p. 175).

The hidden nature of the grieving is compounded by the stigma associated with being childless in a pro-natalist society. Several authors comment on this aspect of the phenomenon. Alexander and colleagues' study of older women found that: "these women's regrets were shaped and formed in the context of a culture that defines womanhood predominantly through childbearing and that forces women to evaluate themselves continually against the pressure of this cultural prescription" (Alexander et al., 1992, p. 618). Given the pro-natalist pressures and social expectations, infertility is a "secret stigma" for many women who experience it (Whiteford & Gonzalez, 1995, p. 28). The sense of stigma implies a level of shame leading to involuntary childlessness being a taboo subject. As Jody Day, founder of Gateway Women, wrote in 2012, "like all taboos, the way its policed is that talking about it is seen as shameful and embarrassing" (Day, 2012, p. 86). The shame is associated with a strong sense of having failed as a woman: "the lived experience is all too often one of failure, the failure of the treatment and the failure of the woman" (Whiteford & Gonzalez, 1995, p. 35).

The impact on identity or sense of self can be devastating, particularly for women who have postponed childbearing as "generally, they are people who feel they have control over their lives, who believe that hard work and determination will produce desired results" (Glazer & Cooper, 1988, p. xx). Their inability to control their fertility and achieve the expected outcome is not only devastating but also strikes at the heart of a sense of self: it has been described as an "identity shock" (Matthews & Matthews, 1986, p. 645). For many women and their partners then, part of the grieving process involves rebuilding a central aspect of their identity, in many cases, as individuals and as a couple.

Several studies explore the process of moving forward from the despair of involuntary childlessness, either through the decision to stop infertility treatment or to terminate attempts to become pregnant through natural conception. A number of authors provide practical advice for those struggling to come to terms with their new reality. These include coping strategies in the short term, the creation of alternative nurturing outlets, and alternative parenting (Anton, 1992; Black & Scull, 2005; Daniluk, 2001; Day, 2012). Central to the process of moving forward seems to be being able to "reconstruct a meaningful life vision that did not include biological children. This reconstruction involved a re-evaluation of their beliefs, needs, and priorities" (Daniluk, 1996, p. 95). There is also an awareness of the likely long-term impact. This leads Letherby to argue that the process is one of adaptation to the new reality rather than resolution: "resolution is inappropriate not least because as the life course continues, 'infertility' and 'involuntary childlessness' may take on a different significance" (Letherby, 2002, p. 285). While the existing literature contains a wealth of information about pregnancy loss, involuntary childlessness, and, to a lesser extent, the impact of postponing pregnancy, there is no study which explores the relationship of all three.

Participants

Given that the issues under investigation were specific in nature, I undertook purposive sampling. My inclusion criteria were women who had experienced a pregnancy loss at a late stage of fertility (aged thirty-five plus), those who had delayed starting a family, were in a place to be able to reflect on their experiences, did not have a biological child, and were based in the UK and fluent in English. Six women, who fulfilled the criteria, participated in the research. Pseudonyms were agreed with each individual to ensure confidentiality (Table 2.1).

Data collection

Given the sensitive nature of the research, a qualitative research approach was utilised. Face-to-face semi-structured interviews were

Table 2.1. Details of participants in the research.

Name	Age	Summary of experience
Colette	47	Colette became pregnant at forty and miscarried at eleven weeks. She became pregnant for a second time at forty-one and went through labour at eighteen weeks. She took the decision at forty-three to stop trying to conceive.
Maria	44	Maria conceived naturally at thirty-five and miscarried. She went through four cycles of assisted reproduction but did not become pregnant again.
Sarah	46	Sarah became pregnant at forty and miscarried. She has not become pregnant again.
Sylvia	50	Sylvia had four cycles of assisted reproductive technology in her mid-thirties and became pregnant at age thirty-six on the final cycle. She miscarried. Following gynaecological problems, she had a hysterectomy.
Tessa	56	Tessa became pregnant at age thirty-six and miscarried. She became pregnant a second time at thirty-eight but had an ectopic pregnancy. Tessa has gone through the menopause.
Zaina	47	Zaina became pregnant at age forty-one. She miscarried at twelve weeks. She was diagnosed with endometriosis and has been taking a low dose contraceptive to help with the pain.

conducted in mutually convenient locations. The interviews were based on the following questions.

- Can you reflect on reasons why you delayed starting a family?
- When did you decide you wanted to try to get pregnant?
- Can you tell me about the process of trying to become pregnant?
- Can you tell me what happened?
- How would you describe the impact of the losses upon you?
- Can you tell me where you are now in relation to the specific loss(es) you experienced?
- Can you tell me how you feel knowing you will not give birth to your own child?

The interviews were digitally recorded, transcribed, and analysed. Informed consent was obtained and the participants had the opportunity to read through the transcript prior to the analysis stage.

Findings

Three superordinate themes were identified: each had three subordinate themes (Table 2.2).

Superordinate theme 1: Hope and loss

This theme emerged from the participants' experiences of deciding to become pregnant, being pregnant, and experiencing pregnancy loss. Hope was connected not only to the desire for a child with their partner, but also for a particular future as a mother. As well as grieving a specific pregnancy loss, therefore, participants also mourned the loss of an anticipated, expected future.

Table 2.2. Emerging themes.

Superordinate themes	Hope and loss	Isolation and belonging	Rewriting the future
Subordinate themes	Right time Intensity Shattered expectations	Hidden grief Hard to bear Connection	Self Control Living with loss

Subordinate theme 1.1: Right time

All of the participants spoke of their decision to start trying for a family in the context of it being the right time, albeit for different reasons. For four of the participants, the issue of central concern was finding the right partner. Colette explained, "So it was really meeting John and ... him pushing the question ... and then actually thinking yeah, maybe this is something I want to do." For the other participants, there had been a desire for a child prior to meeting their partner: "It had always just been, I was at some point going to have children and when I met my husband ... he triggered in me a really strong maternal instinct. I desperately wanted a child as soon as I met him" [Sylvia]. For Tessa and Maria, respectively, the timing was connected to career and financial stability. Tessa recalled, "Towards the end of my career, things changed and I thought, well, I am getting older, I would like a family and so now it's time to think about what I am going to do about this." For Maria, the issue was that "we didn't have much money ... we can't afford it" and so they delayed starting a family until they were financially secure.

Subordinate theme 1.2: Intensity

Intense emotional attachment was experienced throughout the process for all the participants. As Tessa noted, speaking of her second pregnancy: "Because I now knew what it was to imagine that thing inside you growing, the minute I knew I had conceived, I was imagining what size it was, its organs." Zaina talked about "the attachment you have right from the start when you find out." The level of attachment at the early stage of pregnancy was felt to be significant in making sense of the huge loss, at whatever stage of the pregnancy, as Sylvia explained, "With the miscarriage, the common thing that people say is, 'Well, how far gone were you?' And I wanted to say it doesn't bloody matter. The fact is that I lost something that you will never understand what it meant to me."

Powerful extremes of emotions were experienced. Tessa spoke of being "absolutely off the planet. I mean I kept redoing the pregnancy test every five minutes. I kept retouching my boobs to make sure they were sore. I couldn't believe it. Is it real? I was terrified something was going to go wrong." For Sylvia, who had experienced successive fertility treatments before becoming pregnant, the overwhelming feeling was fear: "I felt so precarious, everything was precarious when I was pregnant . . . I didn't want to move anywhere or do anything. I just wanted to stay safe." Zaina described her experience in stark terms: "It was devastating because we knew, well I knew, it was our only chance, you know, getting pregnant at forty, forty-one . . . I knew that and I just felt as if I had been given a gift, a miracle, but in fact, it wasn't, it was actually a curse."

Subordinate theme 1.3: Shattered expectations

Two of the participants married later in life and had been accepting of life without children until they became pregnant. Zaina explained, "I thought, OK, you know the child thing is off the menu because I haven't met anybody . . . and that is when I actually met my husband . . . and that's when I became pregnant, you know, and lost the baby. And I think that's when I struggled." Regardless of how and when the participants had come to the view that they would like a child, the expectation that it would occur became part of their imagined future. As Sarah explained, "When you are younger and you are expecting to have children, everything you think about your future includes children, just automatically, without really recognising that is what you are doing." The struggle to come to terms with the loss of that future was devastating for participants. Maria explained, "All I ever wanted to do was have a family and that hasn't happened."

Superordinate theme 2: Isolation and belonging

This theme emerged from a powerful sense of the participants' aloneness in the aftermath of pregnancy loss and childlessness. The feeling that nobody could understand their experience or the magnitude of their grief was overwhelming and compounded the pain of the losses. The hidden nature of the grief reinforced the sense of isolation. Many of the participants sought ways of connecting with others as a way of gaining support and validation.

Subordinate theme 2.1: Hidden grief

The intense pain of grief at the losses incurred was both confusing and hidden: there was nowhere to place it and participants struggled to name it. As Maria recalled, "It's something you lost but you never had and that is difficult to explain . . . how can you grieve it so much?" For Sarah, hearing Jody Day (Gateway Women) on the radio, "saying that it's grieving and I knew it was grieving but actually having someone say, you are grieving for your children . . . that sort of acknowledged how difficult it was which was really helpful. It didn't stop me being angry but it helped me understand, you know, why I was feeling the way I was feeling." As well as the confusion, there seemed to be no place for the grief, so it often remained hidden. As Tessa recalled, "So this awful, awful pain I went through—I can't tell you how many times I was crying before work because I didn't want to see other people's children; oh, it was awful." The experience of the participants powerfully suggests they struggled to recognise or name their grief. This was heightened by the fact that they felt their feelings were not acknowledged or validated by others.

Subordinate theme 2.2: Hard to bear

While seeing other women pregnant was difficult, participants spoke of being able to distance themselves if the friends were not particularly close: it was much harder with good friends and family. As Tessa remarked in relation to her close friend's pregnancy, "And, you know, I am very happy for her, but I went backwards . . . because I just had a complete relapse into that uncomfortable place." Zaina, whose sister-in-law was pregnant at the time of the research, explained she "didn't want to engage in the 'oh, how is she doing? How many months is she?' I don't even know how many months pregnant she is because I just didn't want to know." For Maria, it was her cousin's pregnancy that helped her to become aware of the depth of her own grief: "I kept thinking that should be me. I am eleven years older than her and that should be me and it affected me a lot, so much that I couldn't see her. It brought everything back . . . it actually hit me very, very hard."

Subordinate theme 2.3: Connection

The sense of "massive isolation" [Colette] was a strong element in the testimony of many of the participants. For the two participants whose husbands had had children from a previous marriage, there was an honest recognition that they could not understand the depth of their partner's grief: as Sarah remarked, "Although my husband is really supportive and lovely, he would admit I don't really understand because I have got the boys." All of the participants, with the exception of Tessa, whose marriage broke down, spoke of how the experience of loss had strengthened their relationship. As Maria explained, "It was very, very difficult and I think we have got a strong marriage anyway and I think it only strengthened it going through that . . . it did gel us together even more." Despite the support and love of their husbands, many of the participants felt that no one really understood what they were going through. As Sylvia poignantly recalled, "I needed someone to hear me and I think that is the thing, that the whole way through the process, there wasn't really anybody who could understand." Zaina described her experience with her family: "But all they asked was, 'Are you OK?' and I said, 'Well, no, not really, it's quite hard' and then it just goes quiet and the conversation starts about something else . . . because I think they were embarrassed. They didn't know what to say." The isolating experience with family and friends enhanced the desire among a number of participants to find a connection with others who could understand the multi-layered sense of loss. Four participants mentioned online communities as supportive. Colette talked about desperately seeking a place where her experience would make sense and her relief in finding it: "It was really helpful to me to hear other people, kind of just their stories and feeling that I wasn't alone and that other people knew how I felt."

Superordinate theme 3: Rewriting the future

This theme emerged as participants reflected on how their pregnancy loss had affected them, how they had struggled to cope with the new reality of their lives and, in some cases, how they had begun gently to step into a different future. The subordinate themes engage with the complex emotions felt as the past is relinquished and a new, unexpected future is tentatively approached.

Subordinate theme 3.1: Self

This subordinate theme emerged in three different guises throughout the research. Participants spoke about the loss of self, how they protected themselves, and how they were changed by their experience. The loss of self was inextricably linked with a sense of failure: as Sylvia noted, "I felt as if I had failed at the most... profound and fundamental level, at being a woman." Tessa explained, "I am still the only person I know who wanted a baby and didn't get one... because actually the few people I know who had problems, they managed it." The loss of identity, the questioning of one's purpose and role in life is encapsulated in Sarah's comment: "If I am not a mother, why am I here?"

Part of the grieving process participants described related to the development of strategies (conscious or otherwise) to protect themselves. Tessa, whose job involves working with children, spoke about how she had "anaesthetised myself to the pain" and developed a "thick skin". Colette is aware that while she has moved on, the "one thing I still can't do is I can't go to a baby shower... This is just too painful to contemplate." The ability to find ways of coping with the reality of pregnancies appeared to be about survival and recognition that "the world is going to keep getting pregnant" [Zaina].

For those who have emerged from the rawness of their grief, there was a sense of a changed, different self. Sarah, who explained, "You go through the fire and all the extraneous bits are burnt away and you are left with the essence, you are left with you", most powerfully recounted this. Other participants spoke about recognising that, despite their grief, they were able to take on new challenges. Sylvia explained, "I also feel quite free. There is a part of me which feels I wouldn't be able to do the things I am doing now, um, if I had had children." The creative aspect of the different self was significant for three of the participants. Several spoke about the growing and deepening level of empathy they felt had developed as a result of experiencing their losses: as Colette explained, "I know what it means to have your heart broken... I know what it means because I had all of those physical sensations along with the emotions but it does mean, I hope, that I can use that to support people." Using the experience of their own pain to help others was also recognised by Sylvia, "I think it is healing and maybe it is healing for me as well knowing that maybe I can make a difference in some way."

Subordinate theme 3.2: Control

Part of moving through grief for the participants was about retaking some control over their bodies and their future. This was related to the significant feeling of losing control engendered by the experience of pregnancy and loss. As Sylvia recalled in relation to her cycles of fertility treatment, it was "as if it was lurching from one attempt to the next of treatment . . . I was living from one attempt to the next. It was the only hope I saw." Sarah described it as being out of control: "And I knew it wasn't healthy but I couldn't do anything. I didn't know what to do to get it under control . . . it was like a sort of raging beast almost, I couldn't think about anything else." Feelings of powerlessness also emerged when reflecting on the loss, as Sylvia recounted: "I remember shouting 'stop this, please stop this' and of course, there is nothing you can do." In recounting her loss, Colette spoke about her disbelief: "You felt you were in a, in a theatre play or a soap opera . . . You were acting something out. It wasn't real and any minute the credits were going to roll and the world was going to go back to normal."

Regaining some control was a significant element for those participants who were in a position to make a decision. Colette explained, "Well, we made the decision, because it had been four years of just stress and pain and torture." Sarah spoke in similar terms: "I realised very strongly that I couldn't just wait to have children and not do anything else." For Sylvia, taking control freed her to accept her emotions: "I decided to take charge of it rather than coasting and that makes me feel as if the anger that I have from time to time is OK." Tessa was able to retake control through focusing on her passion for her work: "I think where I am fortunate over many other women is that I did have a career, a vocation, something I still enjoy." She described it as her "anchor" and her "saviour".

Subordinate theme 3.3: Living with loss

Many of the participants knew they had experienced movement away from the raw stage of grief. For Sylvia, "Rather than a searing knife wound that I used to feel, I feel a kind of hmm, it's like something pressing, it's like a fist pressing in my, you know, inside." The journey metaphor was used by two of the participants. As Sarah stated, "I do still get upset yes, but I know that I am sort of several miles further down the road." Colette talked about having reached "landmarks" in her grieving journey as she recognised her growing ability to cope with her grief.

The struggle to move forward is captured by Colette's description of "cycling through mud" and Sylvia's view that it was like "wading through treacle". An additional element of living with the loss is that the participants recognised the pain of childlessness is likely to re-emerge in a different guise in the future. Anxieties were expressed around grandchildren: "The grandmother thing is probably going to be quite a big thing" [Colette]. For Maria, there is a concern about "What's going to happen when we get old, we are not going to have anyone so it sort of rolls on, it's this constantly roll on effect because it affects everything." While participants recognised their grief had "changed shape" [Sylvia], there was a poignant awareness that it would be a life-long companion.

Bringing together the literature and the findings

Findings indicated that postponing pregnancy was not a conscious choice for the majority of the participants: the desire to have a child with the right partner was the core explanation for the delay in starting a family. Having a child was not seen to be a decision that had been consciously postponed, but one which had not happened until later in life due to reasons outside of their control: in this context, there were very few regrets. These findings concur with Cooke and colleagues, whose recent qualitative study demonstrated both the lack of control women felt in their own reproductive process and the need to find the right partner (Cooke et al., 2012). Of the two respondents who had made a conscious choice to postpone pregnancy, only Maria expressed some regrets for delaying for financial reasons. However, she countered this by explaining she and her husband had wanted to be responsible and provide for their child. Tessa was the only participant who had delayed pregnancy due to her career: this was primarily for the physical impact pregnancy could have had on her dancing. She did not express regrets, but accepted the choices she had made to focus on her career at an earlier age. These findings contradict the majority of studies which suggest education and careers are the predominant reasons why women postpone pregnancy (Bhrolchain & Beaujouan, 2012; Wu & MacNeill, 2002).

The intense emotions experienced by participants on finding they were pregnant and then experiencing loss is discussed in previous studies, although these have tended to focus on the shock of the loss (Maker & Ogden, 2003). Given that participants had often struggled to become pregnant, the combination of joy and fear is understandable. In particular, the findings demonstrate the fear of loss expressed by the participants, who were aware of the precariousness of their pregnancy, due either to age or fertility challenges. While this aspect is generally not covered in the literature, Swanson does recognise there might be additional concerns experienced by older women who are trying to become pregnant (Swanson, 2000). This study demonstrates there is an additional layer of emotional intensity for pregnant women who are childless and, due to their age, aware of limited future chances of successful conception.

The intensity of attachment to the growing foetus was a strong factor in the level of grief experienced by the participants. This is supported in the literature (Hutti, 1992; Peppers, 1989; Robinson et al., 1999; Shreffler et al., 2011). Given the maternal age and childless status of the participants, the additional meaning inherent in, and hope for, a positive outcome suggests further devastation is experienced when the pregnancy is lost. While previous studies have noted the grief experienced by childless women who suffer a pregnancy loss, they have not considered the double impact of advanced maternal age and childlessness. These findings suggest an additional level of grief when women do not have the opportunity to conceive another child. As Bansen and Stevens found in their study of women who experienced a miscarriage, "several women were at least reassured by the fact that they had been pregnant and thus believed they would be able to conceive again" (Bansen & Stevens, 1992, p. 88). This option is usually not available to older women.

Participants' awareness that their pregnancy losses at the end of fertility signified a future childless status shattered expectations about how their lives would unfold. This was the case even for those women who had reconciled themselves to being childless until they became unexpectedly pregnant. Previous studies of involuntary childlessness have discussed the extent to which it affects identity, confidence, and assumptions about the world (Daniluk, 2001; Pfeffer & Woollett, 1983). In addition, these findings suggest the need to explore the impact as traumatic. This perspective could provide insight into the multi-levelled nature of the loss and consequent readjustments required to construct a meaningful future. While pregnancy loss has been studied in relation to post traumatic stress (Engelhard et al., 2001), the same lens has not been applied to the double impact of pregnancy loss and childlessness (Schwerdtfeger & Shreffler, 2009). Janoff-Bulman's work could provide insight in this regard. He argues that trauma shatters three core assumptions that the majority of people hold to be the case: the world is benevolent (generally, people believe the world is a good place), the world is meaningful (there is a relationship between a person and what happens to him or her), and the self is worthy (Janoff-Bulman, 1992, p. 6). The experience of pregnancy loss and involuntary childlessness can shatter assumptions on all three levels and, in doing so, call into question issues of self, justice, order, and meaning.

The findings concur with previous research that grief is an expected outcome of pregnancy loss (Lok & Neugebauer, 2007). In line with other studies, the participants' experience also demonstrates the disenfranchised nature of the grief (Anton, 1992; Cooper & Glazer, 1994; Cooper-Hilbert, 1998; Daniluk, 1996). Given the continuing taboo surrounding both pregnancy loss and childlessness, the participants experienced real challenges in being able to name their grief and openly acknowledge it in an environment where it could be heard and understood. Sylvia's comment that there "was no place for it" highlights the confusion and despair arising from the experience. While many of the participants could share their feelings with their partners, there was a real desire to find other women who could truly understand the depth of their pain. The sense of disappointment that those closest, particularly family members, were unable to understand, were embarrassed, or made inappropriate comments, added significantly to the sense of being alone in their grief. This sense of isolation and embarrassment is recognised in previous studies (Bagchi & Friedman, 1999; Bansen & Stevens, 1992; Daniluk, 1996). The need for participants to have some acknowledgement of the intense emotional impact of their loss was a strong theme emerging from the research. Although other studies have recognised this, it appears that the taboo which surrounds pregnancy loss and involuntary childlessness continues to silence women in their pain (Corbet-Owen, 2003).

The challenges that participants faced when a family member or close friend became pregnant have been discussed in previous studies (Cooper & Glazer, 1994; Houghton & Houghton, 1984). However, the findings demonstrate more specifically how a close friend or family pregnancy can have an impact on a woman's grief and loss: for Maria, Colette, and Tessa, it acted as a trigger for them to recognise or re-access their own pain. In this sense, the findings demonstrate the lingering pain of childlessness and the difficulty of negotiating the pain within the context of family and close friends.

The desire for understanding and connection emerged very strongly from the participants' experience of isolation: these findings are supported by previous studies (Corbet-Owen, 2003; Van, 2012–2013). Forums where women could share their stories, find others who understood their pain, or where they could support other women, were very beneficial for Colette, Tessa, and Maria. This is supported by two other studies which found internet forums to be supportive arenas for women dealing with pregnancy losses (Lafarge et al., 2013; Sejourne et al., 2010). The forums seemed to provide a space where it was possible for participants to break their silence, knowing that those hearing their voice would not feel awkward or offer inappropriate and ultimately unhelpful comments: a sense of belonging appears to have been gained via the online communities.

These findings demonstrate how pregnancy loss and involuntary childlessness strike at the heart of how the participants perceived themselves. There was a profound sense of having failed as a woman because they were not able to give birth to their child. Terms used by the participants, such as "not real", "not worthy", "non-identity", point to a sense of an incomplete self. For women who are used to having control over the direction of their lives, the experience of failing at what appears to be the most natural and basic role of a woman, to be a biological mother, was deeply destabilising. This sense of personal failure is inextricably connected to wider social norms: as Ireland writes, "there is an implicit assumption that motherhood is intrinsic to adult female identity. This assumption necessarily implies an 'absence' for any women who is not then not a mother" (Ireland, 1993, p. 1). The sense of personal failure is compounded by Zaina's feeling of "not belonging" in wider society, or, as Sylvia described it, being "on the edge".

All of the participants spoke movingly of their attempts to protect themselves from the pain of their losses and the reality of other women's pregnancies and children. Deeply aware of their vulnerability, all of the participants recalled moments when they had had to withdraw in order to survive emotionally. They were also aware there are still situations that are too painful to contemplate. Reflecting on these participants' experiences demonstrates that even in the midst of an existential life crisis, an aspect of the self is able to access internal resources and strength as part of developing resilience and retaking some measure of control. While other studies discuss coping strategies, these findings demonstrate how women intuitively know what is manageable at different moments in their grieving process and they seek to ensure they do not push themselves beyond what they can cope with.

That growth comes from grief and pain is acknowledged in literature on bereavement and loss (Attig, 2011). What emerges from the findings is the sense that those participants who were sufficiently far enough along in their grieving processes had worked hard to find some meaning in their experience of loss: Colette's determination to ensure it was not a "waste of an experience" profoundly demonstrates this. The emotional turmoil was described as having led to the development of deeper empathy with others who were in pain, although both Colette and Sarah rejected the view that this was the "purpose" of their experience. Being able to support other women in the midst of their suffering was important to Tessa, Colette, and Sylvia, to ensure other women were not so isolated in their loss. Another aspect of offering this support appeared to be connected to having an opportunity to validate their own losses and integrate the experiences into their changed self: this was openly acknowledged by Sylvia. Colette, Sarah, Sylvia, and Tessa spoke about how they had been able to view their childless status as bringing some benefits to their lives, allowing them to know themselves more deeply and, on a practical level, freeing their time and ability to explore other aspects of themselves, especially in the creative arena. Arriving at this place had clearly taken time and a great deal of reflection, whether alone, with other women, or through counselling: it had been a struggle, as Colette's metaphor of "cycling through mud" graphically demonstrates. These women demonstrate the amount of grief work that is required to move out of the pain of loss into a new reality.

Studies of infertility highlight the overwhelming loss of control experienced by women who are trying to conceive naturally or through medical intervention (Houghton & Houghton, 1984). These findings support previous research and highlight the total feeling of powerlessness and helplessness the participants felt in the face of their inability to conceive or to stop the pregnancy loss. Sarah defined her lack of control as a "raging beast" within her, powerfully suggesting her total inability to control what was happening to her: it is as if she was possessed. Colette's description of her pregnancy losses suggests her sense of disorientation: these heart-breaking experiences were not part of her life script. For older women, many of whom have educational or career successes behind them, the loss of control can be more disempowering than for younger women: this is particularly the case when there is an awareness that this is likely to be the final chance to be a biological mother. This came through strongly in the research, confirming the challenge of dealing with a multi-layered sense of loss.

Taking control was an important aspect of the grieving process and this has been recognised in previous studies (Pfeffer & Woollett, 1983). For Colette, the decision was framed as a positive one: it was ending a process of "stress and pain and torture". Sarah and Sylvia knew they had to regain control in order to survive and move forward. Doing so freed their energy to be able to contemplate a different future and, in Sylvia's case, allows her to accept her anger when it re-emerges. Tessa had a slightly different experience: her career had always been a central aspect of her life and when she had to face the reality of a childless future, she had an alternative future already in place. She acknowledged her "luck" in having this option available.

Living with loss involves acknowledging the extent of the pain and finding ways to integrate it within the self. While participants were at different stages in their grieving process, they all acknowledged that it continued to have an impact on them in different ways. The physicality of the pain was mentioned by Sylvia and Colette, who also acknowledged they knew their pain was diminishing because the physical sensations were less intense. Having an awareness of how the grief shaped their responses and lives was evident from all the participants, as was the recognition of how hard they had had to work to move through the grieving process. As well as integrating the loss, participants were also aware that their childlessness might re-emerge in different guises in their futures. Colette, Sylvia, Tessa, and Maria all mentioned their concerns about how they would feel when their peers became grandparents. Research undertaken by Wirtberg and colleagues with women twenty years after unsuccessful fertility treatment demonstrates the painful impact of being "grandchildless" (Wirtberg et al., 2007, p. 602). These findings confirm Letherby's argument that infertility and involuntary childlessness is not resolved, but, rather, "adaptation" takes place (Letherby, 2002).

Conclusion

This chapter has contributed to deepening an understanding of the existential crisis that faces women who experience pregnancy loss at an advanced maternal age and remain childless. The findings are based on the lived experience of six women who bravely recalled a deeply painful time in their lives. While they have each had unique experiences, a set of common themes has been distilled. This process necessarily leads to omissions in that it cannot capture the nuances of their individual journeys. What it has done, however, is shed light on a taboo issue and, in doing so, raised awareness of the grief and pain associated with these hidden and multiple losses. A number of significant findings have emerged. First, the women in this study did not consciously delay childbirth, but, rather, they waited for the right person with whom they wished to have a child. This finding is a departure from previous studies that assume delay is connected to conscious choices around career and education. Delaying childbirth, given that it is not a conscious choice, therefore does not seem to have additional impacts on the depth and nature of the losses experienced. Second, the experience of pregnancy is fraught with emotional turmoil for childless older women: they desire to become biological mothers, feel they might have achieved their aim when they become pregnant, only to experience the devastation of the loss. Acknowledging that childless women of advanced maternal age experience additional fears about their pregnancy is a significant finding. Third, being childless is a lifelong state. The rawness of grief usually recedes but it is replaced by a lingering sadness and an awareness of the need to self-protect: all of the participants were aware that pain is likely be triggered in the future. The study highlights that while it is possible to move from devastating loss to a place of calm, growth, and healing, it is a huge struggle that takes strength, determination, and time. Being able to find a renewed sense of purpose and accept the new reality of the present and the future can emerge from the disappointment and pain.

A number of implications for practice emerge. First, it is essential that women are offered access to good counsellors, preferably those who have an understanding of fertility-related distress. A number of participants were not offered any form of professional support following their pregnancy loss, which led to further isolation. Having access is seen to be even more significant given the continuing social awkwardness that surrounds pregnancy loss and childlessness. Second, raising awareness of the existential pain associated with losing a pregnancy and involuntary childlessness could enhance practice: the need for women who are going through this emotional turmoil to be acknowledged and heard is vital. Facilitating women to access and name their grief, to recognise that their feelings are valid, and to hear the multiple levels upon which loss can be felt is a significant aspect in the healing process. On a final, practical note, sharing information with clients about the online support forums could facilitate the process of healing and recovery.

References

Alexander, B. B., Rubenstein, R. L., Goodman, M., & Luborsky, M. (1992). A path not taken: a cultural analysis of regrets and childlessness in the lives of older women. *The Gerontologist, 32*(5): 618–626.

Anton, L. H. (1992). *Never to be a Mother. A Guide for all Women Who Didn't—or Couldn't—Have Children*. New York: HarperCollins.

Attig, T. (2011). *How We Grieve. Relearning the World*. Oxford: Oxford University Press.

Badenhorst, W., & Hughes, P. (2007). Psychological aspects of perinatal loss. *Best Practice and Research Clinical Obstetrics and Gynaecology, 21*(2): 249–259.

Bagchi, D., & Friedman, T. (1999). Psychological aspects of spontaneous and recurrent abortion. *Current Obstretics and Gynaecology, 9*: 9–22.

Bansen, S. S., & Stevens, H. A. (1992). Women's experiences of miscarriage in early pregnancy. *Journal of Nurse-Midwifery, 37*(2): 84–90.

Bhrolchain, M., & Beaujouan, E. (2012). Fertility postponement is largely due to rising educational enrolment. *Population Studies: A Journal of Demography, 66*(3): 311–327.

Black, R., & Scull, L. (2005). *Beyond Childlessness. For Every Woman Who Wanted To Have a Child and Didn't*. London: Rodale International.

Brier, N. (2008). Grief following miscarriage: a comprehensive review of the literature. *Journal of Women's Health, 17*(3): 451–464.

Cooke, A., Mills, T. A., & Lavender, T. (2012). Advanced maternal age: delayed childbearing is rarely a conscious choice. A qualitative study of women's views and experiences. *International Journal of Nursing Studies, 49*: 30–39.

Cooper, S. L., & Glazer, E. S. (1994). *Beyond Infertility. The New Paths to Parenthood.* Lanham, MD: Lexington Books.

Cooper-Hilbert, B. (1998). *Infertility and Involuntary Childnessness. Helping Couples Cope.* New York: W. W. Norton.

Corbet-Owen, C. (2003). Women's perception of partner support in the context of pregnancy loss(es). *South African Journal of Psychology, 33*(1): 19–27.

Daniluk, J. C. (1996). When treatment fails: the transition to biological childlessness for infertile women. *Women and Therapy, 19*(2): 81–98.

Daniluk, J. C. (2001). *The Infertility Survival Guide. Everything You Need to Cope with the Challenges while Maintaining Your Sanity, Dignity and Relationships.* Oakland, CA: New Harbinger.

Daniluk, J. C., & Koert, E. (2013). The other side of the fertility coin: a comparison of childless men's and women's knowledge of fertility and assisted reproductive technology. *Fertility and Sterility, 99*(3): 839–846.

Day, J. (2012). *Rocking the Life Unexpected. 12 Weeks to Your Plan B for a Meaningful and Fulfilling Life without Children.* Seattle, Washington DC: Createspace.

Dick, E., & Wimpenny, P. (2012). Perinatal bereavement. In: P. Wimpenny & J. Costello (Eds.), *Grief, Loss and Bereavement: Evidence and Practice for Health and Social Care Practitioners* (pp. 160–174). London: Routledge.

Doka, K. (1989). *Disenfranchised Grief. Recognising Hidden Sorrow.* Lanham, MD: Lexington Books.

Engelhard, I. M., Hout, M. A., & Arntz, A. (2001). Posttraumatic stress disorder after pregnancy loss. *General Hospital Psychiatry, 23*: 62–66.

Franche, R.-L., & Bulow, C. (1999). The impact of a subsequent pregnancy on grief and emotional adjustment following a perinatal loss. *Infant Mental Health Journal, 20*(2): 175–187.

Friedman, T., & Gath, D. (1989). The psychiatric consequences of spontaneous abortion. *British Journal of Psychiatry, 155*: 810–813.

Geller, P. A., Kerns, D., & Klier, C. M. (2004). Anxiety following miscarriage and the subsequent pregnancy: a review of the literature and future directions. *Journal of Psychosomatic Research, 56*: 35–45.

Glazer, E. S., & Cooper, S. L. (1988). *Without Child. Experiencing and Resolving Infertility.* Lanham, MD: Lexington Books.

Harris, D. L. (2011). Infertility and reproductive loss. In: D. L. Harris (Ed.), *Counting Our Losses: Reflecting on Change, Loss and Transition in Everyday Life* (pp. 171–181). New York: Routledge.
Hewlett, S. A. (2003). *Creating a Life. What Every Woman Needs To Know About Having a Baby and a Career*. New York: Miramax
Houghton, D., & Houghton, P. (1984). *Coping with Childlessness*. London: George Allen and Unwin.
Hutti, M. H. (1992). Parents' perceptions of the miscarriage experience. *Death Studies, 16*: 401–415.
Iles, S., & Gath, D. (1993). Psychiatric outcome of termination of pregnancy for foetal abnormality. *Psychological Medicine, 23*(2): 407–413.
Ireland, M. S. (1993). *Reconceiving Women. Separating Motherhood from Female Identity*. New York: Guildford Press.
Jaffe, J., & Diamond, M. O. (2011). *Reproductive Trauma: Psychotherapy with Infertility and Pregnancy Loss Clients*. Washington, DC: American Psychological Association.
Janoff-Bulman, R. (1992). *Shattered Assumptions. Towards a New Psychology of Trauma*. New York: Free Press.
Keefe-Cooperman, K. (2004–2005). A comparison of grief as related to miscarriage and termination for fetal abnormality. *Omega, 50*(4): 281–300.
Kennell, J. H., Slyter, H., & Klaus, M. H. (1970). The mourning response of parents to the death of a newborn infant. *New England Journal of Medicine, 283*(7): 344–349.
Kersting, D. M., & Wagner, B. (2012). Complicated grief after perinatal loss. *Dialogues in Clinical Neuroscience, 14*: 187–194.
Kersting, D. M., Kreulich, C., Reutemann, M., Ohrmann, P., Baez, E., & Arolt, V. (2005). Trauma and grief 2–7 years after termnation of pregnancy because of fetal anomalies – a pilot study. *Journal of Psychosomatic Obstetrics and Gynaecology, 26*(1): 9–14.
Korenromp, M. J., Page-Christiaens, G. C. M. L., van den Bout, J., Mulder, E. J. H., Hunfeld, J. A. M., Bilardo, C. M., Offermans, J. P. M., & Visser, G. H. A. (2005). Psychological consequences of termination of pregnancy for fetal anomaly: similarities and differences between partners. *Prenatal Diagnosis, 25*: 1226–1233.
Lafarge, C., Mitchell, K., & Fox, P. (2013). Women's experiences of coping with pregnancy termination for fetal abnormality. *Qualitative Health Research, 23*(7): 924–936.
Leff, P. T. (1987). Here I am Ma: the emotional impact of pregnancy loss on parents and health-care professionals. *Family Systems Medicine, 5*(1): 105–114.

Letherby, G. (2002). Challenging dominant discourses: identity and change and the experience of 'infertility' and 'involuntary childlessness'. *Journal of Gender Studies*, 11(3): 277–288.

Lok, I. H., & Neugebauer, R. (2007). Psychological morbidity following miscarriage. *Best Practice and Research Clinical Obstetrics and Gynaecology*, 21(2): 229–247.

Maheshwari, A., Porter, M., Shetty, A., & Bhattacharya, S. (2008). Women's awareness and perception of delay in childbearing. *Fertility and Sterility*, 90(4): 1036–1042.

Maker, C., & Ogden, J. (2003). The miscarriage experience: more than just a trigger to psychological morbidity? *Psychology and Health*, 18(3): 403–415.

Mann, J. R., McKeown, R. E., Bacon, J., Vesselinov, R., & Bush, F. (2008). Predicting depressive symptoms and grief after pregnancy loss. *Journal of Psychosomatic Obstetrics and Gynecology*, 29(4): 274–279.

Matthews, R., & Matthews, A. M. (1986). Infertility and involuntary childlessness: the transition to nonparenthood. *Journal of Marriage and the Family*, 48: 641–649.

McCreight, B. S. (2004). A grief ignored: narratives of pregnancy loss from a male perspective. *Sociology of Health and Illness*, 26(3): 326–350.

Menning, B. E. (1988). *Infertility. A Guide for the Childless Couple* (2nd edn). New York: Prentice Hall Press.

Monach, J. H. (1993). *Childless: No Choice. The Experience of Involuntary Childlessness*. London: Routledge.

Moulder, C. (1998). *Understanding Pregnancy Loss. Perspectives and Issues in Care*. Basingstoke: Macmillan.

Neugebauer, R., & Ritsher, J. (2005). Depression and grief following early pregnancy loss. *International Journal of Childbirth Education*, 20(3): 21–24.

Neugebauer, R., Kline, J., O'Connor, P., Shrout, P., Johnson, J., Skodol, A., Wicks, J., & Susser, M. (1992). Determinants of depressive symptoms in the early weeks after miscarriage. *American Journal of Public Health*, 82(10): 1332–1339.

Office of National Statistics (December 2013). Cohort Fertility, 2012. Available at www.ons.gov.uk/ons/dcp171778_340636.pdf.

Office of National Statistics (2014). Births in England and Wales, 2013. Available at www.ons.gov.uk/ons/dcp17171778_371129.pdf.

Peppers, L. G. (1989). Grief and elective abortion: implications for the counselor. In: K. J. Doka (Ed.), *Disenfranchised Grief: Recognising Hidden Sorrow* (pp. 135–147). Lanham, MD: Lexington Books.

Petersen, G. (1994). Chains of grief: the impact of perinatal loss on subsequent pregnancy. *Pre and Perinatal Psychology Journal*, 9(2): 149–158.

Pfeffer, N., & Woollett, A. (1983). *The Experience of Infertility*. London: Virago.
Robinson, M., Baker, L., & Nackerud, L. (1999). The relationship of attachment theory and perinatal loss. *Death Studies*, 23: 257–270.
Schwerdtfeger, K. L., & Shreffler, K. M. (2009). Trauma of pregnancy loss and infertility among mothers and involuntarily childless women in the United States. *Journal of Loss and Trauma*, 14: 211–227.
Sejourne, N., Callahan, S., & Chabrol, H. (2010). Support following miscarriage: what women want. *Journal of Reproductive and Infant Psychology*, 28(4): 403–411.
Shreffler, K.M., Greil, A. L., & McQuillan, J. (2011). Pregnancy loss and distress among US women. *Family Relations*, 60: 342–355.
Stirtzinger, R., Robinson, G., Stewart, D., & Ravelski, E. (1999–2000). Parameters of grieving in spontaneous abortion. *International Journal of Pyschiatry in Medicine*, 29(2): 235–249.
Swanson, K. M. (2000). Predicting depressive symptoms after miscarriage: a path analysis based on the Lazarus Paradigm. *Journal of Women's Health and Gender-Based Medicine*, 9(2): 191–206.
Tonelli, M.. (2006). Perinatal loss and adolescents. *Journal of Pediatric Adolescent Gynaecology*, 19: 247–248.
Tough, S., Tofflemore, K., Benzies, K., Fraser-Lee, N., & Newburn-Cook, C. (2007). Factors influencing childbearing decisions and knowledge of perinatal risks among Canadian men and women. *Maternal Child Health Journal*, 11: 189–198.
Tromans, N., Natamba, E., Jeffries, J., & Norman, P. (2008). Have national trends in fertility between 1986 and 2006 occurred evenly across England and Wales? *Population Trends*, 133: 7–19.
Van, P. (2012–2013). Conversations, coping and connectedness: a qualitative study of women who have experienced involuntary pregnancy loss. *Omega*, 65(1): 71–85.
Van, P., & Meleis, A. I. (2003). Coping with grief after involuntary pregnancy loss: perspectives of African American women. *Journal of Obstetric, Gynaecologic and Neonatal Nursing*, 32(1): 28–39.
Whiteford, L. M., & Gonzalez, L. (1995). Stigma: the hidden burden of infertility. *Social Science and Medicine*, 40(1): 27–36.
Wirtberg, I., Moller, A., Hogstrom, L., Tronstad, S.-E., & Lalos, A. (2007). Life 20 years after unsuccessful infertility treatment. *Human Reproduction*, 22(2): 598–604.
Wu, Z., & MacNeill, L. (2002). Education, work and childbearing after 30. *Journal of Comparative Family Studies*, 33(2): 191–213.

CHAPTER THREE

If only: adult reflections on being an only child

Caroline Fletcher

Introduction

What is it like to go through life as an only child? How does this single biographical fact shape people's lives and the way in which they view the world? My central research question is: for counsellors who are only children, how has the experience of growing up without siblings affected their view of themselves, their relationships, and their approach to counselling practice? In this chapter, I explore the lived experience of being an only child, trying to understand the thoughts and feelings of individuals as they reflect upon what being an only child means to them.

My study poses a number of supplementary questions to the central research question, including: what impact do stereotypes and external assumptions about only children have on the self-concept? I also explore connections between only child experience and counselling. While looking for common themes, I have tried to capture the "essence" (Smith et al., 2009) of the experience and to honour the uniqueness and complexity of individual lives.

McLeod (2011, p. 182) talks of the personal nature of qualitative research. In my study, the choice of topic, as well as the approach, is essentially personal: I am an only child, the daughter of an only child, and the mother of an only child. As I trained to become a counsellor, the "only child" element of my personal history came into sharper focus, leading me to question its meaning more deeply. It was part of an unfolding process of increasing self-knowledge and self-awareness that is "integral" (Rose, 2012) to counsellor training. Rogers (1961) talks of the tension between the internal and external locus of evaluation and I wondered about the meaning of external evaluation for only children when the identity of "only child" is the subject of external assumptions and generalisations that seem to ossify into stereotypes (Falbo, 2012). Does this hinder the nurturing of what Rogers describes as the "organismic self"? It certainly seemed to be connected to my own reluctance to admit to others the fact that I was an only child, and to a defensiveness that persisted despite my perception that external assumptions were wide of the mark. It seemed like an altogether misplaced sense of shame, and I wanted to explore further what the personal experience (and external evaluations or stereotypes) had meant for others who had been brought up, and continue to live, without siblings. I came to believe that trying to understand the real lived experience of those who grew up without siblings was, in itself, a valid and fruitful subject for psychological research as "an attempt to understand more adequately the human condition as it manifests itself in lived, concrete experience" (Spinelli, 2005, p. 131).

This chapter, therefore, aims to explore in depth the personal lived experience of counsellors who are only children and to reach an understanding of what it means for each individual to be an only child, hoping that the exploration will offer a further insight into the human condition. I hope, too, that capturing the essence of this experience might challenge some of the formulaic, socially conditioned ideas about only children.

What the literature says

I was surprised at the sheer volume of literature concerned with the only child, much of it generated by research on the effects of China's "one child policy" and an ensuing debate about the implications of this policy for Chinese society and future generations. It seemed that this debate had almost reinforced and magnified some of the stereotypes surrounding the only child. "Little emperors" had become another unflattering soubriquet for only children.

Such a momentous social change justified looking again at only children in order to evaluate the likely advantages and disadvantages in terms of their personal and social development. It was almost a licence for sociologists to generalise. Only children became topical and a category apart—a category labelled "problem" or "potential problem". Reading some of this research strengthened my motivation to carry out a qualitative study exploring the unique perceptions of adult only children about their experience. It also created a sense of conflict about the objectives of my own project: would the search for themes inevitably lead to more generalisation?

Falbo (1984) states that the psychologist, Brill, warned of a predisposition to neuroticism in only children, and, going further, said, "It would be best for the individual and the race that there were no only-children". Winnicott (1958), in a lecture given in 1945, talked of the "immeasurable disadvantages" of growing up without siblings (although he also states that, if these are understood, they can be alleviated to some extent and he even finds some value in the possibility of an uncomplicated infancy). Winnicott (1958) also points to the capacity to be alone (in which an only child is likely to have some practice) as an aspect of emotional maturity.

The most prevalent stereotype, of being "pampered" and "spoiled"—the recipient of undiluted attention from parents—seems to originate largely from the work of Adler (1962) on the significance of birth order on children's overall development. Generalised characteristics were attributed to all birth orders, but the less positive tendencies identified by Adler (1962) in eldest, middle, or youngest children do not seem to have become entrenched in popular perception in the same way as those in respect of only children. Messages about only children have proved powerful and enduring. In their study of stereotyping, Von Hippel and colleagues (1995) point out that stereotypes provide perceivers with background information so that they do not pay as much attention to the individual. This seems to go to the heart of the insidious kind of depersonalisation involved in categorisation. In the case of only children, I think that this means that they may frequently meet an unconscious social schema (Fiske, 1993) in others; a kind of short-cut to understanding. Many quantitative researchers have offered other undesirable qualities of the only child, such as unsociable behaviour (Claudy, 1984), egocentrism (Jiao et al., 1986), and even a disproportionately high incidence of mental health problems (Howe & Madgett, 1975). It would seem that such works have been influential in perpetuating some fairly unattractive stereotypes and negative cultural assumptions. I wondered if thinking in terms of archetypes rather than stereotypes was more helpful. In her wide-ranging and perceptive work on only children, Sorensen (2008, p. 166) identifies themes that, according to her research, make up the only child archetype:

- lack of connectedness;
- loneness and space;
- specialness;
- self-esteem;
- lack of sibling opportunities;
- triangular relationships;
- enmeshment;
- separation and individuation;
- the effect of the only-child stereotype;
- shame.

On her website, Richardson (1998) offers a positive archetype based on the only child being: "independent, capable, reliable, a good friend to others, sensitive, thoughtful, considerate, organised and responsible". Both Sorensen and Richardson offer more searching and layered ideas, but I was still unsure whether an archetype of the only child is any more illuminating than a stereotype. I came to the conclusion that there is no helpful distinction between them.

Falbo (1984) has been prominent in seeking to counter some of the negative publicity for only children with her own quantitative research. Her findings suggest that singletons are, broadly speaking, no different from children with siblings in terms of adjustment, character, sociability, achievement, and self-esteem—except that they tend to score higher in self-esteem, intelligence, and achievement (Falbo & Polit, 1986). She has also joined the debate (Falbo, 1984) about the social implications of China's one child policy. According to Falbo's (2012) overview of the research, many of the findings suggested that any differences were minor and, where there were differences, the comparisons were, in fact, favourable to only children. Ostensibly, her research offers comfort for the only child as it denies any disadvantageous difference. Yet, the advantageous findings for only children still seem to be adding to the generalisations and the tendency to treat the only child as a class apart.

Mancillas (2006, p. 268) identifies the need to challenge old beliefs and labels—that the only child is "lonely, spoiled and maladjusted"—and urges mental health professionals, teachers, and parents to make "unbiased" decisions about only children. Rosenberg and Hyde (1993, p. 269) refute the old negative stereotypes, saying that only children are "not a homogenous category". I felt disappointed that they then go on to identify "three distinct sub-categories or types of only-child". Categorisation still seems to be irresistible and, it seems to me, to illustrate just how deep-seated these stereotypes are. Dunn's (2002) research casts doubt upon the negative stereotypes, suggesting that there is not any real difference between the social adjustment of only children and that of those with siblings. She believes that it is tenuous to make an equation between a child's ability to get on with his contemporaries, and whether he has siblings. The environmentalist, McKibben (1999), who made the choice to have a single child for environmental reasons, argues that cultural stereotypes around the only child are false, adding his voice to the argument that, essentially, only children are very much the same as anyone else.

Somewhat discouraged by the underlying premise of much of the research, I wanted to hear from some only children themselves—only children talking about their experience rather than being the subject of analysis. I found two websites devoted to being an only child: *onlychild.org.uk* and *beinganonly.com* both offering a forum for adult only-children to share their richly varied stories throughout the life-span. My searches also revealed numerous press articles written by "onlies" recounting their own experiences, but, again, all placed firmly in the context of negative assumptions about only children. Consequently, the writers set out (sometimes humorously, sometimes bitterly or sadly, often positively and defensively) to tell their stories to illustrate why being an only child was a good, or a bad, thing. Just a few of the many titles give a flavour:

"Only need not mean lonely" (Blinkhorn & Shah, 2005)
"The lifelong pain of being a lonely only" (Murray, 2013)

"Advice for only children: invent a sibling so you can pass for normal" (Archer, 2013)
"Yes, I'm an only child and, no, I'm not depressed – or beastly" (Gillan, 2013)

Each individual's story seemed somehow overshadowed (and weakened) by a stated or implicit desire to prove or disprove some received ideas. Ironically, a study devoted to interviewing over sixty only children in depth (Pitkeathley & Emerson, 1994) seemed to me to perpetuate and solidify stereotypical thinking. Interesting and moving reflections of interviewees are contained within a glib narrative of overcoming problems, a kind of self-help for only children complete with useful tips for partners in "how to cope with the situation"—the "situation" being the perceived faults and idiosyncrasies of the only child. An example (by no means unrepresentative) will perhaps illustrate the tone: "Don't be afraid to point out to your partner times when he is being self-centred. (Most only children are very worried about this, and keen to correct it if they can)" (Pitkeathley & Emerson, 1994). That the authors of this work are themselves only children seems only to deepen the irony of the powerful categorisation at work in this book.

Sorensen (2008) writes very differently about her own qualitative research into only children, dealing tentatively with themes that emerge: a sense of something missing, feelings of difference and separateness. Her exploration of the subject, and acknowledgement of distinctive experiences of only children, seem qualitatively different— empathic rather than evaluative. Grayling (2002, p. 166) points out the potential significance of things that are missing: "Absence is a large presence". Sartre (1956) also identifies things that are absent being as important as those that are present in defining who we are and how we see the world. An only child is defined in a very literal way by what is missing—defined by the absence of siblings. He or she misses the opportunity to develop psychosocial skills (Dunn & Slomkowski, 1992), emotional support (Brody, 1998), and learning opportunities, to name but a few "absences". While parental presence and attention seems to be prominent in the literature, usually as the source of perceived problems, I wondered if it could sometimes compensate for the absence of siblings. Not according to Coles (2003), for whom parental attention is only half the story: the absence of siblings is a crucial gap in the emotional life of a child. In a family of one child and two parents, the child is in the minority, which might tend to result in that child becoming a "little adult" (Sorensen, 2008, p. 21), growing up too soon and missing out on the freedom simply to be a child. Besides the company of peers within the home, only children miss out on important opportunities to rehearse some of the more complicated aspects of relationships within (usually) a safe environment. The sheer complexity of sibling relationships can, in itself, be valuable as "a way of learning to love and hate the same person" (Mitchell, 2003, p. 225). As Rowe (2007) points out, for most people, sibling relationships—described as "painful, wonderful and extraordinary"—are likely to be the longest lasting relationships of their lives. Only children never experience these peculiarly rich and complex relationships, and also miss out on important witnesses and sources of validation throughout the course of their lives. As an only child counsellor, Sorensen (2008, p. 204) identifies validation as an important aspect of her work with clients who are only children: "This is what I offer as a therapist and researcher: the importance of existential validation of the onliness in the lives of only-children". This seems important to me: that a significant element of an adult client's life—the "onliness"—should be explored and acknowledged, and that this kind of witnessing could, in some small way, compensate for the missing siblings who, in addition to their many other roles, act as witnesses in the life course.

I feel less attracted by Sorensen's use of an archetype to identify issues that an only child client is likely to bring to counselling. It does not seem to sit well with the person-centred approach and seems conducive to a kind of bias or predisposition, something Stewart (2004) calls the "Aha" phenomenon that can lead a clinician to interpret selectively based on ideas about birth order. Stewart gave therapists identical vignettes about a client that differed only in respect of the client's supposed birth order; his study found that therapist assumptions about the client were heavily influenced by archetypal ideas about a particular birth order. I wonder whether such assumptions threaten to undermine the entire counselling relationship. It seems to be at odds with the idea of entering a client's frame of reference and the "as-if" quality of empathic sensitivity that Mearns and Thorne (2013, p. 57) describe as "crucial" to the professionalism of the counsellor. I, therefore, doubt that the archetypes put forward by Sorensen and Richardson are conducive to deeper understanding of only child clients. They seem related to the use of personality tests (such as the Myers–Briggs type indicator) in counselling as an aid to understanding clients. Douglas (2010, p. 34) states that these stable views of personality—which lead to categorisations of personality disorder—are giving way to a postmodern view of personality as "more fluid, intersubjective and embedded in relationship". Perhaps this postmodern approach can extend to the only child who has long been identified and discussed in terms of a fixed personality type.

Briefly, I feel that the literature on the subject provides quite a narrow, enclosed context for my research. There are some distinctive, personal voices expressing feelings and thoughts about what it means to be an only child. Yet, those voices seem almost to be drowned in the clamour of those seeking to pass judgement on, or to defend, the only child as a type. The literature seems almost stifling in the way it is pulled back irresistibly to the subject of stereotypes and the debate about whether, in crude terms, the only child is a "good" or a "bad" thing.

Participants

I decided to interview participants who had reached at least mid-life, who had lived long enough to have experienced being an only child at different stages of their lives and, particularly, a fairly long period of being an "only child" as an adult. The other stipulation for "my" only children was that they should be qualified counsellors. There were two main reasons for this. First, I was interested in insights gained through training to become a counsellor, and, second, I wanted to explore what links there might be between being an only child and being a counsellor or, at least, what connections the participants might make. Accordingly, I advertised for participants and made informal enquiries that resulted in finding four only child counsellors who were willing to share and reflect upon their experience. The participants who responded to my advert were:

Adam, who is in his late forties, married with three children. He was brought up by both parents, with whom he had an easy relationship. Remembering a comfortable, secure childhood—"like a flat plane"—he is nevertheless aware of missing out on some of the "camaraderie" and "chaos" of family life.

Susanne, who is in her early sixties, divorced with three adult children. Her parents split up when she was two and she was brought up principally by her mother. She described feelings of loneliness in childhood and a longing for siblings.

Christine, who is in her early fifties, single with no children. Brought up by both parents, she recalls a happy, "fun-filled" childhood. This strong base made her feel "grounded", able to function in groups yet able, also, to be on her own. As an adult, she has perhaps more sense of being an only child and what that means for her.

Rachel, who is in her late fifties, divorced with two adult children, living with her long-term partner. She was brought up by her mother without knowing her father. Her memories of childhood seem to be suffused with a sense of absence—"the missing mother". She struggled with feelings of loneliness, boredom, and a sense of being different.

Data collection

The data collection was by semi-structured interviews that were based on the following open-ended questions, intended mainly as a basis for each participant to reflect on and talk about their experience:

1. Describe your relationship with your parents as you grew up? How was this relationship affected by the fact that you were an only child? Did you wish that you had siblings? How did you develop social and emotional relationships with other children? What was your awareness of external perceptions (and negative stereotypes) of the "only child"? What is your adult sense of and reaction to negative stereotypes of the only child?
2. How do you feel that the experience of growing up without siblings affected your development of a self-concept?
3. In thinking about your relationships as an adult, what significance do you attach to the fact that you were raised as an only child? What personal qualities (positive and negative) do you attribute to the fact that you were raised as an only child? As an adult, do you wish that you had siblings?
4. How do you think your ideas about the concept of family have been informed by the fact of being an only child?

5. Have there been times in counselling sessions (either as counsellor or client) when the fact of being an only child (either counsellor or client) has been directly in your awareness or even played a part in the dialogue?

Findings

Four superordinate themes with subsequent subordinate themes were identified (Table 3.1).

Superordinate theme 1: Parents

The relationship with parents was the starting point for each interview and was identified as a superordinate theme with two subordinate themes.

Subordinate theme 1.1: Attention

Christine had the most positive memories of parental attention: "I was a daddy's girl, my dad did all of the fun things . . ."; ". . . my mum was . . . the disciplinarian and my dad was more tactile than my mum . . ."; ". . . when I had a real problem in my life, I talked to my mum." She felt "a real closeness to both but very . . . very different . . ."; ". . . so, I felt I grew up quite grounded because I had everything from . . . both influences that wasn't diluted or . . . you know, shared in a way that was detrimental to me." She values the nurturing attention she received and seems to appreciate the fact that it did not have to be shared with siblings. For Rachel, the picture was very different: ". . . my mum,

Table 3.1. Emerging themes.

Superordinate themes	Parents	Missing siblings	Identity	Counselling
Subordinate themes	Attention	Being part of a group	Stereotypes	Training
	Responsibility	Rivalry, conflict, and other stereotypes	Self-concept	Practice
		An adult world		

I guess was missing . . . in some ways because she was struggling as a single mum . . ."; "my mum was individuating which was like, in teenage years, Erikson's stage five or whatever, that she was struggling with relationships, work, getting on at work . . ."; ". . . she was preoccupied perhaps through no fault of her own . . . with becoming the person she is or negotiating life . . ." ". . . I think she struggled with self-esteem and . . . schooling and that sort of thing, so I think my mum had sort of got by and then she was doing her thing, so it was that, maybe lack of connection, I don't know, I don't know." Looking back, she seems to have had little sense of anyone paying her attention: ". . . there was like . . . a gap of . . . nothingness. I can remember my . . . it's the central theme is that lack of . . . I was very aware that I wasn't the focus . . . and I think you want to be as a child." She seems to have an acute sense of the absence of parental or adult attention and there is a yearning in her words: "Why was this missing?"

As a child, Susanne also seems to have enjoyed little nurturing or empathic attention from her parents, both of whom, for different reasons, seemed to lack emotional attunement to her needs. She felt unable to say anything to her mother about a specific "heart-breaking" experience that was "the end of the world", about being bullied in a new school, or about her general sense of loneliness and isolation: "Even then I picked up that, if I told my mum, there would be no sympathy, no empathy . . . Keep it inside. Don't say anything." Her father, too, seemed beyond her emotional reach. He was: "very, very quiet . . . exceedingly quiet." Going to stay with him felt "very, very constrained: . . . he was too insular and I used to get homesick."

Adam described an easy, harmonious relationship with his parents: "We were a little group of three." However, within this small group, parental attention did not become too intense: "I didn't get the sense that I was the focus of everything for them and that they had all the expectations of me. I didn't have any of that sense at all . . .". The only child generalisation does not fit, and Adam goes further: "I felt almost the opposite—almost to the point in hindsight where I think we . . . perhaps there should have been more pressure . . ."; "I was usually brought into some kind of discussion. So I remember that as being a good thing, but perhaps they should have pushed me into some things . . ." He does not describe the kind of ideal balance Christine perceived, but expresses quite a gentle, reflective sense of whether more pressure might have helped him, and he is left wondering about how the balance should be struck as he brings up his own children.

Subordinate theme 1.2: Responsibility

In different ways, all participants expressed a strong sense of responsibility towards their parents in later life. Christine continued to feel driven to make her parents proud of her: "And I always had that sense of whatever I try to do . . . I try to make them proud . . ." She has no children and talks of this in terms of disappointment for her parents: "I do think it's such a shame that they never had grandchildren . . . because of me being an only child and an only child that was gay, you know, if I'd have had brothers and sisters, they'd have had that . . ." She links this, tentatively, to the desire to make them proud: "And whether that was me making up for not giving them grandchildren, I'm not particularly sure . . ." There is a sense of wanting to protect her parents from all disappointment, including disappointment arising from her own "onliness". A need to protect her father (by this time widowed and in bad health) from disappointment and disruption contributed to delay in ending her long-term relationship: ". . . some of my friends who I spoke to about my relationship—'well, why are you still with her?' So, they would never understand, 'well, I don't want to disappoint my dad'."

Adam felt a great sense of responsibility as an only child when his father died: ". . . that was absolutely the . . . biggest driver for me, was that I kind of felt, there's just me . . ." This drive of sole responsibility seemed to gather momentum, from making funeral arrangements to a kind of responsibility for his widowed mother's happiness, "an urge to somehow get it all neatly sorted somehow." He wanted to ". . . make it better in some way and to fix it . . . 'cause I guess in a way the triangle of you know . . . supportive adult, calm, whatever you want to say, but that was broken at that point . . . so maybe there was a deeper need for me to somehow make it all better." His words reflect a sense of longing, loss, and helplessness as he tries "in some way" and "somehow" to make things better. Following his mother's death (five days before the birth of Adam's youngest son), Adam described a feeling of relief, mixed with all the other emotions experienced during a "blurry time": "The other thing that came with all of that was actually a sense of relief . . . you know, that these . . . this huge sense of responsibility ... well, the only responsibility now is to get stuff sorted with houses and technical things rather than ... a person." He feels that, if he had siblings, he would not have felt "a complete sense of responsibility ... that's a big thing, I think ..."

Susanne felt a responsibility for her mother's loneliness in later years and was unable to resist her mother's increasing possessiveness: "... wanting to be involved in everything and making sure she was involved in everything and I couldn't say no at that time, wanting to say no but I couldn't." "She'd come on the phone ... it felt like hours, but she was lonely and I understood that." Like Adam, Susanne felt a kind of impotent compulsion to make her mother's life better: "... her feeling lonely and me coming up with all these suggestions—go to this ... could go to that, join the church, I'll come with you. No." This difficult period, and her mother's subsequent illness and death, highlighted, again, Susanne's sense of loss around being an only child: "As an only child—although I've got my children—it's not like having a sibling when you can share it."

Rachel is the only participant who has a parent still alive. Her mother, now in her eighties, lives with Rachel and her partner. Rachel did not talk explicitly about feelings of responsibility towards her mother and yet she has assumed great practical responsibility by inviting her mother to live in her home. There seems to be an irony in the "missing mother" of childhood now living in her adult daughter's home. Her mother has expressed regret for not being there for Rachel as a child, but Rachel's attitude seems to be one of acceptance and "a rueful humour": "She's expressed guilt and regret that she wasn't there with me at that young age ... but no one can do anything about that now"; "I take some of the stuff she says with a pinch of salt ... and some with a rueful humour, because I think, 'bloody hell, you didn't do that for me!'"

Superordinate theme 2: Missing siblings

If an only child is defined by the absence of siblings, how do only children experience this absence? Is it possible to miss something we have never had and to experience it as a kind of loss? The absence of siblings emerged as a superordinate theme with three subordinate themes around the meaning that this gap in their lives had for the participants.

Subordinate theme 2.1: Being part of a group

Both Rachel and Susanne express intense feelings of loss around their childhood in general, including a sense that the presence of siblings would have made life less difficult. Rachel describes a lack of companionship arising from a combination of family circumstances: "It was not easy to have a friend . . . and I don't think that was so much because I was an only child . . . but because I was different." "And it would have been great to have a brother or a sister to be able to go out because I had no friends on that estate and I went to school with people who lived so far away . . . it was just like purgatory really." The idea of a sister was powerfully attractive—as a passport to a social or sociable life and to being part of a family set-up where children were noticed and valued. She recalls an incident when she and a friend fell over on some ice and the parental concern devoted to her friend seemed to accentuate all that was missing in Rachel's life: ". . . and her parents made such a fuss and . . . were kind and paid her attention and it was like, where was anybody paying me any attention?"; "I was extremely jealous of people with sisters." Rachel had sensed—in contrast to popular thinking—that the presence of a sibling would have given her more (rather than less) of the adult attention she craved. Susanne also responded strongly when asked if she had wished for siblings: "Always. Always thought, 'Why haven't I got a brother or sister?'" Something of her vulnerability as a child and a feeling of being exposed comes through in her words: "When you're an only child, you've got nobody to hide behind . . . *nobody* to hide behind."

Adam, too, while not having wished for siblings—"it didn't really occur to me"—is aware of that sense of being in some way exposed, of missing out in not being part of a group: "Whereas the only-child is not . . . one of anything, except a sort of two adults and child type of triangle . . . You're not really part of . . . a sibling group." Both Adam and Susanne express some level of discomfort as a child arising from not being part of a group of siblings—a sense of missing, among other things, an opportunity to experience some of the solidarity and security that comes from being in a group.

As a child, Christine had no sense of missing out: "I sailed through my childhood . . . I was never in and I was always out playing, I was always out playing with other kids." She had a large extended family and remembers Sunday lunches and holidays spent with "a whole bigger clan." She felt no desire or need for siblings. However, this is changing in adulthood. There is some sense of loss, despite the existence of "a great network of friends" and her extended family: "I've felt it more . . . as I've got older and going through, you know, relationship break up, that's when I've felt it." She goes on, ". . . yes, I've got loads of cousins, but I don't think it's the same bond as some of my friends who've got . . . with their sisters and brothers and even though they might . . . fight like cat and dog, when the chips are down, you know . . . that you've got family, and being single and not having any children and not having any brothers and sisters, that I think, is a . . . is sometimes a challenge for me, especially when I . . . you know, with what I see in my job and, you know, while I try not to think about death and dying, you do wonder if, unless I meet somebody, who's going to be there?" Her words suggest a sense of anticipatory loss and existential isolation, but it seems as if she is touching on, rather than exploring, some difficult thoughts and feelings. Adam expresses some sense of loss as an adult—the absence of someone who knows and has shared his past: "There's nobody to talk to . . . who was there" and "It feels quite lonely . . . or it's kind of internalised, the memories that I have and I can't really check them out." Memories of the past, because they are not truly shared, cannot seem to find a proper place in the present. Being "internalised", it feels that they are elusive, almost unreal.

Subordinate theme 2.2: Rivalry, conflict, and other learning opportunities

Two participants identified the absence of conflict as something missing from their own childhood and something they had learned to deal with when they had their own children. Susanne had been keen to avoid having only one child, but was initially quite startled by the "squabbling" between her three: "And, as an only child, I had no rivalry. I didn't know about rivalry until I had my children. I thought, what on earth is going on?" Adam did not set out to avoid having an only child, but having three children has brought a sense of valuing some of the more "chaotic" side of family life: ". . . so I think my ideas about what a family, a good family or something like that, is supposed to be like, I think they've shifted . . . Not that my . . . not that being the only-child family was a bad thing . . . but there's lots of good things about other kinds of families where there might be more ... you know, stuff going on generally speaking ... whether it's emotional stuff or just people running about or whatever it is, just general chaotic stuff ..." He speculates about his own adult responses to his wife's family dynamics, linking his responses to lack of familiarity with the "chaotic stuff" of family life or lack of "rehearsal" in his own upbringing: "So I think I didn't get that rehearsal really within the family anyway. But I can see it in other people's families, it's happening all the time. And for me, it's almost like a comedy, but I think that's probably just me ... being defensive about it ..."

Subordinate theme 2.3: An adult world

The idea of an only child growing up too soon and becoming a kind of honorary adult is quite prominent in the literature. Only two participants in my study identified a sense of being in some way and to some extent a "little adult". Adam and Susanne described very different childhoods but both identified a sense of fitting into an adult world. Susanne was "always hearing adult conversations when I would stay with my dad". She played an "adult role" when she became a carer for her mother when she was fifteen. Adam described his childhood as "very ... adult as well: I wasn't ... you know, capering around with my brothers or sisters sort of thing causing chaos." He says, "... somehow I had to be a good boy and ... you know ... fit in with the adults and not mess around and not do stuff like that." For me, there is a kind of sadness and sense of loss in these simple, matter-of-fact words.

Superordinate theme 3: Identity

The master theme of "Identity" produced two subordinate themes: "Stereotypes" and "Self-concept".

Subordinate theme 3.1: Stereotypes

All four participants felt that the stereotypes associated with the only child did not apply to them. Only one seemed to show any real interest in the idea of the stereotype. Both Susanne and Christine identify the stereotype of being spoilt with having material possessions and feel that their own economic circumstances in childhood precluded this: "I think people think you're spoilt. You're an only child and you've got everything, which isn't true . . . So, no, I wasn't spoilt" [Susanne]. Christine says, "I just think . . . it is what it is, it's a stereotype and it doesn't fit." However, Christine almost goes on to transfer the stereotype to those with siblings: "Looking back . . . the kids I grew up with, you know . . . some of them were more spoilt, you know . . . younger boys, first born, last born and all this." Adam also rejects the stereotype of the only child: "That's not how I am", and has a sense that, as a child, he was "almost the opposite of the . . . sort of spoilt brat" in that he was expected to behave like an adult. But he acknowledges some engagement with the idea of the stereotype: "I sort of remember feeling a bit, you know, like I've got to stick up for it really." He talks of wanting to "challenge" the stereotype, demonstrating his own authentic difference from the stereotype, but goes on, "As well as wanting to challenge it, I kind of laugh at it really" and "it's no big deal". He goes on to speculate on the possibility of stereotypes operating unconsciously, wondering if his own views of himself have perhaps been influenced in some way. He wonders about his sense of liking to be alone: ". . . maybe that's partly a product of . . . you know, the messages about only children that I've internalised about only children or how people said I appear to be as an only child." Rachel is aware of some unfair assumptions that were made by adults about her own situation but feels that her position was "hugely complex" and any stereotyping that might have been applied to her as a child was due to other factors besides being an only child.

Subordinate theme 3.2: Self-concept

Overall, Christine is unsure how far the only-child factor has contributed to her own sense of self, but concedes that it has played a part. Rachel talks of the difficulty for her in building her own sense of self: "It's all about the self-concept and you build it by people . . . they're your mirrors that witness you, value you, feed back to you your conditions of worth stuff . . . so, if you don't have those mirrors . . . it's harder to form it." She describes a kind of existential feeling of isolation, a feeling of being adrift in the absence of adult attention and experiencing a kind of "free for all". Yet, even without those important mirrors, she was able, eventually, to turn a "fragile self-concept" into something more robust and to develop secure attachment despite the "insecure attachment" and "avoidant" patterns in childhood. There is a kind of existential assumption of responsibility for her own life—"I had my own self-drive"—that has enabled her to make good some of the deficits of childhood, to overcome a fearful sense of isolation and to accept the "less than ideal" that life has to offer: "I'm responsible for my life and you can't look or blame . . ."

Susanne has also faced a kind of existential aloneness, a raw sense of enduring adversity alone that has left her with a sense of becoming a "character".

Adam describes himself as someone who makes friends easily but who likes his own space. A sense of "keeping something back" in his friendships seems to be rooted in his only-child experience. Three participants specifically identified "resilience" in terms of what they had gained.

Susanne talks of resilience and adaptability forged through having to cope alone with her distress in childhood. She feels that she is "so resilient in some ways". She is acutely aware of being an only child and the way that has shaped her, saying: "I had to deal with all this myself and I think it's made a character of me." Christine talks of "resilience" and "resourcefulness" arising from coping with the death of a parent on her own. Adam talks of "resilience" and "acceptance" but is unsure about "strength": "I sort of think there's a resilience in that actually. I think there is a . . . I was going to use the word strength, but I'm not sure about that, but there is a . . . an acceptance as well . . . something actually that is positive in a way, I think." Rachel talks of "coping mechanisms", "acceptance" and "self-determination": "I'm responsible for my life." Two participants talked of the ability to be alone: "Being an only child has given me that . . . confidence that I quite like my own company . . . but I can work . . . I'm quite comfortable in groups . . ." [Christine]. Adam is perhaps less enthusiastic: "I don't mind being on my own." Susanne, on the other hand, says: "I like being quiet but I don't like being alone."

Susanne talks of some of the "benefits" of being an only child, identifying her ability to "go with the flow" and "to adapt quickly" and: "I think it's helped me to be quite a caring person." Christine talks of being "grounded" and "placid" and feels that there is some connection with being an only child: "And I can't say it was the significance of . . .

directly being an only child, but I think some of the qualities that I developed are as a result of being [one]. But equally other people develop them in different ways, don't they?"

Superordinate theme 4: Counselling

All participants made links between counselling and their only-child experience. The superordinate theme of "Counselling" seemed to divide into two areas: training and practice.

Subordinate theme 4.1: Training

Adam embraced the opportunities that were offered: "It felt like something that would, that was good for me to do, as an only child, but challenging as well, in many ways, but also because I was an only child." Although apprehensive about the challenges he would face, challenges to his sense of privacy, and tendency to "keep something back", he sensed positive possibilities: "I'll need to be opening up a little bit more . . . so this is . . . whoa . . . but I suppose also I kind of welcomed it." The training and personal development work seemed to fulfil expectations: "It wasn't a[n] . . . overly scary or difficult experience. It felt like it was, you know, almost what was needed." I sensed that he felt a kind of relief, almost liberation, in finding something life-enhancing that had previously been missing. He felt as if the process helped him "to develop a deeper relationship with people".

Susanne also found that training gave her something valuable in terms of personal development, enabling her to be more open: "It was all about a person-centred way of being—Carl Rogers and all that. It suited me and I was able to open up and talk about things much more openly." Previously, she had not confided in anyone, no matter how painful her experiences had been: "I've been very, very quiet about my background over the years but when I did the counsellor training, I think I opened up more than I thought I would. I felt like I was on a journey."

Neither Christine nor Rachel talked about the attractions of counsellor training, apart from Christine feeling a general sense of having the "right way of being to be a counsellor". Yet, both identified some powerful learning. For Christine, conditions of worth came into sharp focus: ". . . when you do your training and you . . . some of the things you recognise, the traits . . . you know, I wrote a lot about people pleasing . . . and conditions of worth and being a daddy's girl." The personal development work in training helped her to realise that her relationship of thirty years "had run its course" and to act on that insight. For Rachel, training was almost a natural progression from her early interest as a child in "all sorts of psychological stuff". It seems to have helped her to make sense of her early life: "But, latterly, I understood so much—especially through training and theory." She goes on, "I'm now an adult looking back with all this counsellor training."

Subordinate theme 4.2: Practice

All participants talked of the importance of keeping their own experiences (including any ideas arising from being an only child) separate from whatever clients were bringing to therapy. Rachel specifically linked this to what she had learnt as an only child: "I suppose part of my learning as an only child is you don't project your stuff on to people . . . you know, you keep your stuff away." Also, she recognises that she has dealt with issues of her own that might otherwise intrude: "So I'm not aware of the only-child thing in as much as I think I'm OK with it, that it doesn't tip me in one way or another." At present she is working with an only-child client and describes, tentatively, how her own only-child experience might, to some extent, enhance her work with this client, might prompt her to: ". . . ask a different question, have a curiosity about something that is something that they may not be aware of, but still following their lead . . . they might make a different connection."

Adam is conscious of the need to resist assumptions or a temptation to identify with clients who may be only children: "It's hanging on to them as the individual only child who maybe has a very different experience to the one that I had. But it's certainly there in my mind." Sometimes there are echoes and feelings of recognition, such as when only-child clients talk about confidence and esteem. It feels "a bit like familiar territory" and he reminds himself, "This is them. It's not me." Often, he is aware of differences when clients with siblings are talking; he notes contrasts with the calmness of his own experience: ". . . things happening which are out of my experience of family . . . This will pull me up as well . . . I think, yes, this is something . . . very different to what I experienced. So I think it's there . . . it's there all the time."

Christine, a bereavement counsellor, states that she often does not know whether clients are only children or not. However, she does go on to say of her own only-child experience and her counselling practice, "I mean . . . I think it helps me to empathise with . . . people . . . who haven't got a significant group of family they can rely on . . . but it's not . . . it doesn't impact me in any way." She adds, "When I'm working with people who . . . haven't got anybody in their life, haven't got brothers and sisters and are quite sort of isolated . . . I do think, oh . . . it does resonate, but not . . . you know, I can't allow it to impact anyway because it's their frame of reference." Like Adam and Rachel, Christine is aware of resonance with some client material but very clear about the need to keep this separate and remain within the client's perceptual world. Besides issues of isolation, she notices similarities with clients who feel "the weight of that responsibility"—that is to say, the burden of responsibility she assumed for her father in his last years, a responsibility that could not be shared with a brother or sister.

Susanne makes strong links between her present work with families and children and her own painful childhood—in general, rather than specifically in terms of being an only child. She seems very much to see her work in terms of the "wounded healer": ". . . the intuitive side of me could actually understand and be empathic with these young ones who were really upset and in pain. So, I think you get to the point as the hurt and wounded one where you can actually help." It seems, too, as if her own reluctance or inability to confide in others as a child has given her a kind of heightened, protective sense of a child's right to privacy: ". . . they may never, ever open up. I never push children . . . it's got to be safe to come out and they've got to be able to feel that safety." There seem to be echoes from her own childhood. Susanne and Adam both mention links between their only-child experience and the satisfaction they derive from their counselling practice. Susanne talks of offering something distilled from her experience and ability to empathise, but also says that she feels "fulfilled" to do so. Adam continues the theme of going deeper that he had welcomed in training: "I've come to the idea that what it's about is emotional connections, that's what it's about and I think as an only child, that's attractive, that's an attractive thing." He makes a specific link between the drive towards emotional connections and the fact that he is an only child. A sense of valuing the counselling relationship comes across in his words. Although conscious that he is being more adventurous in exploring deeper feelings, he is aware also of doing this in a kind of controlled environment within the counselling room. It is "*still* a sort of safe . . . safe way, in a way, to engage in strong and perhaps difficult emotions." It is almost as if he wonders if he has, after all, strayed so very far from his calm, comfortable upbringing. He welcomes the mutuality of counselling. As well as helping the client, ". . . there's something for me in this as well, definitely." Each participant reveals a clear sense of his or her own life experience in terms of being an only child. It is an important aspect of who they are, even if the rich diversity of personal experience and interpretation means that, at times, the connecting thread in their narratives is difficult to discern. On concluding the interviews and analysis, I had a strong sense that being an only child is a deeply significant part of each participant's sense of self.

Discussion

My findings did not reflect the dominance of stereotypes and archetypes identified in the literature—spoilt, overprotected, lacking social skills, etc. (Sorensen, 2008). Neither did my participants exhibit any of the emotional responses to those stereotypes that feature prominently in the literature. Indeed, the gulf between literature and lived experience is striking in this small study. All participants believed that there *is* stereotyping of the only child; all identified the primary component of the stereotype in terms of being spoilt; and all believed it to be inaccurate in their own case. Yet, belief in the inaccuracy of an unflattering perception did not translate into an emotional response, say, of anger or a strong sense of injustice (although Adam acknowledged some desire to "challenge" it). Perhaps, also, there is some implicit resentment when Christine, in rejecting the stereotype for herself (possibly), projects the stereotype on to other birth orders.

The Adlerian premise of 200% parental attention in childhood, which seems to be influential in the formation of the "spoilt" stereotype, simply does not apply in three of the four accounts given by my participants. Two felt a painful absence of parental attention and the third wondered whether there could perhaps have been more attention. Where the idea of 200% attention does, arguably, apply, in the account given by Christine, it is not experienced as something that might "spoil" her development. Instead, it is experienced in a nurturing, life-enhancing, and empowering way that seems to support some of the contentions of those trying to lobby for more positive images for the only child. Even if participants are not offended by stereotypes or engaged in a debate about those stereotypes, it is my sense and belief, based on lived experience, that their existence must affect the way only children perceive themselves as well as the way others perceive them. Sorensen's research (2008) seems to support this view, and yet most of my participants made no link between stereotyping and their own sense of self. Only one (Adam) seemed to engage with the idea, talking about the possibility that he may have "internalised" the views of others as well as feeling inclined to "challenge" the stereotype.

In my encounters with participants, I did not experience any sense of the relevance of an archetype. Sorensen (2008) offers her model of an only-child archetype tentatively, as a set of characteristics that are likely to relate to the lived experience of only children. This is rooted in qualitative research, and yet it did not seem applicable in my study. Certainly, some of the elements were recognisable: a lack of a sense of connectedness (Adam); issues around responsibility (all participants); a need for personal space (Adam); the experience of shame (Rachel, Susanne). However, these individual elements were very far from comprising a complete "set" of characteristics for any of the participants.

In terms of counselling practice, my participants seemed to endorse Stewart's findings (2004) that labelling, or thinking in terms of archetypes or prototypes, is unhelpful for practitioners. I noted (and preferred) Adam's emphasis on the importance of hanging on to "the individual only child", being attuned to elements of a client's sense of his or her "onliness", and separating his own sense of "familiar territory". It seems to suggest a person-centred approach that is more conducive to achieving relational depth (Mearns, 1996). I was also struck by Rachel's subtle, nuanced "take" on counselling an only child, using her awareness of her own experience in a tentative way, being sensitive to echoes while remaining very much in the client's frame of reference. She talked of "curiosity" born of personal experience. It is a long way from the world of archetypes and defining characteristics. It seems much closer to the "as-if" quality of empathy (Mearns & Thorne, 2013), combining an ability to "bracket off" personal experience while, paradoxically, allowing that experience to heighten the counsellor's own ability to "walk alongside" the client.

Counsellor training proved to be a powerful experience for all participants and I wondered if there was scope for further research into the meaning of this training experience for only children. Is there a link between what may be experienced as "missing" in only children's experience and something that is to be found in the intensity of most training programmes? Adam seemed to make this connection, finding something "powerfully attractive" for the only child in the opportunity to relate at a deep level. Yet, other participants did not talk in these terms and, again, it seemed difficult to identify any unifying "only-child" theme in their responses on the subject of counsellor training. Nevertheless, I was left with a sense that each participant's experience during training had, to some extent and in some way, ameliorated some of the more negative aspects of their only-child experience: dissolving conditions of worth (Christine); achieving a profound, intellectual understanding (Rachel); making a deeper connection (Adam); a realisation that early distress could be turned into a source of strength (Susanne).

Husserl (1927) believed that we can only reach the essence of a phenomenon if we rigorously examine our own experience of the world in relation to that phenomenon. I have assessed my findings, partly, at least, in the context of my own emotional and intellectual responses to the material as well as in the context of published literature. There is no doubt that the theme of "responsibility" has a particular resonance for me on an emotional level. I am reminded of the intensity of feeling responsible—"completely responsible" [Adam]—for the happiness of parents in later life, which three of my participants describe so movingly. Above all, there is a sense of seeking the impossible, taking on responsibility for another's happiness in a quest that is really doomed to failure as we strive to negate, or compensate for, the effects of old age and death. There is a sense, too, of a futile attempt to compensate for the other children that our parents did not have, as expressed by Christine in the strength of her longing not to disappoint her parents. I share also the sense of sadness expressed by Adam as he reflects on being the only keeper of family memories. It is part of the journey from being the only "child" to being the only surviving member of the birth family that most only children will travel. The absence of someone who understands and (at least, partially) shares our story is indeed a "large absence". Conversely, the only child might be fortunate to miss the intensely destabilising experience of invalidation that occurs, according to Rowe (2007), when siblings have conflicting memories of a shared past. And, for me, this last sentence expresses some of the limiting aspects of discussions about only children and their missing siblings: the conversation is constantly pulled back by an "at least" thought: at least they did not have to endure the pain of sibling rivalry; at least they did not have to share their toys; at least they did not have to fight for parental attention . . . And yet, this pulling back seems to miss an important aspect of how the only child experiences the absence. By offering a sensible, consolatory kind of counter-balance, it almost seems to diminish the only child by claiming that he or she has been fortunate to escape from some of the richness and complexity—what Adam terms "the chaotic stuff"—of life.

Returning to the theme of something missing and "a large absence", I wondered again about the experience of missing something we have never had. I believe that we can indeed miss what we have never had and I think that the absence of siblings can be felt as a kind of unacknowledged loss throughout life. Barnes expresses his own sense of missing something that he believes was never present: "I don't believe in God, but I miss him" (Barnes, 2008, p. 1). Presumably, these words suggest a kind of longing (for faith), a longing heightened by a feeling of being excluded from something important. For me, and, I sense, for my participants, the desire for siblings is a similar kind of longing: it is heightened (if not caused) by a sense of exclusion, a sense of being cut off from something experienced by others. In a society where there is widespread idealisation of the family, we only children are aware that our own small family group might be found to be deficient in some way.

In existential terms, I am conscious of my participants having a kind of heightened sense of the isolation that, ultimately, faces all of us, no matter how close our relationships. Perhaps the only child is better prepared, more practised at confronting the fact of being alone, more able to show the emotional maturity that Winnicott associates with the capacity to be alone. Fromm (1963) goes further, stating, "Paradoxically, the ability to be alone is the condition for the ability to love" (p. 93). I am reminded of Susanne's words: "there's nobody to hide behind . . . *nobody* to hide behind", and it is as if the early necessity of facing life alone has strengthened her by revealing a truth that might not be revealed so early to others. This is the "truth", in existential terms, as described by Yalom (1991, p. 12): that we are born alone and die alone. Perhaps the only child has had more opportunity to come to terms with this truth and, consequently, has a greater sense of the "tension between our awareness of isolation and our wish for contact, protection and to be part of a larger whole" (Yalom, 1991, p. 10). I felt that, in their very different ways, each participant had wrestled with a sense of being alone, even if they would perhaps not adopt my interpretation of existential isolation. I am thinking, particularly, of Susanne, whose strong religious faith was evident throughout our interview and who would, presumably (this was not explored), have a very different view of the sense of isolation that she experienced in childhood. Still reflecting in existential terms, I had a strong sense that each participant had accepted the responsibility for shaping one's own life that comes with the "given" of freedom. Each participant, either explicitly or implicitly, has become, in Sartre's terms (cited in Yalom, 1991), the "author" of his or her own life, accepting personal responsibility for the choices they have made and the way they have lived (and are living) their lives. Frankl (1985, p. 98) reflects on existential responsibility: "Life ultimately means taking responsibility to find the right answer to its problems and to fulfil the tasks which it constantly sets for each individual". So, the tendency to accept responsibility even, as in Adam's case, for those things over which we have no real control, might find expression in a readiness also to take full responsibility for our lives. I was left with a strong sense of the way in which each participant's story was marked by insight and an awareness of decision-making in the way their lives had been shaped. There was a complete absence of self-pity or a feeling of being defined by early family circumstances, even when, as in the case of Rachel and Susanne, those circumstances had been particularly difficult. Yet, I was brought back, once again, to the unanswerable question of how much this was attributable to being an only child. Have other factors been just as influential—or even more influential—in producing the unflinching narratives of my participants? Still, I felt convinced by the link that participants make between only-child experience and what amounts to resilience and an ability to confront the existential challenge of freedom.

Most counsellors believe in the value of story-telling, both as a means of understanding experience and as a therapeutic aid to personal growth: "Each of us is a biography, a story. Each of us is a singular narrative, which is constructed, continually, unconsciously, by, through and in us" (Sachs, 1985, as quoted in Sugarman, 2004, p. 69). Narrative therapy is recognised as a counselling approach in its own right by McLeod (2003), who talks of personal experience and reality being "constructed" through the process of telling stories. Shaping the narrative becomes an aspect of the client taking responsibility for his or her own life, facing up to existential freedom or, as characterised by Rogers (1951), taking the opportunity to write or rewrite the narrative of identity. As I interviewed participants, each one seemed to make sense of experience through telling his or her story. And story-telling was what they were being asked to do, having only one hour to encapsulate a life's experience and, just to add to the difficulty of the task, trying to view past, present, and future through the lens of what it means to be an only child. It was demanding. I was also conscious of the transience and the nuances of oral story-telling, how the stories we tell about ourselves are fluid and changing. Yet, my participants' stories would become fixed; for the purposes of this study, they would become a kind of life script to be read and re-read before being analysed. I would then become the narrator of the stories of others. Despite these misgivings, in a final act of reduction and interpretation, I have tried, in the paragraphs that follow, to distil a meaning that I have taken from each story, hoping that this does not do too much injustice to the "real" narrators of the stories and their complex narratives of identity.

Rachel's story is of an only child who has used intellectual strength and personal fortitude to compensate for what was missing in her childhood and to create something very different for her own children.

Christine's story is of an only child who enjoyed a nurturing, sociable upbringing and whose confident sense of self has enabled her to end a relationship lasting more than thirty years and to face life alone—albeit with strong, supportive friendships—in her fifties.

Susanne's story is of an only child who has developed strength out of childhood adversity and whose religious faith and family of three children have helped her to create a very different life for herself in adulthood.

Adam's story is of an only child who has reached a deep understanding of himself in relation to being an only child, an understanding that seems evident in a calm acceptance of what might have been missing, combined with an appreciation of the more populated family life he now enjoys as an adult.

As I approached the conclusion of my study, trying to understand where the process had left me, it was the complexity and humanity of these stories that lingered as a powerful memory.

Conclusion

This study is on a small scale, involving interviews with only four participants. By contrast, the subject seems vast, complex, and, at times, elusive. I asked participants to capture their subjective sense of what it means to be an only child. As they reflected over many years, trying to distil the "only-child" element in their lives and ways of being, I was aware of the difficulties in this process of disentangling. As one participant (Christine) said, "It's who I am." I was initially troubled by the fact that two participants had been brought up by only one parent each, and this seemed to preclude some of the dominant themes in the existing literature, that of the sometimes intense nature of the two parents–one child relationship. Indeed, in a single parent household with one child, the "only" part of "only child" is diluted in that the other family member is the "only adult". There are two "onlies". Still, I hoped that those differences might prove to be a source of strength as well as a limitation, and I now believe this to have been the case. My study led me to believe that the link between only-child experience and the impact of counsellor training might justify further research. Such research might usefully explore ways in which counsellor training can enhance understanding of an only child's sense of something "missing" that seems to feature in each narrative. Despite my resistance to any treatment of only children as a separate category (ironic in the context of my choice of my topic), I believe that qualitative research into the real, lived experience of only children might, in fact, serve as something of a corrective to the prevalence of stereotypes. It might even facilitate "knowledge of the other" (McLeod, 2011, p. 3) which could be useful in terms of self-awareness of trainees and useful, too, for counsellors and counselling tutors, leading them beyond stereotyped views of their clients or students.

In concluding my study, I was pleased that an initial hope—that my findings might represent a challenge to the stereotype—was, in my view, fulfilled. Ideas around a stereotype or archetype seemed irreconcilable with the people whom I encountered, and with the narratives that I heard. My participants' own lack of engagement with ideas around stereotyping was entirely unexpected and gave me pause for thought. Mostly, I felt encouraged that only children—or at least, "my" four only children—seemed to treat harsh stereotypes with a kind of dismissive shrug. I reflected on the way that I, along with so many researchers and writers, seemed to have a rather less healthy response, feeling some indignation about the kind of casual, insidious prejudice that surrounds this subject. Initially, I felt a little chastened by the views of participants. Was I, perhaps, taking things too personally? Yet, reflecting on the study, I found myself returning to the feeling that, even if the prejudice involved in stereotyping does not have a direct or measurable impact on the lives of only children, it is still "wrong" in more than one sense of that word: both inaccurate and morally suspect.

References

Adler, A. (1962). *What Life Should Mean to You*. London: Unwin.
Archer, G. (2013). Advice for only children: invent a sibling so you can pass for normal in group outings. *Telegraph*, 26 August.
Barnes, J. (2008). *Nothing To Be Frightened Of*. London: Jonathan Cape.
Blinkhorn, A., & Shah, D. (2005). Only need not mean lonely. *Sunday Times*, 7 July.
Brody, G. H. (1998). Sibling relationship quality: its causes and consequences. *Annual Review of Psychology, 49*: 1–24.
Claudy, J. G. (1984). The only child as a young adult: results from project talent. In: T. Falbo (Ed.), *The Single Child Family* (pp. 211–252). New York: Guilford Press.
Coles, P. (2003). *The Importance of Sibling Relationships in Psychoanalysis*. London: Karnac.
Douglas, B. (2010). *Disorder and its Discontents, Handbook of Counselling Psychology*. London: Sage.
Dunn, J. (2002). In Freeman, H. (2002). Sole Survivors. *Guardian*, 5 June.
Dunn, J., & Slomkowski, C. (1992). Conflict and the development of social understanding and aggression. In: C. U. Shantz & W. W. Hartup (Eds.), *Conflict in Child and Adolescent Development* (pp. 70–92). Cambridge: Cambridge University Press.

Falbo, T. (1984). *The Single Child Family*. New York: Guilford Press.
Falbo, T. (2012). Only children: an updated review. *Journal of Individual Psychology*, 68(1): 38–49.
Falbo, T., & Polit, D. (1986). Quantative review of the only-child literature: research evidence and theory development. *Psychological Bulletin*, 100: 176–189.
Fiske, S. (1993). Controlling other people: the impact of power on stereotyping. *American Psychologist*, 48: 621–628.
Frankl, V. (1985). *Man's Search for Meaning*. New York: Washington Post.
Fromm, E. (1963). *The Art of Loving*. New York: Bantam Books.
Gillan, A. (2013). Yes, I'm an only child and, no, I'm not depressed—or beastly. *Guardian*, 22 August.
Grayling, A. C. (2002). *The Reason of Things: Applying Philosophy to the 21st Century*. London: Weidenfeld & Nicolson.
Howe, M. G., & Madgett, M. E. (1975). Mental health problems associated with the only child. *Canadian Psychiatric Association Journal*, 20: 160–165.
Husserl, E. (1927). Phenomenology. In: *Encyclopædia Britannica* (14th edn.), vol. 17 (pp. 699–702). Chicago, IL: Encyclopædia Britannica.
Jiao, J., Ji, G., & Jing, Q. (1986). Comparative study of behavioural qualities of only-children and sibling children. *Child Development*, 57: 357–361.
Mancillas, A. (2006). Challenging the stereotypes about only children: a review of the literature and implications for practice. *Journal of Counselling and Development*, 84(3): 268–275.
McKibben, B. (1999). *Maybe One: A Case for Smaller Families*. New York: Plume.
McLeod, J. (2003). *An Introduction to Counselling*. Maidenhead: Open University Press.
McLeod, J. (2011). *Qualitative Research in Counselling and Psychotherapy*. London: Sage.
Mearns, D. (1996). Working at relational depth with clients in person-centred therapy. *Counselling*, 7(4): 306–311.
Mearns, D., & Thorne, B., with McLeod, J. (2013). *Person-centred Counselling in Action*. London: Sage.
Mitchell, J. (2003). *Siblings: Sex and Violence*. Oxford: Polity Press.
Murray, J. (2013). The lifelong pain of being a lonely only. *Daily Mail*, 23 March.
Pitkeathley, J., & Emerson, D. (1994). *The Only Child*. London: Souvenir Press.

Richardson, A. (1998). www.ann-richardson.co.uk. Accessed 1 October 2015.
Rogers, C. (1951). *Client-centered Therapy.* London: Constable.
Rogers, C. (1961). *On Becoming a Person.* London: Constable.
Rose, C. (2012). *Self-awareness and Personal Development.* Basingstoke: Palgrave Macmillan.
Rosenberg, B., & Hyde, J. S. (1993). The only child: is there only one kind of only? *Journal of Genetic Psychology, 154*(2): 269–282.
Rowe, D. (2007). *My Dearest Enemy, My Dangerous Friend.* Hove: Routledge.
Sachs, O. (1985). *The Man who Mistook his Wife for a Hat.* London: Duckworth.
Sartre, J.-P. (1956). *Being and Nothingness.* New York: Washington Press.
Smith, J., Flower, P., & Larkin, M. (2009). *Interpretative Phenomenological Analysis.* London: Sage.
Sorensen, B. (2008). *Only Child Experience and Adulthood.* Basingstoke: Palgrave Macmillan.
Spinelli, E. (2005). *The Interpreted World: An Introduction to Phenomenological Psychology* (2nd edn). London: Sage.
Stewart, A. E. (2004). Can knowledge of client birth order bias clinical judgment? *Journal of Counselling and Development, 82*: 167–176.
Sugarman, L. (2004). *Counselling and the Life Course.* London: Sage.
Von Hippel, W., Sekaquaptewa, D., & Vargas, P. (1995). On the role of encoding processes in stereotype maintenance. *Advances in Experimental Social Psychology, 27*: 177–253.
Winnicott, D. W. (1958). *The Capacity to be Alone in The Maturational Processes and the Facilitating Environment.* London: Hogarth Press.
Yalom, I. (1991). *Love's Executioner and Other Tales of Psychotherapy.* London: Penguin.

CHAPTER FOUR

Processing perceived parental rejection through personal development

Tracey Clare

Introduction

Perceived parental rejection in childhood is a topic of interest to me based on personal experience. While training to be a person-centred counsellor, my sense of self was profoundly affected by the personal development (PD) aspect of the course. I had previously been attached to the idea that any change in my feelings about self would result from a cognitive process of intervention, which I had self-implemented in the form of goal-setting over a period of years, with some degree of success. However, when problems in my life arose, I found myself once again bound in a cycle of self-rejection and self-loathing, typified in the research by Rohner (1986). The turning point for me occurred during the process of engaging in PD groups and personal therapy, purposefully choosing to work towards my own self-growth. I was often frustrated by the lack of cognitive control I felt throughout this process, but I gradually began to understand and accept the nature of my feelings and to listen to them and give them voice. I was not to know at the time that the sensitive listening of others, and their warm acceptance of me, would be so incredibly life changing, leading to a reintegration of my sense of self and the development of greater inner autonomy (Rogers, 1980). Unexpectedly, feelings of self-acceptance, self-compassion, and positive self-regard slowly unfolded and I began tentatively to realise that I could learn to trust in the process of the actualising tendency (Rogers, 1980).

It is from my own intensely rewarding experience that I felt compelled to study the experience and outcomes of others, and to consider, in context, where their meaning making of parental rejection and PD converged and differed in timbre. My aim was to investigate the effect of PD on perceived parental rejection, specifically asking, "Does the experience of personal development in counsellor training impact on residual adult feelings derived from perceived parental rejection in childhood?" There are empirical studies which unfortunately demonstrate adverse outcomes for participants involved in PD groups (e.g., Back, 1988; Irving, 1993), and it is with this knowledge that I do not assume that my own experience is the experience of others. I do hope, however, that this chapter stimulates more professional interest in, and awareness of, the outcomes of perceived parental rejection and a renewed interest in providing support and care for those adults and children who continue to suffer the effects.

What the literature says

Maternal and paternal acceptance–rejection

It is widely acknowledged in the literature that a fundamental need of every infant is the provision of an emotionally responsive mother (e.g., Ainsworth, 1989; Baumrind, 1989; Bowlby, 1969; Rohner, 1975, 1986; Winnicott, 1964), capable of understanding and accepting her infant's needs (Dunn et al., 1987; Miller, 1997b; Monti et al., 2014), in a dialogue informed by developmental readiness (Spitz, 1963). The "initial mutual intimacy" (Miller, 1997b, p. 33) enjoyed by mother and child provides a secure base for the child's development (Bowlby, 1988), and such availability of maternal warmth is predictive of emotional health in offspring (Chen et al., 2000). In contrast, perceived maternal rejection, whereby the mother is experienced as a hostile force in the environment, can have devastating effects on the child's emotional development (Dwairy et al., 2010). Miller (1997b) asserts that "a small child feels he is in deadly danger if he loses the love of the person closest to him" (p. 96), arousing not only fear, but also more complex feelings of anxiety, shame, self-blame, and hopelessness (Thomas, 1999).

Paternal acceptance has been shown to correlate with healthy emotional development in offspring also (Veneziano & Rohner, 1998), and paternal rejection has been linked to psychopathology (Dwairy et al., 2010). Another study, however, suggested that maternal acceptance mediates outcomes for offspring in relation to paternal acceptance (Lila et al., 2007). On reflection, the complex dynamic of the relationship between parents means it is likely that paternal behaviour is influenced by maternal behaviour (McBride et al., 2005), and vice versa. For example, fathers who provide relief to mothers as the primary carer are more likely to raise children who feel accepted by their mothers, and mothers who dominate childcare to the extent that fathers spend little time with their children are likely to produce children who feel rejected by their fathers (Rohner, 1986). Research demonstrates that the quality of the mother–father bond also has an impact on behavioural outcomes for offspring, suggesting that an unsatisfactory partnership is one causal effect of inadequate mothering (Osborne & McLanahan, 2007). It follows, then, that the provision of a warm, nurturing mother is more probable if the father plays a role in childcare and the relationship between the mother and father is emotionally satisfying to both.

It is certainly the case to date that the literature has paid more attention to the role of the mother than the role of the father in relation to the rearing of offspring. Although, as societal patterns of child care change and fathers increasingly take on the role of the main carer, an increase in funding for studies exploring the effects of paternal acceptance–rejection has been made available by the International Society for Interpersonal Acceptance and Rejection (ISIPAR) (www.isipar.org/index.html), and bodies such as the National Fatherhood Initiative (www.fatherhood.org/). The reigning paradigm, however, suggests that the biggest cause of emotional disturbance in young children is an effect of perceived rejection in relation to the primary attachment figure (Dwairy et al., 2010), and, therefore, most often the mother.

Outcomes for rejected children

The ability of the primary attachment figure to express "warmth, love and acceptance" (Schmitt, 1980, p. 237) is a crucial proponent of healthy emotional development in children. Cross-cultural studies (Rohner et al., 2003) suggest that children who perceive such attitudes tend to demonstrate healthy psychological adjustment in adulthood, whereas those who experience a hostile parental environment demonstrate emotional disturbance in adulthood (Khaleque & Rohner, 2002; Rohner, 1975, 1986, 2004). Specifically, perceived parental rejection in childhood is acknowledged as a causal factor of adolescent and adult aggression, hostility, dependent-type behaviour, diminished self-esteem and self-adequacy (Khaleque & Rohner, 2002; Rohner, 1975, 1986), heightened feelings of anxiety and insecurity (Rohner, 1986; Rohner & Rohner, 1980) and difficulties in relation to self and others, manifesting in feelings that are "intensely painful" (Rohner, 2004, p. 833). Miller (1997a) asserts that the experience of rejection in the early years "damages a human being for life" (p. 160). Longitudinal research conducted by Valliant (2012), however, found that adult male offspring who perceived maternal rejection as a child no longer suffered the intense effects over the age of fifty. Valliant (2012) proposes that compensatory life events are capable of exerting a therapeutic effect enabling personal growth and psychological adjustment.

Rohner (1986) acknowledges that unexpressed feelings of rejection result in symbolic behaviours that manifest in a disconnected expression. He gives an example of children who are typically discouraged from expressing feelings of anger, growing up to internalise or externalise it. Rohner (1986) and Rogers (1951) agree that cultural values generally dictate parental acceptance or rejection of emotional expression in offspring. Rogers (1951) proposes that parental conditions of worth elicit desirable behaviour in children and, for him, the resultant disintegration and separation of the Self is the cause of internalised and externalised harmful behaviour. Fernald (2000) concurs, theorising that enforced behaviour has the effect of producing "a split between organismic experiencing and self" (p. 173). A child's emotional needs, thereby, remain unmet, causing incongruence and a diminished sense of self (Murphy, 2009).

Rejection as pain and the loss of self

It is instinctive for a child to believe that they are to blame for parental rejection and to introject parental attitudes towards themselves (Hamilton, 1989), making it difficult to appropriately express the pain they feel, out of fear of total parental abandonment (Miller, 1997b). Inevitably, "the child must suppress his rage to survive in a hostile environment, must even stifle his massive overwhelming pain in order not to die of it" (Miller, 1997a, p. 162). Fernald (2000) recognises the visceral "organismic experiencing" (p. 172) of the body, and, for a young child without the skills of cognitive interpretation, the pain is perhaps felt as a very real sensation. For ethical reasons, research into a child's feelings regarding parental rejection is restricted, and, where it has been possible, parental consent is usually a prerequisite of such studies (Carroll-Lind et al., 2006), compounding difficulties in effectively examining the topic. Additionally, research into the phenomenology of rejected children might not always be fully understood. McAdams and colleagues (2011) postulate that rejected children, "often include unrealistic and exaggerated themes of personal failure, self-blame, and inadequacy, themes that define not only their life experiences but also their views of themselves" (p. 34). Such objective descriptions of phenomenology suggest that researchers could struggle, or fail to engage adequately, with the meaning making of rejected children. An alternative method of studying the topic is to interview adults who experienced the pain of perceived parental rejection in childhood.

Research suggests that the pain of rejection in childhood is either felt intensely and internalised (e.g., Rogers, 1951; Rohner, 1986; McAdams et al., 2011), or blocked from awareness and inflicted on others as the child matures (Miller, 1987; Rogers, 1951; Rohner, 1986). Ainsworth and colleagues (1978) assert that where rejection is felt sporadically, the child strives to win parental acceptance in a bid to feel that they are safe and wanted, and where rejection is severely perceived, the child withdraws and attempts to self-nurture. In essence, the child becomes either more dependent on the parent or defensively independent (Khaleque & Rohner, 2002; Rohner, 1975, 1986, 2004). Both responses are illustrative of dependency behaviours that stunt the growth of emotional independence and leave the child lacking in self-nurturing behaviours (Rohner, 1986) and the ability to self-soothe (Gallop, 2002). It can also be argued that both are a result of introjected conditions of worth, coercing accordance with another's values or eliciting reactions in defiance of them (Rogers, 1961).

Dependency is recognised as a risk factor in a variety of psychological maladaptive conditions (Greenberg & Bornstein, 1988). One outcome of emotional over-reliance on others is the loss of a sense of self (Hoogstad, 2008), and the then corresponding development of an external locus of control (Rogers, 1951). Strickland (1978) proposes that individuals who exhibit an external locus of control experience lower levels of emotional stability and psychological health, and those with an internal locus of control are much more aware and accepting of feelings relating to self. Suicide ideation (Williams & Nickels, 1969) and suicide attempts (Melges & Weisz, 1971) are found to be significantly higher in those with external loci of control, suggesting a lack of self-acceptance and the ability to self-nurture. In contrast, perceived parental acceptance has been found to significantly correlate with internal loci of control in children (Rohner et al., 1980), indicating that parental warmth and acceptance is perhaps related to inner autonomy in offspring. The role of nurturant mothers, in particular, was found to predict internal loci of control in female offspring (MacDonald, 1971), implying emotional independence and a sense of self in daughters are positively affected by maternal warmth.

Rejection sensitivity

Rejected children can be extremely wary of forming relationships with others. Erikson (1998) ascribes the ability to trust and form relationships, to the successful meeting of a child's needs in infancy. Conversely, the unsuccessful resolution of the initial psycho-social stage of development produces a feeling of hopelessness in regard to trusting others (Erikson, 1998). Rohner (1986) asserts that "the most outstanding and consistently found trait among rejected children is their inability to form warm attachments to others" (p. 84). This behavioural reaction is possibly one of rejection sensitivity, which can be understood as "the tendency to anxiously expect, readily perceive, and intensely react to rejection" (Kross et al., 2007, p. 945), and the perceived threat of abandonment by significant others (Özen et al., 2011). Bowlby (1969, 1973) theorises that infants build a relationship schema informed by the primary attachment relationship they experience. Consequently, rejecting behaviour by the significant attachment figure leads to a belief in the child that they are unworthy of love (Özen et al., 2011). The resultant expectation of interpersonal rejection or abandonment becomes a self-fulfilling prophecy (Merton, 1948), as rejected children learn to adopt behaviours that subliminally encourage further rejection from people in their social environment (Dozier, 2003), compounding their initial experience (Sroufe, 1990).

The literature acknowledges friendships as an important factor in developing feelings of self-worth and self-acceptance (Rubin et al., 2004). Rejected children typically shy away from friendships (Rohner, 1986), and, thus, negate developing positive feelings towards self in this way. Feelings of unworthiness (Özen et al., 2011; Rohner, 1986), introjected from a rejecting style of parenting, then become self-reinforced (Rosenberg, 1962), compounding the isolation and loneliness that often stems from rejection sensitivity (Rohner, 1986). The failure of the significant attachment figure to meet the needs of the child has a snowball effect on the psychosocial stages of development, and, thus, by the time the child has reached young adulthood, a crisis is likely to occur that is unsuccessfully resolved (Erikson, 1998). Buber (1957) maintains that the embedded mistrust of others negates any genuine meeting of another in relationship.

Rejection and the transition into adulthood

Arnett (2007) suggests that this period of the life span is the most "heterogeneous" and "least structured" of all (p. 69), which can cause real difficulties for isolated and lonely young adults, bereft of emotional support (Sugarman, 2001). The childhood trauma of parental rejection, in combination with the later effects of poor attachments in friendships (Kobak, 1999), serves to increase vulnerability at this stage, and the triggering effect of the transition intensifies the acting out of attachment behaviour formed in childhood (Riggs & Han, 2009), often resulting in mental health issues (Arnett, 2007). Rohner (1986) agrees that outcomes for rejected children climax during this transitional period into adulthood. For McAdams and colleagues (2011), it is the unexpressed grief of childhood rejection that contributes to outcomes concerning mental health. The term "chronic sorrow" (Roos, 2002), usually attributed to illness or disability, describes grief that exists in an unresolved state, due to the loss of self in response to a life-changing event (Weingarten, 2012). Arguably, then, an individual, who as a child perceived parental rejection, may be said to psychologically suffer because of chronic sorrow. The cumulative effects of unprocessed grief are recognised as degenerative in nature

(Jacobs, 2004), causing a downward spiral of mental health during adolescence and into adulthood.

The literature suggests that attachment style is a predictor of outcomes for young people during this transitional stage. Bowlby (1973) argues that an anxious style tends to result in feelings of unworthiness and dependency behaviours, while aloofness and lack of trust in others are indicative of an avoidant style. Rohner (1986) stipulates that dependency, as an outcome of rejection, is consistent with an anxious attachment style; however, the array of projected outcomes (Khaleque & Rohner, 2002; Rohner, 1975, 1986, 2004; Rohner & Rohner, 1980) correlate with a range of outcomes predicted by both attachment styles.

Newer research by Bartholemew (1990) introduced the idea of an adult attachment style referred to as "fearful avoidant" (p. 147). This conceptualises the craving for intimacy in adulthood, but avoidance of it, based on feelings of unworthiness and a belief that they, as an adult, are unlovable. Thus, the need for intimacy remains unmet, in the self-defeating cycle of rejection sensitivity that prevents the experience of it. There appears to be much cohesion between outcomes for fearful avoidant adult attachment (Bartholemew, 1990) and those postulated by interpersonal perceived acceptance–rejection theory (IPARTheory) (Rohner, 2004). The characteristics of aloofness, passivity, insecurity, inability to trust and rely on others, and feelings of unworthiness (Bartholomew & Horowitz, 1991) closely mimic hostility, dependency, anxiety, and insecurity, difficulties in relation to others, and feelings of self-inadequacy (Khaleque & Rohner, 2002; Rohner, 1975, 1986, 2004; Rohner & Rohner, 1980). It is perhaps at this crucial stage of development that an attachment style is most closely resonant with the emerging adult's experience of rejection in childhood.

For Erikson (1998), this difficult transitional stage is the struggle for identity *vs.* role confusion, and intimacy *vs.* isolation. If the rejected adolescent emerges from the former in a state of identity confusion, having no clear sense of self, the inevitable result is that the young adult matures into a being without facility for intimacy (Sugarman, 2001). Thereafter, the prognosis for relationship with self and others is poor, unless an intervention of therapeutic value succeeds in having a transformative effect (Bartholemew & Horowitz, 1991).

Rejection and personal development

Bartholemew and Horowitz (1991) concluded that life-enhancing experiences, such as marrying a supportive partner, are capable of moderating the effects of problematic attachments. It is the aim of this chapter to explore the role of PD, as experienced on a person-centred training course, as a way in which complex emotional effects of perceived parental rejection might be processed.

A core value of the person-centred approach is to fully enter into the phenomenology of the other, and work in a non-directive way, at the pace of the client, and only with the material that is brought (Joseph, 2005), fully respectful of how a person has interpreted their past experiences and how, as a result, they experience their life in the here and now. Psychopathology, a possible outcome of rejection, is reinterpreted as "a fragile process" in person-centred terms (Warner, 1991), acknowledging that an individual might struggle to form relationships because of a propensity to perceive rejection or threatening behaviour where none is intended (Crisp, 2011). In such circumstances, it might be necessary that pre-therapy (Prouty, 1998) be engaged initially to establish the conditions in which psychological contact could be made. If an individual demonstrates the ability to make psychological contact in therapy, Rogers (1957, 1959) argues that an individual's perception of the remaining necessary and sufficient conditions will enable the release of visceral feelings trapped within the body. This shift in emotion is thought to be demonstrative of irreversible change in the Self (Rogers, 1961). Bohart and Tallman (2010) support the argument that the ability of the actualising tendency to self-heal rests on the provision of Rogers' (1957) six necessary and sufficient conditions of therapeutic change.

Mearns (1997) acknowledges a person-centred training community as a therapeutic environment committed to supporting the individual growth of all trainees on their journey towards practising person-centred therapy. Although there is no definitively agreed definition of what PD is (Donati & Watts, 2005), and no scope here to enter into that debate, the core focus is on a thorough exploration of self and the facilitation of the same for others. Johns (2012) describes it as "a consistent and continual striving for self and other awareness, knowledge, understanding and acceptance" in a "purposeful process" (p. 17). Thus, it is with intent that the trainee sets out to accomplish an awareness and understanding of his or her personal fears, and "experiment" with "fearless relating", in a process that differentiates PD from personal therapy (Mearns, 1997, p. 94). By this, it is meant that thoughts and feelings relating to self and others are fully admitted into awareness without distortion or denial (Rogers, 1951), in a flow of full organismic experiencing. Josselson (1996) underlines the significance of developing a transparent relationship with self and others in an environment of empathy, genuineness, and unconditional positive regard. For Fernald (2000), such an environment releases the force of the actualising tendency whereby the process of PD is enabled.

An intimate therapeutic environment might, however, pose a threat to the adult trainee rejected as a child, as self-disclosure carries strong expectations of abandonment (Özen et al., 2011), even though there is often an overwhelming desire for intimacy in relationships (Özen et al., 2011). Mearns (1997), however, cites congruent relating within a PD group as an experience demonstrative of the resilience of the Self, in that the Self survives without annihilation. Therefore, if a trainee is able to experiment with "fearless relating" (Mearns, 1997, p. 94) in self-disclosure, it is hoped that rejection sensitivity can be gradually overcome and the sense of self reintegrated (Rogers, 1951).

In large community groups there is often conflict and criticism (Gillon, 2007) that emerge out of the "psychological hunger" of members of groups (Houston, 1990, p. 55) in a cry for acceptance disguised by defensiveness. Group process is the developmental evolution (Johns, 2012) of the whole journeying to accept its parts. Each member strives not only for self-awareness and self-acceptance, but also for other-awareness and other-acceptance, that all members may grow towards authenticity (Thorne, 1991). For Fey (1955) the development of self-acceptance not only enables the acceptance of others, but also creates the perception of acceptance by others. Rogers (1961) too found that the growth in self-acceptance correlates with the growth of other-acceptance. The effective facilitation of groups is dependent on a self-accepting facilitator and their ability to express the attitudes of warmth, acceptance and genuineness towards others, enabling individual members of the group to feel both connected with each other, and an integral part of the whole (Johns, 2012). For Thorne (1991), this process leads to the condition of mutuality. Rogers (1951) asserts that only by experiencing these conditions can the actualising tendency become fully trusted and personal growth be achieved. The group, struggling towards cohesion, is reflective of the struggle of the individual towards integration.

Dedicated personal development groups are smaller than community groups, and, therefore, perhaps offer more emotional security (Johns, 2012). They provide a forum that can be used to explore personal issues in more depth, with supportive feedback from other members (Gillon, 2007), interwoven with the core conditions. Similar to personal therapy, the purpose is for the trainee to experience the "deathly" fear of their authentic self (Rogers, 1951, p. x). The reflective mirroring of self-disclosure by others provides an "exquisite witness" to the previously blocked and unexplored emotional pain (Jeffreys, 2005, p. 127), enabling the integration of the past experience. Weingarten (2012) argues that catastrophic experiences in life are not overcome, but are processed in the compassionate and empathic presence of another. When integration is achieved, it is usual for a person to feel an increase in autonomy (Rogers, 1951), which is symbolic of the growth of an internal locus of control. For Erikson (1998), group work facilitates the reintegration of the fragmented parts of the self, where previously incongruence of emotion, cognition, and self in relation to others are experienced.

The process of personal therapy provides the opportunity of a relationship for the trainee with a qualified professional, who is detached from the group and who offers a space for feelings to be explored and expressed in a therapeutic alliance, understood to be central to successful therapy (Mearns & Cooper, 2005). Briere (2002) attributes the intimate relationship of client and therapist as especially powerful in the building of a safe attachment and the ability to trust. The expression of the core conditions by the therapist is the central tenet that the relationship is built upon and the vehicle by which it is hoped a trainee can fully immerse herself in the engagement of her feelings, congruently admitting to feelings which also arise in response to the therapist (Mearns, 1997). The non-judgemental attitude of the therapist encourages an end to denial and distortion of past and present experience, enabling fuller organismic experiencing in the growth towards becoming a more fully functioning organism (Rogers, 1980).

In the successful engagement of PD, the trainee uses the therapeutic relationships he forges as agents for growth. Trainees learn to connect with themselves and with others in an environment of intimacy, a construct that Houston (1990) believes equates to love (p. 55).

Murphy (2009) proposes that the relational values upheld by the person-centred approach and the central focus on phenomenology qualify it as therapeutically effective for adults suffering from the psychological effects of unresolved childhood pain. Evidence-based practice also indicates that the therapeutic supporting of the grieving process is particularly benefited by the person-centred approach (Boelen et al., 2007). For McAdams and colleagues (2011), the expression of the grief caused by the rejecting experience is the key to processing and resolving the pain.

This chapter does not aim to add to the universalistic field of IPARTheory. My personal communication with Rohner confirmed that interpretative phenomenological approach is not a research method typically utilised by ISIPAR. The preferred method of data collection is from nomothetic studies of experience (Rohner, 2004; Rohner, et al., 2005), that "tend(s) to emphasise the phenomenological perspective" (Rohner, 2004, p. 831). Rather, this chapter aims to examine the phenomenology of a small sample of adults who have experienced perceived parental rejection in childhood, and, in some degree, gauge to what extent personal development in counsellor training helped to process that experience. The idiographic lens of the study hopes to unfold more fully the lived experiences behind the statistical data traditionally analysed.

Participants

The inclusion criteria specified that participants had perceived parental rejection in childhood and had also followed a programme of PD within a person-centred counselling training course. It was also necessary that participants had access to either a therapist or a clinical supervisor. This method of targeting a specific group of people, known as "purposive homogenous sampling" (Smith et al., 2009, p. 49), was aimed at recruiting participants with a uniformity of broad experience of PD and a capacity to assess its impact on processing perceived parental rejection, whereby convergence and divergence of idiographic experience could be recorded, measured, and interpreted (Smith et al., 2009). A flyer was created that specified the aforementioned criteria for participation in the study and permission was then sought from a small number of health and social care agencies, each based in the North West of England and North Wales, to circulate the flyer among person-centred counsellors working in those establishments, in both paid employment and a voluntary capacity. I was unable to consider any participants previously known to me, as dual relationships potentially cause bias within interviews and analysis (Bond, 2004), unintentionally skewing results.

Five respondents met the inclusion criteria and all were sent a copy of the proposed interview questions to facilitate a more informed decision about participation. One counsellor then decided not to participate, as, on reflection, she felt she did not meet the inclusion criteria. The four remaining counsellors agreed to volunteer, three of whom were female and one male. Ages ranged from thirty-five years to sixty-five years. All were of white British ethnicity. Each was qualified to Diploma level; three had qualified more than five years ago and one had recently qualified. All were working as counsellors in a voluntary capacity.

Data collection

Research data would be abstracted from disclosures during the interview process, and for this reason a substantial amount of time was taken to construct the questions in such a way that material could be elicited to the degree deemed necessary for effective research, while also upholding the principle of non-maleficence (BACP, 2013). A set of questions was produced that addressed the issue of sensitivity and would sufficiently prompt the elicitation of lived experience.

Prior to meeting any of the participants, a pilot interview was conducted with a colleague who met the full criteria of the study. This was a valuable experience in that it provided feedback concerning interview technique, and provided experiential insight into the difference between conducting a practitioner research interview in contrast to a counselling session. This distinction is necessary if unbiased material is to be collected and the aim of the research fulfilled (McLeod, 2003).

One-to-one interviews were conducted with each participant in order to elicit and capture the full essence of each related experience. Consent to audio-record each interview was obtained from each participant. This meant that disclosures could be tracked and monitored moment by moment, and any confusion I experienced could be addressed without delay. Questions were of a semi-structured format and open-ended. Each interview lasted between thirty-five and seventy minutes and audio-recording ceased at the end of each interview. The questions were as follows:

- Tell me about your childhood experiences with your parents, the ones that still stand out for you.
- Which experiences did you feel were most rejecting?
- How did those experiences make you feel about yourself?
- Do you feel it had any impact on your development?
- In which ways do you think it had an impact on you emotionally and psychologically? For example, your friendships and relationships with others, how you performed at school, etc.
- What was your experience of personal development during your training? For example, reflective journal writing, group work, personal therapy, etc.
- How did PD impact on your self-understanding and self-acceptance?
- Has your personal development had an impact on your current relationship with your parents, or how you now feel about your experiences in childhood?

As recommended by Smith and colleagues (2009), prior to the interview process I reflected deeply on my own experience of perceived parental rejection in order to pre-empt any confusion of my own experience with that of a participant. While interviewing, I consciously attempted to bracket off my own material in order to focus more fully on the participant's experience. I occasionally veered from the interview schedule only in response to disclosures that seemed particularly salient to a participant. I hoped that my minimal input would encourage the free flow of experience, without unnecessary hindrance or intrusion. I further hoped to hear each participant without judgement or undue comment, but, rather, with respect and recognition of their experience. On completion of each recording, participants spent some time reflecting on their interview, before being asked to sign a declaration of informed consent. In compliance with ethical guidelines (Bond, 2004), I advised each to speak to their clinical supervisor or counsellor about any painful feelings they might experience as a result of the process.

What was discovered

Each transcript unearthed many emergent themes and, after detailed analysis, these were collectively grouped to form superordinate themes. It was with careful deliberation that the following universal superordinate themes and sub-themes were chosen, as these appeared to best represent a holistic picture of experience common to all participants (Table 4.1). In unison with O'Connell and Kowal (1995), direct quotations were replicated without superfluous sounds such as "um" and "er" to produce textual coherence.

Superordinate theme 1: The child's experience

Subordinate theme 1.1: The pain of maternal abandonment

It seemed important to present the initial pain of rejection that each participant recounted, and the depth of explicit and implicit emotional turmoil that each alluded to. For Sue, Richard, and Mia the initial sense of rejection was the terror and devastation of physical maternal abandonment, whereas for Sally it was the sense of abandonment by her mother into an abusive situation beyond her control. For all, the abandonment was experienced as a young child. "I went into hospital ... I can remember screaming my head off ... I can remember lying in bed absolutely paralysed with fear" [Sue]. "I'd been abused by my dad's friends for a number of years, sexually, and when I told my

Table 4.1. Superordinate and subordinate themes.

Superordinate themes	The child's experience	Self in relation to others	The healing journey
Subordinate themes	The pain of maternal abandonment	Unworthy of acceptance	Acknowledging and feeling the pain
	The cry for parental acceptance	Issues with trust	Finding self-acceptance
	Transition into adulthood	Isolation and loneliness	Developing an internal locus of control
		Connecting with others	

mum about it, she'd said I'd made it up, said I was a liar, he was probably just drunk and didn't know what he was doing and so it just continued" [Sally]. "Somewhere my body remembers that ... that's inside me and the fear, that fear can kill you" [Richard]. "I was aware of fear but I wasn't feeling it, I was just aware of fear, manic, intense fear and the thought was, is that fear would kill you and then the next thought was, I've been as frightened as that" [Richard]. "She told me she was going out for a loaf of bread and then she didn't come back. That pretty much devastated me, really devastated me" [Mia]. "I used to cry myself to sleep a lot because I just wanted to live with her" [Mia].

Subordinate theme 1.2: The cry for parental acceptance

There was a universal theme of an intense striving for acceptance against the backdrop of parental rejection. For Sue, there is a sense that she perceived she would never be acceptable no matter how hard she tried, and for Sally, there was a yearning to win parental warmth, until the moment of realisation that she would never do so. Richard is hurt by the rejection of his father and the understanding that neither of his parents ever understood or accepted him. Mia presents evidence that she was a "good girl", and by implication should have been accepted. ". . . it was all around the not being good enough and it was all around my sister being, meant to be clever and I wasn't, and my cousin, and it was almost as if the planet I lived on wasn't good enough" [Sue]. "I always pretended, I kind of lived out this life, I started living out this life that I felt would please the relatives, my mum and her sister" [Sue]. "I always felt as though I had to try harder and harder and harder" [Sue]. "I've actually never been good enough for her. It's only later on in life, much later on in life that I've stopped trying to please her, you know, stopped trying to be good enough, stopped trying to get her approval" [Sally]. "I just always wanted their approval, I wanted to be good enough for them" [Sally]. "I loved this, it was great, but he only came for about six weeks and then he started to say, I'm too busy, you go on your own, and then I didn't like it" [Richard]. "They couldn't accept you [me], nothing, you know the disapproving stare on everything really, so it was like my parents don't even know me, and yet they think they do. They have no idea who I am, no idea at all in my eyes, because they couldn't accept me" [Richard]. "I was a good girl, so I didn't ever need to be pushed to do homework, I always did my homework and got all my work done" [Mia]. "I was high achieving at school and well behaved" [Mia]. "Was I just that unlovable?" [Mia].

Subordinate theme 1.3: Transition into adulthood

Each participant related difficulties in relation to becoming an adult and, in many ways, each appeared unprepared for the transition. Sue did not attain independence, Sally felt that she had to physically escape, and Richard and Mia suffered emotional distress. "My mother had chosen my job, she'd chosen my husband, you know, I never had a choice" [Sue]. "I just wanted to get away. I ended up running to London at seventeen" [Sally]. "I left school, completely unprepared for the adult world, like a basket case really . . ." [Richard]. "I got stuck trying to get into adulthood, couldn't do it, and I became depressed" [Mia].

Superordinate theme 2: Self in relation to others

Subordinate theme 2.1: Unworthy of acceptance

There was a common undercurrent that participants had an expectation of interpersonal rejection within their wider community. Sue, Sally, and Mia are convinced that nobody would want to be with them because they are unworthy, and Richard is incredulous that somebody would want to befriend him. "I didn't think that people, that anyone, would really want to know me if they really knew me" [Sue]. "I didn't think I was good enough for anybody" [Sally]. "When you've been rejected as a child you never feel good enough" [Sally]. "That was kind of just, just impossible that it happened, just impossible" [Richard]. "It's lunchtime, I'll go and be on my own because they couldn't possibly want to spend time with me, is what's underlying it all, they couldn't actually like me enough to be with me" [Mia]. "I want to be friends with women who don't necessarily want to be friends with me" [Mia]. "I'm surprised if people like me, and I expect people not to like me" [Mia].

Subordinate theme 2.2: Issues with trust

The topic of trust was endemic in the transcript of two participants, brought up in a third, and implied in the fourth. Sue alludes to her difficulty in trusting her personal counsellor. Sally speaks of her earlier difficulty in trusting men because of her early childhood experiences. Richard reports that he is unable to fully trust anyone. Mia admits that she has to test people for trustworthiness, in an implied process of self-protection. "I didn't feel able to sort of even share with her a great deal really, I was always a bit guarded and I'd kind of operate from my guarded self" [Sue]. "I didn't trust men; I thought they were all violent" [Sally]. "I don't trust people, nobody, even people I'm close to. I've noticed that. I'll watch everybody for what they do, I'm always waiting for something where they will let me down" [Richard]. "If you can't trust your parents as a kid, you can't trust anybody" [Richard]. "It's a very difficult thing to trust, it's huge" [Richard]. "I need to be able to trust people, so I have one, two good friends, I don't do a whole load of people" [Mia]. "If you're not safe to have as a friend, so if you're not transparent, if I can't trust you completely, I'm not interested" [Mia]. "I make people jump through hoops, I set standards very, very high and I judge them on that and make them jump through hoops and if they fail I'm not interested in them" [Mia].

Subordinate theme 2.3: Isolation and loneliness

The topic of relationships created a sense of each child and young adult feeling very much on their own. Sue speaks of a time where she had not one friend. Sally remembers having few friends. Richard reflects on how he felt alone and afraid in the world, and Mia states a preference for loneliness, implying it is preferable to the threat of rejection. "There was a two year gap where I didn't have a friend and that was devastating, that was huge" [Sue]. "I was very shy, quiet, always in the background, didn't have many friends" [Sally]. ". . . just like afraid of the world and isolated and lonely and at fourteen, fifteen, probably properly depressed then" [Richard]. "I spend quite a lot of time on my own and I'd rather be on my own than in an environment where I feel insecure" [Mia].

Subordinate theme 2.4: Connecting with others

A theme common to all was the finding of a person or people that they could trust and to whom they could form an attachment. For Sue and

Richard, friends came to symbolise family and transformed how they functioned in the world. For Sally and Mia, an attachment figure provided a transformative relationship. "I started making friends who were on their own journey so that was, that became my family really, I can really be who I am" [Sue]. ". . . a turning point for me was when I met my husband, who is a wonderful man, very loving and strong and really loves me" [Sally]. "Friends are important to me because they are probably like my family" [Richard]. "It just ended up he was my mate . . . and I kind of came out of my shell, you know, I was confident and I put weight on, I felt different, it was great. He set me up really, he set me up, yeah, so that was kind of just, just impossible that it happened, just impossible . . ." [Richard]. "I'd become attached to this woman as a mother-figure and couldn't, didn't want to leave her . . ." [Mia].

Superordinate theme 3: The healing journey

Subordinate theme 3.1: Acknowledging and feeling the pain

Each participant described the process through which they were enabled to face their emotional pain. Sue and Sally share their experiences of reliving the pain through self-disclosure. Richard and Mia talk about accepting the pain as part of the healing process. "Shedding the tears was the thing for me" [Sue]. "We went on the weekend away . . . and everything just fell out, there it was on the floor really" [Sue]. "It's unfashionable to talk about counselling being a healing process, but I do think it is, and I think when I've cried about something, you watch films on the telly don't you and that triggers stuff that you're not quite aware of really and I just go with any of those . . . because I know that some of it will be healed" [Sue]. "My massive turning point was on the course . . . I just decided that I was going to tell the truth, what my life had been like, you know, all the horrors really, and I can remember shaking from the top of my head to the bottom of my feet, just shaking as I was saying it all . . . but just feeling so cathartic after, lighter. It was just wonderful to get it out there" [Sally]. ". . . to get used to the kind of pain, it won't destroy me . . ." [Richard]. ". . . pain I think annihilates me, I'm afraid of being destroyed completely . . . it feels like it could destroy me . . . I guess it's getting used to knowing that's not what's going on, you're not going to get destroyed"

[Richard]. "I just sat with this feeling for about four months, I acknowledged it and I recognised what it was and I gave it a name of depression and I didn't take any medication for it, I just let it run its course, and since I did that I feel much calmer, I think there's more self-acceptance" [Mia].

Subordinate theme 3.2: Finding self-acceptance:

Through the process of PD, the ability to find a degree of self-acceptance emerged as a common outcome. Sue shares how she feels she has been through a healing process that has led to self-understanding. Sally, Richard, and Mia directly refer to feelings of self-like. All portray satisfaction with the person that they identify themselves to be. "I worry less about whether people want me or don't want me, because I kind of understand myself better now" [Sue]. ". . . it took me forty years to get to the point where I could say, Sally you're good enough, a nice person" [Sally]. "It's all OK, it's all OK and I like myself. I don't want to be anyone else, I'd rather be dead" [Richard]. "I think that piece of work led to self-acceptance. I can remember looking in a shop window and actually seeing myself as I was, I think I was about twenty-three and thinking, yeah, I like that person" [Mia]. "I can integrate me; I can be me and be a parent and not feel I'm going to leave. Yeah, I think there's self-acceptance there as well really" [Mia]. "I am quite accepting of that's who I am" [Mia].

Subordinate theme 3.3: Developing an internal locus of control

There was a sense that each had moved from a position of dependency towards one of independence. Sue indicates that she has taken self-responsibility and changed the balance of power in her life. Sally speaks of a pivotal point where she decided to also assume self-responsibility. Richard implies that he now has a sense of where he is, rather than existing in confusion, and Mia feels able to rely on herself. "It's all been like a silent revolution really" [Sue]. "Nobody is going to sort this lot out for me, it's going to be up to me" [Sue]. "I'm in charge of me now" [Sue]. "I deal with situations" [Sue]. "I took control and that was it" [Sally]. "I just woke up one day and thought do you know I'm sick of trying to please her and I'm not going to do it any more" [Sally]. "I have a sense of where I am" [Richard]. "I generally don't believe what I am told (haven't since my mother told me she was going out for bread and didn't come back), know my own mind, and draw my own conclusions" [Mia].

Strong themes emerged from the transcripts and these were generally supported in the existing literature. The experience of rejection for each was qualitatively different, but a theme of abandonment emerged from each interview, as did the need for parental acceptance. The transition into adulthood seemed especially difficult for all participants and each had a unique experience at that stage in the life span. The topic of relationships was introduced by an interview question and the experiences that emerged converged at several points. Participants reported issues with trust, feeling unworthy of relationships, being alone or lonely, and then experiencing connection with another. A core theme of pain arose out of the experience of PD and this was experienced in idiosyncratic ways, both explicitly in groups and privately acknowledged in relationship with self. Although the pain of rejection was still palpable for each participant, as reflected in the transcripts, the intensity had diminished for some. All had the experience of facing the pain. Each alluded to greater self-acceptance in the interview and the development of an inner autonomy, not previously experienced.

Bringing together the literature and the findings

It is evident from the phenomenology related by all four participants that each experienced deeply rejecting experiences in their childhoods, which continued to affect them over the course of the life span. Many of the outcomes they related are supported in the relevant literature. Research points to transformative experiences capable of facilitating lasting change in adults rejected as children (Bartholomew & Horowitz, 1991; Valliant, 2012), and this was the experience of all four participants. Significant growth was evident in how they are now able to relate to self and others. In this discussion, I shall attempt to explore the similarities and differences between each participant's experiences and define to what extent PD enabled the processing of feelings relating to perceived parental rejection. Three major themes were identified from the narratives and ten subordinate themes. Together, these captured the essence of ideography and the greater shared experience.

At the outset of each interview participants were prompted to relate a significant event in their childhood history. Each story was pervaded with a strong sense of maternal abandonment, and their experiences of that resonate with the literature. All implied through their dialogue that it was the mother whom they identified as the primary attachment figure and the person primarily responsible for the experience of abandonment. The perceived withdrawal of maternal love is a traumatic event for a child, and a cause of emotional disturbance (Dwairy et al., 2010). For Miller (1997b), maternal rejection is always internalised by a child as abandonment. Sue remembered very clearly the terror she felt at being left by her mother in the unfamiliar surroundings of a hospital. Richard's embodied memory of being abandoned in a hospital came back to him as an adult in an altered state of consciousness, which Rogers (1980) describes as a type of portal enabling a "flood of experiencing at a level far beyond that of everyday living" (p. 123). At that moment of awareness an "intense fear" consumed Richard with a certainty that, "that fear can kill you". For Richard, it was the first time he had been separated from his mother. Miller (1997b) acknowledges that the historic practice of hospital separation occurred out of "ignorance" (p. 33) and has the effect of deeply traumatising a child.

The experiences related by Sue and Richard imply that the experience of abandonment is to experience "deadly danger" (Miller, 1997b, p. 96). Thomas (1999) suggests that survival of abandonment brings with it feelings of powerlessness and hopelessness that affect the continued development of a child. Although self-blame was not articulated by any participant, Hamilton (1989) asserts that this is the inner response of a child in reaction to behaviour perceived as parental rejection. From the phenomenology described by all participants, it seems that each experienced behavioural outcomes classified as emotional disturbance (Khaleque & Rohner, 2002; Rohner, 1975, 1986, 2004), meaning they possibly no longer felt able to place their trust in their self or a parent. The intensity of pain caused by rejection in childhood (Rohner, 2004) is purported to be viscerally discerned (Fernald, 2000; Miller, 1997a). The embodied experiences articulated by Sue and Richard attest to this. The inherent shock of abandonment alluded to by all four participants, and the need for continued dependency on parents as carers, is indicative of a split in organismic experiencing and the self (Fernald, 2000). In such hostile circumstances the self must necessarily move from the infantile capacity to live and trust in experience, to the erroneous belief that it is an "untrustworthy organism" (Rogers, 1980, p. 168).

Although abandonment was expressed in terms of maternal behaviour, the theme of seeking acceptance applied to both parents for half of the participants. The literature suggests that there is a proclivity for children to seek parental acceptance, although it is phrased in a variety of ways. For Bowlby (1969, 1973), there is an instinctive need to maintain attachment bonds in order to survive, and for Rogers (1961, 1980), the actualising tendency strives towards self-enhancement, which, of course, rests on the ability of the child to receive care. Miller (1997a) asserts that the feelings culminating from parental rejection must necessarily be suppressed in the child to achieve parental acceptance in the future. All theories are suggestive of an innate drive that strives for survival, although Ainsworth and colleagues (1978) suggest that parental acceptance is only sought where there is a perception that it may be provided, and severe experiences of rejection result in a child's withdrawal from the parent.

For Sue "the planet I lived on wasn't good enough". This suggests that Sue perceived herself as an alien in her mother's world and, thus, created a persona ("I always pretended") whereby she could appear to fit in. This took an incredible amount of effort to keep up the pretence ("I had to try harder and harder"). Sally explained that "I've actually never been good enough for her [her mother]". This did not stop Sally striving for acceptance ("I just always wanted their approval, I wanted to be good enough for them"). Richard yearned for time with his father, but felt as if he was brushed aside. As well as suffering paternal rejection, a contributory factor in emotional disturbance (Dwairy et al., 2010), he reported a total lack of parental acceptance, to the extent that his parents never knew him. Mia describes herself as "a good girl" and "high achieving ... and well behaved", but was still "unlovable". In such circumstances of striving for acceptance and meeting rejection, it is typical for a child to believe that she is at fault and consequently suffer from extreme feelings of unworthiness (Dwairy et al., 2010; Hamilton, 1989; Özen et al., 2011). For each, it is also likely that organismic experiencing would have to be negated in favour of striving to meet parental conditions of worth, causing a psychological distancing from the self as a more acceptable self-concept was necessarily created. This is a typical response to a traumatic experience (Crisp, 2011; Fernald, 2000; Murphy, 2009; Rogers, 1961, 1980; Weingarten, 2012). The striving for acceptance implies dependency on the rejecting figures, in contrast to a growth in the ability to self-nurture (Rohner, 1986) and self-soothe (Gallop, 2002). The literature reflects that dependency tends to result in the loss of self (Hoogstad, 2008) and an externally placed locus of control (Rogers, 1951).

Sue disclosed in her interview that on the cusp of adulthood she conformed to the conditions of worth imparted by her mother. She reported, "I never had a choice". The younger Sue had created a persona in her strive for acceptance, a reaction typical in a child that perceived such an opportunity to win back feelings of safety and security (Ainsworth et al., 1978). It is possible, however, that, at this stage, a congruent connection with self had been lost in an effort to maintain her self-concept. The disintegration of the self in such circumstances is supported in the literature (Murphy, 2009; Rogers, 1951). In contrast, Sally chose to "get away" and left her parents. Ainsworth and colleagues (1978) propose that the reaction of withdrawal is a last resort in a climate of total rejection. Sally's behaviour is resonant of the outcome of defensive independence (Rohner, 1986), whereby bids for parental acceptance cease to be made because of the expectation of further rejection. During this period, Richard felt like a "basket case", sharing that he was "completely unprepared for the adult world". The reflection on the negative state of his mental health implies a lack of control over himself and his situation. Echoing Richard's experience, Mia "got stuck trying to get into adulthood", and she became "depressed". Resultant mental health issues during this transitional stage are highlighted in the literature (Arnett, 2007; Jacobs, 2004), and are perhaps symbolic behaviours of unexpressed rejection in childhood (Rogers, 1951; Rohner, 1986), and consequent unprocessed grief (McAdams et al., 2011).

All four participants related narratives suggesting they were "typically reluctant or unable to become involved with other people" (Rohner, 1986, p. 84). Sue was convinced that no one would really want to know her "if they really knew me". Richard shares how "impossible" it was that he found friendship and acceptance, revealing his fundamental belief that he was not worthy of either. Mia acknowledged that nobody could "actually like me enough to be with me", betraying the continuing presence of this belief. For Sally, "when you've been rejected as a child you never feel good enough". The child's reinforcing belief that they are unloved is applied to all future potential relationships (Rosenberg, 1962), negatively affecting the formation of intimate friendships (Kobak, 1999). That mind-set is iterated in the literature by Rohner's (1986) postulation that one possible outcome for a rejected child is a negative worldview, which is thought to perpetuate a cycle of interpersonal rejection (Dozier, 2003).

According to Buber (1957), if we believe that people do not like or value us we will consequently have no capacity for trust. Sue did not feel able to fully share her feelings with her personal therapist, confessing that "I'd kind of operate from my guarded self". It may be inferred from Sue's behaviour that she did not perceive the necessary and sufficient conditions of therapeutic change (Rogers, 1957). Although the reasons why cannot be assumed, it is possible that Sue's experience of trauma created a "fragile style of processing" (Warner, 1991, p. 41) more suited to sessions of pre-therapy (Prouty, 1998). Sue's interaction with her therapist and the use of the word "guarded" are indicative of a perceived threat to the self, suggestive of a fragile process (Crisp, 2011). For Rogers (1957), this first condition of establishing psychological contact must be met if a therapeutic intervention is to occur, and Crisp (2011) disputes that this condition can always be met in a traumatised person.

Sally reported that she was unable to trust men, as her experience taught her that they were all violent. Richard tellingly states "if you can't trust your parents as a kid, you can't trust anybody". Both experiences resonate with the abstract construction of an internal model of relationships based on an initial attachment figure (Bowlby, 1969, 1973). Richard shares that it is "very difficult" to trust still. For Mia, trust is the backbone of a relationship and she screens people for this quality. She is adamant that she cannot have people in her life that she does not trust. The inability to trust appears to prevent the development of intimacy in relationships (Bartholomew, 1990; Buber, 1957; Rohner, 1986; Sugarman, 2001) and the associated development of positive feelings towards self (Rubin et al., 2004) is thwarted. Feelings of unworthiness (Özen et al., 2011; Rohner, 1986), combined with trust issues, produce a self-reinforced cycle that can have the effect of isolating a rejected child (Rosenberg, 1962), and that typically continues into adulthood (Bartholomew, 1990).

One participant spoke directly of isolation and loneliness and each of the others alluded to it. Sue speaks of a period as a child where she did not have a friend and testifies that it was "devastating"; Sally remembers that she was "always in the background"; Richard was "afraid of the world" and "felt isolated and lonely"; Mia implies that loneliness is preferential to feeling "insecure" in relationship with others. For Rogers (1980), the most severe experience of loneliness is the "complete separation from one's autonomous organism" (p. 174), and that estrangement from self leads to "more feelings of isolation from others" (p. 171). It is intimated that without an authentic relationship with self, there can be no true relationship with another.

A pivotal event in the life of each was connecting with others. Each related how one or more individuals demonstrated acceptance, an attitude that Rogers (1980) equates to "liking". Sue's fellow peers on the counsellor training course became her "family" because she could "really be who I am". Richard also sees his friends as his family. He speaks in particular about one friend who made a great impression on his life, imbuing him with confidence. Sally met her husband-to-be and he was able to demonstrate that he loved her in a way that she could perceive. Sally calls this connection "a turning point". Rubin and colleagues (2004) credit shared intimacy in friendships as generating feelings of self-worth and contributing towards feelings of self-acceptance. The effects of friendship, therefore, appear to create the conditions of self-growth. Mia speaks about the connection she was able to make with her personal therapist, coming to know her as a "mother-figure". Mia infers that she was able to form an attachment in this relationship, and the idea of a mother is figurative of responding to the need for nurturance (Winnicott, 1964). Rogers (1980) suggests that it is when we experience people who are "being what they are" (p. 61) that we then dare to be who we are. Additionally self-accepting individuals tend to demonstrate acceptance towards others (Fey, 1955). Each participant appeared to experience a degree of "healing through meeting" (Buber, 1957) in the extended presence of such people.

The large group experience was where Sue experienced the pain of her past. It was expressed metaphorically, as though it "fell out . . . on the floor". Sue's choice of the word "fell" suggests it was almost an accidental exposure of self, as if the time had come where the pain of childhood could no longer sustain containment (Miller, 1997a). Sue described how she still sheds tears, alluding to a trust in her bodily capacity to self-heal. The embodied process of self-healing is widely acknowledged in the literature (Bohart & Tallman, 2010; Fernald, 2000; Miller, 2005; Rogers, 1980). Sally also experienced disclosure in a large group. She articulated in her interview that "I was going to tell the truth". She physically experienced her fear in her shaking body, and afterwards reported that she felt "lighter". Both Sue and Sally demonstrate an experimentation with "fearless relating" (Mearns, 1997, p. 94), a criteria of self-growth in PD (Mearns, 1997). Richard describes the pain in the present tense, as an annihilating force, "it feels like it could destroy me", but his experience of it is that he can feel the pain and survive it. Similarly, Mia sat with her pain and embraced it rather than resisted it. She "let it run its course". Mia used her fist to pinpoint where her depression resided in her body. These experiences reverberate with Roger's (1980) sense that emotions are viscerally held. For Miller (1997b), depression, fear, and loneliness are the aftermath of "the tragic loss of the self in childhood" (p. 38). Sue, Sally, and Mia indicate that they were able to let go of some residual feelings trapped inside them once they were able to get in touch with their organismic experiencing (Fernald, 2000). Richard learnt that in acknowledging the pain, he was able to tolerate it. In an environment perceived by an individual as therapeutic, emotional pain from the past is perhaps not eradicated, but, rather, processed (Weingarten, 2012), and this has the potential to free an individual from the associated outcomes of rejection.

Asked about the process of PD, Sue said that as a result she was less worried about whether or not others found her acceptable, because she had come to a better understanding of her self. Sally was able to comment that she was now "good enough". Richard and Mia were also able to say that they like who they are, and Mia felt as if she had experienced integration of the self, a phenomenon discussed in Rogers' (1951) fifteenth proposition, resulting in a "unified organism" (p. 514). A core aim of PD is for a trainee to develop both self-acceptance and acceptance of others (Johns, 2012; Thorne, 1991). Fey (1955) postulates that when self-acceptance is felt, it is more likely that acceptance is perceived from others in the social environment, and acceptance of others is then reciprocated. Key to self-acceptance is the willingness to face all aspects of the self (Rogers, 1951), and this appears to be less daunting in an environment permeated with the core conditions (Johns, 2012; Josselson, 1996; Thorne, 1991). The disclosures of all perhaps suggest, then, that they had embarked on a process of engaging in organismic experiencing to discover the hidden aspects of the self.

All participants demonstrated through their dialogue that they had moved from a state of emotional dependency to one of independence, albeit they differed by degree. Sue used the word "revolution" to describe her transformation, suggesting a seizure of power from the hands of another body. For Fernald (2000) the use of metaphor is symbolic of deep organismic experiencing. Clearly, there is a shift in Sue towards self-responsibility. Sally, too, speaks of taking "control", implying there was another force at work that previously had that control. For both, there is a clear move away from seeking parental acceptance, to determining what feels right for them. Richard now has "a sense of where I am", sounding fully grounded in his own experiential world, where organismic experiencing is perhaps now highly valued. Mia reveals through her words that she still has issues with trust, "I generally don't believe what I am told", but speaks of knowing "my own mind" and an ability to "draw my own conclusions". The development of inner autonomy suggests that the processing of perceived parental rejection refutes the existence of external loci of control. It is suggested in the literature that emotional independence and the growth of self engender an internal locus of control (Rohner et al., 1980).

It is evident that the experiencing of therapeutic conditions in relationship with others had a transformative effect on the way that all participants relate to self. The core finding of this small-scale study is that three participants began their healing journey through relationships with accepting others, before they embarked on a journey of PD. This therapeutic experience of intimacy is supported in the literature (Bartholomew & Horowitz, 1991; Valliant, 2012). One participant found accepting others on the counsellor training course. What the experience of PD did seem to add to each experience was the development of personal congruence. This attitude appeared to enable two participants to self-disclose to a PD group, and had the further effect of causing the remaining participants to honestly confront their experiences. Congruent relating to self and others appeared to result in greater self-acceptance. All participants endured the pain and grief of rejection as part of the PD process, and all, it seems, have begun to process the experience of rejection.

Conclusion

The study was limited in fully exploring all themes that emerged from the data and, thus, the research findings are not fully reflective of the participant's experiences. For the sake of brevity and restrictions on time, only the strongest themes could be included in the study. It is perhaps important to note that the methodological nature of the analysis would elicit an alternative set of themes if undertaken by another researcher. The participants attracted by the research title were all white British and, thus, other ethnicities were not represented in the findings.

Bohart and Tallman (2010) argue that it is the client more than the therapist who explains the success of therapy across the spectrum of therapeutic models. In this study, the purposeful intent of each participant to engage in the process of PD suggests that the trainee is a catalytic agent, but, as discussed, the experience of a therapeutic experience appears to be crucial in the process of self-growth. For Warner (1991) the person-centred approach is particularly helpful in working with a "fragile style of processing experiencing" (p. 41). There is a widespread belief in society that time is a great healer, but without the opportunity and space to grieve for what one has suffered there can be no healing. Greater understanding of this particular hurt might serve to enhance awareness and more thought of conciliatory measures.

A recommendation of this research is to conduct a comparable study to explore the phenomenology of adults who perceived acceptance by their parents in childhood. In conducting such a study, a detailed picture of those particular conditions would add to the current body of research currently used to inform practice regarding parenting programmes. Miller (1997a) proposes that "ignorance" about parenting behaviours poses "the great threat to the future of humanity" (p. 148). Only by continued research into the relationships between children and their parents can useful interventions be created to alleviate the suffering of those children who perceive rejection.

References

Ainsworth, M. D. S. (1989). Attachment beyond infancy. *American Psychologist, 44*: 709–716.

Ainsworth, M. D. S., Blehar, M. G., Waters, E., & Wall, S. (1978). *Patterns of Attachment: A Psychological Study of the Strange Situation*. Hillsdale, NJ: Lawrence Erlbaum.
Arnett, J. J. (2007). Emerging adulthood: what is it, and what is it good for? *Child Development Perspectives*, 1(2): 68–73.
Back, K. W. (1988). Encounter groups revisited. *Society*, 26: 50–53.
BACP (2013). *Ethical Framework for Good Practice in Counselling and Psychotherapy*. Lutterworth: BACP.
Bartholemew, K. (1990). An avoidance of intimacy: an attachment perspective. *Journal of Social and Personal Relationships*, 7(2): 147–178.
Bartholomew, K., & Horowitz, L. M. (1991). Attachment styles among young adults: a test of a four-category model. *Journal of Personality and Social Psychology*, 61(2): 226–244.
Baumrind, D. (1989). Rearing competent children. In: W. Damon (Ed.), *New Directions for Child Development: Child Development, Today and Tomorrow* (pp. 349–378). San Francisco, CA: Jossey-Bass.
Boelen, P., de Keijser, J., van den Hout, M., & van den Hout, J. (2007). Treatment of complicated grief: a comparison between cognitive-behavioral therapy and supportive counseling. *Journal of Consulting and Clinical Psychology*, 75: 277–284.
Bohart, A. C., & Tallman, K. (2010). Clients: the neglected common factor. In: B. L. Duncan, S. D. Miller, B. E. Wampold, & M. A. Hubble (Eds.), *The Heart and Soul of Change: Delivering What Works in Therapy* (2nd edn) (pp. 83–111). Washington, DC: American Psychological Association.
Bond, T. (2004). An introduction to the ethical guidelines for counselling and psychotherapy. *Counselling and Psychotherapy Research*, 4(2): 4–9.
Bowlby, J. (1969). *Child Care and the Growth of Love* (2nd edn). London: Penguin.
Bowlby, J. (1973). *Attachment and Loss: Vol. 2. Separation: Anxiety and Anger*. New York: Basic Books.
Bowlby, J. (1988). *A Secure Base*. Abingdon: Routledge.
Briere, J. (2002). Treating adult survivors of severe childhood abuse and neglect: further development of an integrative model. In: J. E. B. Myers, L. Berliner, J. Briere, C. Jenny, & T. Reid (Eds.), *The ASPAC Handbook on Child Maltreatment* (pp. 175–203). Newbury Park, CA: Sage.
Buber, M. (1957). *Pointing the Way*. New York: Harper & Row.
Carroll-Lind, J., Chapman, J. W., Gregory, J., & Maxwell, G. (2006). The key to the gatekeepers: passive consent to and other ethical issues surrounding the rights of children to speak on issues that concern them. *Child Abuse & Neglect*, 30: 979–989.

Chen, X., Liu, M., & Li, D. (2000). Parental warmth, control, and indulgence and their relations to adjustment in Chinese children: a longitudinal study. *Journal of Family Psychology: Journal of the Division of Family Psychology of the American Psychological Association (Division 43), 14*(3): 401–419.

Crisp, R. (2011). Person-centred rehabilitation counselling: revisiting the legacy of Carl Rogers. *Australian Journal of Rehabilitation Counselling, 17*(1): 26–35.

Donati, M., & Watts, M. (2005). Personal development in counsellor training: towards a clarification of interrelated concepts. *British Journal of Guidance & Counselling, 33*(4): 475–484.

Dozier, M. (2003). Attachment-based treatment for vulnerable children. *Attachment & Human Development, 5*: 253–257.

Dunn, J., Bretherton, I., & Munn, P. (1987). Conversations about feeling states between mothers and their young children. *Developmental Psychology, 23*: 1–8.

Dwairy, M., Achoui, M., Filus, A., Rezvannia, P., Casullo, M. M., & Vohra, N. (2010). Parenting, mental health and culture: a fifth cross-cultural research on parenting and psychological adjustment of children. *Journal of Child and Family Studies, 19*(1): 36–41.

Erikson, E. H. (1998). *The Life Cycle Completed.* London: W. W. Norton.

Fernald, P. S. (2000). Carl Rogers: body-centered counselor. *Journal of Counseling & Development, 78*(2): 172–179.

Fey, W. F. (1955). Acceptance by others and its relation to acceptance of self and others: a revaluation. *Journal of Abnormal and Social Psychology, 50*(2): 274–276.

Gallop, R. (2002). Failure of the capacity for self-soothing in women who have a history of abuse and self-harm. *Journal of the American Psychiatric Nurses Association, 8*: 20–22.

Gillon, E. (2007). *Person-Centred Counselling Psychology: An Introduction.* London: Sage.

Greenberg, R. P., & Bornstein, R. F. (1988). The dependent personality: II. Risk for psychological disorders. *Journal of Personality Disorders, 2*(2): 136–143.

Hamilton, G. N. (1989). A critical review of objects relations theory. *American Journal of Psychiatry, 146*: 1552–1560.

Hoogstad, J. (2008). Choice theory and emotional dependence. *International Journal of Reality Therapy, 28*(1): 63–68.

Houston, G. (1990). *Supervision and Counselling.* London: Rochester Foundation.

Irving, J. A. (1993). Personal development group work in counselling training and learning style preferences. Unpublished MSc dissertation: University of Hull.

Jacobs, B. J. (2004). From sadness to pride: seven common emotional experiences of caregiving. In: C. Levine (Ed.), *Always on Call: When Illness Turns Families into Caregivers* (pp. 111–125). Nashville, TN: Vanderbilt University Press.

Jeffreys, J. S. (2005). *Helping Grieving People when Tears Are Not Enough: A Handbook for Care Providers*. New York: Brunner-Routledge.

Johns, H. (2012). *Personal Development in Counsellor Training* (2nd edn). London: Sage.

Joseph, S. (2005). Understanding post traumatic stress from the person-centred perspective. In: S. Joseph & R. Worsley (Eds.), *Person Centred Psychopathology: A Positive Psychology of Mental Health* (pp. 190–201). Ross-on-Wye: PCCS Books.

Josselson, R. (1996). *The Space Between Us: Exploring the Dimensions of Human Relationships*. London: Sage.

Khaleque, A., & Rohner, R. P. (2002). Perceived parental acceptance–rejection and psychological adjustment: a meta-analysis of cross-cultural and intracultural studies. *Journal of Marriage and the Family, 64*: 54–64.

Kobak, R. (1999). The emotional dynamics of disruptions in attachment relationships: implications for theory, research, and clinical intervention. In: J. Cassidy & P. Shaver (Eds.), *Handbook of Attachment: Theory, Research, and Clinical Applications* (pp. 21–43). New York: Guilford Press.

Kross, E., Egner, T., Ochsner, K., Hirsch, J., & Downey, G. (2007). Neural dynamics of rejection sensitivity. *Journal of Cognitive Neuroscience, 19*(6): 945–956.

Lila, M., Garcia, F., & Gracia, E. (2007). Perceived paternal and maternal acceptance and childrens outcomes in Colombia. *Social Behavior and Personality: An International Journal, 35*(1): 115–124.

MacDonald, J. A. P. (1971). Internal–external locus of control: parental antecedents. *Journal of Consulting and Clinical Psychology, 37*(1): 141–147.

McAdams, C. R., Dewell, J. A., & Holman, A. R. (2011). Children and chronic sorrow: reconceptualizing the emotional impact of parental rejection and its treatment. *Journal of Humanistic Counseling, 50*(1): 27–41.

McBride, B. A., Brown, G. L., Bost, K. K., Shin, N., Vaughn, B., & Korth, B. (2005). Paternal identity, maternal gatekeeping, and father involvement. *Family Relations, 54*(3): 360–372.

McLeod, J. (2003). *Doing Counselling Research* (2nd edn). London: Sage.
Mearns, D. (1997). *Person-centred Counsellor Training.* London: Sage.
Mearns, D., & Cooper, M. (2005). *Working at Relational Depth in Counselling and Psychotherapy.* London: Sage.
Melges, F. T., & Weisz, A. E. (1971). The personal future and suicidal ideation. *Journal of Nervous and Mental Disease, 153*: 244–250.
Merton, R. K. (1948). The self-fulfilling prophecy. *Antioch Review, 8*: 193–210.
Miller, A. (1987). *For Your Own Good: The Roots of Violence in Child-rearing.* London: Virago.
Miller, A. (1997a). *Banished Knowledge. Facing Childhood Injuries.* London: Virago.
Miller, A. (1997b). *The Drama of Being a Child: The Search for the True Self.* London: Virago.
Miller, A. (2005). *The Body never Lies: The Lingering Effects of Hurtful Parenting.* London: W. W. Norton.
Monti, J. D., Rudolph, K. D., & Abaied, J. L. (2014). Contributions of maternal emotional functioning to socialization of coping. *Journal of Social and Personal Relationships, 31*(2): 247–269.
Murphy, D. (2009). Client-centred therapy for severe childhood abuse: a case study. *Counselling and Psychotherapy Research, 9*(1): 3–10.
O'Connell, D. C., & Kowal, S. (1995). Basic principles of transcription. In: J. A. Smith, L. Van Langenhove, & R. Harre (Eds.), *Rethinking Methods in Psychology* (pp. 93–105). London: Sage.
Osborne, C., & McLanahan, S. (2007). Partnership instability and child well-being. *Journal of Marriage and Family, 69*(4): 1065–1083.
Özen, A., Sümer, N., & Demir, M. (2011). Predicting friendship quality with rejection sensitivity and attachment security. *Journal of Social and Personal Relationships, 28*(2): 163–181.
Prouty, G. (1998). Pre-therapy and pre-symbolic experiencing: evolutions in person-centered/experiential approaches to psychotic experience. In: L. S. Greenberg, S. Leslie, J. C. Watson, C. Jeanne, & G. Lietaer (Eds.), *Handbook of Experiential Psychotherapy* (pp. 388–409). New York: Guilford Press.
Riggs, S. A., & Han, G. (2009). Predictors of anxiety and depression in emerging adulthood. *Journal of Adult Development, 16*(1): 39–52.
Rogers, C. R. (1951). *Client-Centered Therapy.* London: Constable.
Rogers, C. R. (1957). The necessary and sufficient conditions of therapeutic personality change. *Journal of Consulting Psychology, 21*: 95–103.

Rogers, C. R. (1959). A theory of therapy, personality, interpersonal relationships, as developed in the client centred framework. In: S. Koch (Ed.), *Psychology: A Study of Science, Vol. 3: Formulations of the Person and the Social Context* (pp. 184–256). New York: McGraw-Hill.

Rogers, C. R. (1961). *On Becoming a Person: A Therapist's View of Psychotherapy.* London: Constable.

Rogers, C. R. (1980). *A Way of Being.* New York: Houghton Mifflin.

Rohner, E. C., Chaille, C., & Rohner, R. P. (1980). Perceived parental acceptance–rejection and the development of children's locus of control. *Journal of Psychology, 104*: 83–86.

Rohner, R. P. (1975). *They Love Me, They Love Me Not: A Worldwide Study of the Effects of Parental Acceptance and Rejection.* New Haven, CT: Hraf Press.

Rohner, R. P. (1986). *The Warmth Dimension: Foundations of Parental Acceptance–Rejection Theory.* London: Sage.

Rohner, R. P. (2004). The parental "acceptance–rejection syndrome": universal correlates of perceived rejection. *American Psychologist, 59*: 827–840.

Rohner, R. P., & Rohner, E. C. (1980). Worldwide tests of parental acceptance–rejection theory. *Behavior Science Research, 15*(1): 1–21.

Rohner, R. P., Khaleque, A., & Cournoyer, D. E. (2003). Cross-national perspectives on parental acceptance–rejection theory. *Marriage & Family Review, 35*(3–4): 85–105.

Rohner, R. P., Khaleque, A., & Cournoyer, D. E. (2005). Parental acceptance–rejection: theory, methods, cross-cultural evidence, and implications. *Ethos, 33*(3): 299–334.

Roos, S. (2002). *Chronic Sorrow, A Living Loss.* New York: Routledge.

Rosenberg, M. (1962). The association between self-esteem and anxiety. *Psychiatric Research, 1*: 135–152.

Rubin, K. H., Dwyer, K. M., Booth-LaForce, C., Kim, A. H., Burgess, K. B., & Rose-Krasnor, L. (2004). Attachment, friendship, and psychosocial functioning in early adolescence. *Journal of Early Adolescence, 24*: 326–356.

Schmitt, J. P. (1980). Unconditional positive regard: the hidden paradox. *Psychotherapy: Theory, Research and Practice, 17*(3): 237–245.

Smith, J. A., Flowers, P., & Larkin, M. (2009). *Interpretative Phenomenological Analysis: Theory, Method and Research.* London: Sage.

Spitz, R. A. (1963). Life and the dialogue. In: H. S. Gaskill (Ed.), *Counterpoint: Libidinal Object and Subject* (pp. 154–176). New York: International Universities Press.

Sroufe, L. A. (1990). An organizational perspective on the self. In: D. Cicchetti & M. Beeghly (Eds.), *The Self in Transition: Infancy to Childhood* (pp. 281–307). Chicago, IL: University of Chicago Press.

Strickland, B. R. (1978). Internal–external expectancies and health-related behavior. *Journal of Consulting and Clinical Psychology*, 46(6): 1192–1211.

Sugarman, L. (2001). *Life-span Development: Frameworks, Accounts and Strategies* (2nd edn). Hove: Psychology Press.

Thomas, H. E. (1999). *The Shame Response to Rejection*. Sewickley, PA: Abnel.

Thorne, B. (1991). *Person-centred Counselling: Therapeutic and Spiritual Dimensions*. London: Whurr.

Valliant, G. (2012). *Triumphs of Experience: The Men of the Harvard Grant Study*. Cambridge, MA: Harvard University Press.

Veneziano, R. A., & Rohner, R. P. (1998). Perceived paternal acceptance, paternal involvement, and youths' psychological adjustment in a rural, biracial southern community. *Journal of Marriage and Family*, 60(2): 335–343.

Warner, M. S. (1991). Fragile process. In: L. Fusek (Ed.), *New Directions in Client-centered Therapy: Practice with Difficult Client Populations* (pp. 41–58). Chicago, IL: Chicago Counseling and Psychotherapy Center.

Weingarten, K. (2012). Sorrow: a therapist's reflection on the inevitable and the unknowable. *Family Process*, 51(4): 440–455.

Williams, C. B., & Nickels, J. B. (1969). Internal–external control dimension as related to accident and suicide proneness. *Journal of Consulting and Clinical Psychology*, 33: 485–494.

Winnicott, D. W. (1964). *The Child, the Family and the Outside World*. London: Penguin.

CHAPTER FIVE

The impact of emotional labour on secondary school teachers

Eileen Doyle

Introduction

This chapter focuses on secondary school teachers' experiences of the way in which they are affected by the emotional labour involved in their profession. It is widely accepted that teaching involves a great deal of emotion (Demetriou et al., 2009; Hargreaves, 1998; Nias, 1996; Titsworth et al., 2010) and is an emotionally demanding job (Bakker & Demerouti, 2007). The emotional demands placed on teachers can lead to burn-out (Chan & Hui, 1995; Hakanen et al., 2006), stress (Klassen, 2010; Kyriacou, 1987), and emotional exhaustion (Grayson & Alvarez, 2008; van Dick & Wagner, 2001). Despite recommendations to reduce teachers' workload in order to alleviate stress (PricewaterhouseCoopers, 2001), the number of teachers reporting stress-related illnesses has continued to rise (National Union of Teachers, 2013). While looking at research relevant to this chapter, I found that much of it was quantitative in nature and focused on the manifestations of stress and burn-out, with very little on the day-to-day experiencing of the emotional demands on teachers (Kinman et al., 2011).

My interest in the emotional labour of teaching arises from my own experiences as a secondary school teacher and my decision to leave the profession. As a middle manager in several schools, I was also faced with the task of managing stress-related absenteeism and the return to work of colleagues suffering with stress. Although, as a teacher, I was aware that teaching adolescents meant witnessing and, to some degree, managing the emotions associated with their developmental stage (Erikson, 1968; Jacobs, 1986; Sugarman, 2001), I was unaware that the emotional demands for the teacher could have such significant consequences as exhaustion and burn-out. Therefore, my initial engagement with the literature for the purposes of this chapter had a considerable impact. Although aware through my daily experiencing of the "performing" nature of teaching in the classroom as highlighted by McLaren (1986) and Nias (1989), I felt that the classroom was only one area where teachers experienced this type of emotional labour, yet it was the area given most focus in the research that I came across. My interest lies in the emotional labour associated with other aspects of teaching as well as classroom work, such as relationships with peers and managers, workload, and the impact of educational reform.

What the literature says

In order to place this chapter into a research context, I undertook a review of the literature concerned with the demands of the profession of teaching, and the role of emotional support. Realising that there was such a wealth of relevant research about the emotion work of teaching was reassuring, but also disquieting. Having experienced teaching as an isolating profession for several years, it felt very strange to be suddenly faced with a plethora of books and journal articles which highlighted similar experiences to my own and not only normalised them, but treated them as serious issues. However, I noticed that there was very little research on the role of workplace support for teachers.

Emotion in teaching

It is widely recognised that teaching is a profoundly emotional activity. Emotions "lie at the heart of teaching" (Hargreaves, 1998, p. 835) and it is "highly charged with feeling" (Nias, 1996, p. 293). Often described as a vocation, the accepted wisdom about teaching is that it is more than just a job, with a high level of personal investment in both subject and pupils. Most of the research I came across focuses on the emotion of teaching in general, rather than being specific to the educational phase (i.e., primary, secondary, etc.), although a small number are phase-specific: for example, Hebson et al. (2007), who looked at the emotion work of primary school teachers, and Duffield et al. (2000) whose research focuses on secondary schools. My interest in the secondary phase arises from my teaching experience, which has been solely in secondary education. This is because for secondary school teachers, in particular, dealing with emotion is magnified by the "storm and stress" of adolescence (Hall, 1904) where teachers are also managing the behaviour of children at a particularly vulnerable time in their emotional development. Geving (2007) suggests that because children are reaching a time of transition into adulthood during secondary school, they feel more able to vocalise their dissatisfaction and frustrations with teachers than in primary school. Ultimately, this leads to a more emotionally charged environment for teachers.

Because teachers tend to be emotionally attached to their work, there are many positive feelings that arise from the day-to-day experience of doing their job. Hargreaves (1998) emphasises the passion that teachers feel for their subject, the importance of the emotional connections they make with their pupils, and the pleasure they derive when creativity and challenge are experienced (p. 835). Woods and Jeffrey (1996) point to the emotional bonds that underpin good pedagogic practice, while van Manen (1985) and Eisner (1986) emphasise the role of the teacher's intuition in conjunction with emotionality in creating a positive classroom experience. Since there is such potential for teaching to be emotionally rewarding, this poses the question of why there is so much evidence of negative emotion experienced by teachers (Brackett et al., 2010; Kyriacou, 1987; Travers & Cooper, 1996).

Teacher stress

Research has shown that, given the nature of the teaching role, it invariably involves a substantial level of stress. Therefore, studies of the demands of teaching often look at the causes of teachers' work-related stress. The term "teacher stress" was coined in *Educational*

Review (Kyriacou & Sutcliffe, 1977) and since then there has been a significant amount of both quantitative and qualitative research into teacher stress with the result that it is now widely accepted that teaching is one of the most stressful occupations (Johnson et al., 2005). So, I was surprised to find that very little research exists on the notion of formal support for teachers in the form of counselling, debriefing or supervision. The literature that is concerned with teacher support tends to focus on support from managers (Kyriacou, 2001) or workplace social support (Kinman et al., 2011). Fielding (2001) talks of "mutually supportive endeavour" (p. 700), which is interesting from a person-centred counselling perspective as it echoes Rogers' (1980) and Natiello's (2001) embracing of the notions of mutuality and collaboration. Perhaps because stress is now such a well-used notion in describing teaching, I was reluctant to use it for the title of this chapter. In my opinion, there is a danger that overuse of such commonplace terms can render them meaningless, and there is already a great deal of negative commentary surrounding the profession. For example, Richardson (2012), who quotes Sir Michael Wilshaw, England's Chief Inspector of Schools, as critical of teachers who use stress as an excuse for "poor performance". However, I am aware that considerable focus on the term "stress" in research studies, for example, Travers and Cooper (1993), Greenglass and colleagues (1997), Kyriacou (2001), and Connor (2008), has brought attention to the emotional demands of teaching and highlighted the need for fundamental improvement in teachers' working conditions.

Emotional labour

Having looked at a range of literature on the nature of teacher stress and how this is inextricably linked to emotion, I decided to focus on the concept of emotional labour, how teachers experience this on a day-to-day basis and how this affects them. The concept of emotional labour is described in several journal articles relating to occupational stress and was introduced by Hochschild (1983). It can be defined as "the effort, planning and control needed to express organisationally desired emotion during interpersonal transactions" (Morris & Feldman, 1996, p. 987). Kinman and colleagues (2011, p. 843) state that, "As yet, however, little is known about the emotional demands faced by teachers". Since the notion of emotional labour is of personal interest to me, my curiosity was aroused by this statement and I wanted to find out more about it.

Early research into emotional labour focused on service sector employees: for example, Warr and colleagues (1979), Hochschild (1983), and Wharton and Erickson (1993). Hochschild (1983) identifies two levels of emotional labour: surface acting and deep acting. Surface acting is the pretence usually associated with many day-to-day workplace interactions and involves masking one's true emotion by overtly displaying another. This can be demonstrated using Hochschild's (1983) study of flight attendants. For example, in reassuring passengers during an emergency landing, the calm voice of the flight attendant might belie his or her actual feelings of anxiety and fear. The level termed "deep acting" involves actually modifying emotions rather than suppressing them in order to meet the demands of an organisation. For example, although annoyed by a rude passenger, a flight attendant, in offering assistance, realises that the passenger is anxious because her child is sick. By modifying emotion, the worker starts to empathise with the customer (Hochschild, 1983). Researchers such as Rafaeli and Sutton (1987) and Diefendorff and colleagues (2005) use the term "emotional display rules" to describe the manner in which employees are expected to perform emotional labour. Typically, employees are aware of these expectations because many service sector organisations use explicit means of conveying them, such as corporate mottos, pledges to customers, and mission statements. However, Rafaeli and Sutton (1987) acknowledge that organisations are often ambiguous about their expectations for emotional display rules (p. 24). Bolton and Boyd (2003) expanded the work of Hochschild by classifying emotional labour into four distinct states: "pecuniary", "prescriptive", "presentational", and "philanthropic" (p. 291). The identification of these four states recognises the complexities of the emotional demands of differing workplaces and professions. Since Hochschild's (1983) work focused on the emotional labour experienced by flight attendants, these would fall into the category of pecuniary emotional labour, as the nature of their work ultimately depended on commercial gain for the organisation. The emotional labour of teachers is best represented by the prescriptive state, since it describes feelings that follow institutional or organisational rules and the formation of a professional identity. It also encompasses the altruistic nature of teaching, where motivation for emotional labour is not commercial gain.

Emotional labour in teaching

The Teachers' Pay and Conditions Document (Department for Education, 2014) highlights the importance of emotional labour in teaching in its contractual framework with the requirement for teachers to "maintain good relationships with pupils" (p. 53) and to "establish a safe and stimulating environment for pupils, rooted in mutual respect" (p. 51). In addition, one of Ofsted's requirements is for a "positive climate" in the classroom (Ofsted, 2014, p. 61). Thus, the statutory requirement and the inspection requirement intensify the need for teachers to be seen to be managing emotion correctly in the classroom. This is highlighted by Troman (2000), Fielding (2001), and Perryman (2007).

Since teaching is widely accepted as an emotional and emotionally demanding occupation, it follows that the additional expectation on teachers not only to model appropriate emotions, but also to respond to, and manage, someone else's emotion at a crucial stage in their development means that the emotional labour involved in teaching is markedly more demanding than in other occupations (Brackett et al., 2010). Moreover, teachers' experiences of emotional labour differ from those experienced in other workplaces because of the frequency of their interactions and their longer-term relationship with their "clients" (Morris & Feldman, 1996).

Despite the demands on teachers for the performance of emotional labour, very little research exists on this topic (Brown, 2011). Although there is a wealth of research on the emotional aspects of teaching, most emotional labour research is concerned with the emotional regulation abilities of teachers, rather than how emotional labour is experienced by them (Brackett et al., 2010; Jennings & Greenberg, 2009; Sutton, 2004). Although emotional labour inevitably involves the conscious management of one's emotions, emotional regulation can be defined as, "the process by which individuals influence which emotions they have, when they have them, and how they experience and express these emotions" (Gross, 1998, p. 275). Gross (1998) proposes a model of emotional regulation that describes the way in which employees process their emotional labour. Because both involve the control of emotion, it becomes difficult to differentiate between them. However, there are three distinct differences. First, emotional labour is related to work. Second, the emotional display rules are organisationally determined, and third, emotional labour is focused on another person rather than the self (Brown, 2011).

How teachers experience emotional labour

Research demonstrates that teachers engage in a wealth of emotional labour throughout the working day (Brown, 2011). This takes the form of both surface acting and deep acting (Hochschild, 1983) and can involve interactions with pupils, parents, colleagues, and superiors. Brown (2011) also found that while most respondents' experiences of deep acting were with pupils, most surface acting took place outside of the classroom, that is, in interactions with colleagues and superiors.

The emotional labour involved in teaching is largely seen by researchers through the nature of interactions with pupils, and the image of the teacher as a caring professional is a major aspect of the job (Isenbarger & Zembylas, 2006). Traditional expectations of teachers are as resolvers of conflict (Merazzi, 1983) or "friend, colleague and helper" (Travers & Cooper, 1996, p. 9). These role expectations, along with Fried's (1995) portrayal of "the passionate teacher", demonstrate the positive emotions associated with teaching. However, researchers have found that interactions with pupils can also be a source of negative emotion: for example, Kinman and colleagues (2011), Burke and Greenglass (1995), and Turk and colleagues (1982). Kyriacou (2001) and Travers and Cooper (1996) highlight maintaining classroom discipline as a source of negative emotion, leading to teacher stress. Carlyle and Woods (2002) indicate that managing abusive, stressed, challenging, and aggressive students escalates the degree of emotional labour for teachers with a negative effect. This view is reinforced by Klassen (2010).

Other sources of emotional labour for teachers include the radical change associated with the profession, and Kyriacou (2001) identifies educational change as a source of stress for teachers. Hargreaves (1998) goes further and argues that educational reform, a constant pressure in teachers' lives, makes it more difficult for them to sustain their emotional commitment to pupils. This is echoed by Forrester (2005), who describes the shift away from the caring aspects of the role to the performing aspects of it which is necessary if teachers are to pass inspections and observations. Thus, the notion of playing a role that is the normal expectation of emotional labour in teaching takes on a new dimension. The "standards agenda" (Thrupp, 2001) is highlighted by Hebson and colleagues (2007) as having a major impact on the emotional work of primary school teachers, and this has also extended to secondary schools (Duffield et al., 2000). Kyriacou's (2001) assertion that being evaluated by others is a major source of stress for teachers is emphasised more stridently by Rea and Weiner (1997): "present-day teachers who are 'named and blamed' for the failings of decades of inadequate education recipes and policies" (p. 3), and by Jeffrey and Woods (1996), who describe the extreme emotional labour involved during an Ofsted inspection. Intrinsic to the standards agenda is the notion of outcome measures that have come into effect in secondary schools. Leckie and Goldstein (2009) indicate the limitations of the widespread use of school league tables, while Perryman and colleagues (2011) describe the demoralising effects of such performance measures as a "pressure cooker" for teachers. The emotional labour for teachers in this area is extremely demanding since they have to be seen to be promoting the importance of such standards. Thus, Hebson and colleagues (2007) argue that public sector professionals are being judged by the "alien" standards of pecuniary emotional labour (p. 683). Research has also found that a heavy workload takes an emotional toll on teachers (Chan, 2006; Naylor, 2001; Rothi et al., 2010). In fact, a report commissioned by the Department for Education and Skills (DfES) by PricewaterhouseCoopers concluded that a reduction in teachers' workload was essential in order to improve pupil performance (Department for Education and Skills, 2001). Rothi and colleagues (2010) identified teachers as having higher than average mental health disorders with excessive workload cited as one of the main causal factors. The emotional labour involved in excessive workload encompasses the increased bureaucratisation of teaching (Rothi et al., 2010), where teachers are engaging in needless administrative tasks in an age of accountability (Perryman et al., 2011).

The impact of emotional labour on teachers

The association between teaching and caring has long been recognised (Collinson et al., 1999; Heath, 1994; Noddings, 1992). Isenbarger and Zembylas (2006) recognise the emotional labour inherent in this role of the teacher and argue that this places a significant demand on teachers. However, research shows that there are positive effects of emotional labour on job satisfaction (Brackett et al., 2010; Travers & Cooper, 1993, 1996), and many teachers believe that some degree of emotional labour is essential to their role and, if managed correctly, actually increases effectiveness (Sutton, 2004). For example, teachers feeling that they make a positive contribution to their students' lives (Isenbarger and Zembylas, 2006).

What Hochschild (1983) and other researchers found is that sustained emotional labour can have the effect that workers start to experience exhaustion and/or burn-out, suppress the real self, and suffer from a distorted emotional reality (Hochschild, 1983). Colley (2006) describes the negative consequences of such emotional work as "not a source of human bonding and satisfaction, but of alienation and eventual emotional burn-out" (p. 16). In fact, much of the research on emotional labour also involves the study of burn-out: for example, Roger and Hudson (1995), Grandey (2000), Zhang and Zhu (2008) and Brackett and colleagues (2010). Since the links between emotional labour and emotional exhaustion are widely recognised (Goldberg & Grandey, 2007; Kruml & Geddes, 2000), this indicates that teachers' wellbeing is at risk if the impact of emotional labour is significant. Although widely accepted as an intrinsic part of teaching, little is known about the type of emotional labour that teachers engage in, how they experience it, and what effect this has. By focusing on the day-to-day experiences of teachers, I shall give a qualitative account of teachers' lived experiences, rather than using statistical information.

Participants

Since the area of interest to me was very specific, I elected to use a purposive (non-probability) sampling of five teachers. The inclusion criteria were: UK secondary school teachers with current or recent experience. There was no gender or age bias, or any limitation to employment setting, such as type and size of secondary school. All five participants were women, three of whom had over twenty years' experience in teaching. Two of the participants taught the same subject, and three worked in the same county, although in different schools (Table 5.1).

Table 5.1. Details of the participants.

Participant	Approximate age	Current or recent experience	Number of years taught
Alison	Over 50	Current	More than 25
Becky	Over 50	Current	More than 25
Chloe	40–50	Current	More than 20
Di	40–50	Current	More than 10
Ellie	30–40	Current	Fewer than 10

Data collection

The data was collected using a format of semi-structured interviews. The questions asked are listed below.

- In what way is teaching an emotionally demanding job?
- How often do you have to suppress authentic emotion?
- How important do you feel this is to you? Do you see this as an important part of your job?
- What are the expectations from your school on your display of emotion?
- What are the positive feelings associated with suppressing your true emotions?
- What is the negative impact?
- What coping mechanisms do you use to deal with the suppression of your emotions?
- What support is available to you?
- How did your training prepare you for this aspect of teaching?
- Is there anything more you would like to add?

What was discovered

The findings are presented thematically with three superordinate themes, each with three subordinate themes, and this is represented in Table 5.2.

As part of the hermeneutic circle associated with phenomenological research, the themes I have focused on reflect my interest in the subject matter as well as the universality of the participants' experiences. The quotes used are verbatim extracts from the participants'

Table 5.2. Emerging themes.

Superordinate themes:	The expectation to conform	The focus on outcome measures	The impact in the classroom
Subordinate themes:	The removal of individuality	Targets/improvement	Authentic vs. inauthentic emotion
	The fear of not conforming	The blame culture	Workload issues
	Not having a voice	Collusion	"Them and us"

material and I have used those that capture most fully the significance of these experiences.

Superordinate theme 1: The expectation to conform

Subordinate theme 1.1: The removal of individuality

All five participants talked about the expectation from their managers to behave in an unemotional way. Three used the word "robot" or similar to describe the manner in which they were expected to work. For Chloe, this affected her relationships in the classroom: "I don't think you get the best out of the children if you are just a robot at the front of the room, and I think you have to be human to do it effectively." For Alison, this had an impact on her both in and out of the classroom: "There is an expectation you know, you really are pretending to be this almost robotic type of super, moral, well-behaved, upstanding, no-flaws member of the community for all the time that you're in that role." This view is echoed by Becky: "There is that very clear-cut expectation that you don't show any great levels of emotion." Di took the analogy even further: "I don't think they want diverse. I think they want robotic don't they? It's almost a bit *Nineteen Eighty-Four* sometimes. They're all stood in their blue boiler-suits you know, and they're all saying the same thing at the screen and that's what they want."

Subordinate theme 1.2: The fear of not conforming

For the participants, there was an explicit acknowledgement of the climate of fear apparent in schools. This manifested itself in two significant ways: fear of being deemed inadequate as a teacher, and fear of losing one's job. The fear of failure appeared to outweigh the fear of financial loss. Chloe spoke about her main fear very early in the interview: "You want to get things right as regards to pleasing your leadership team. You don't want to be seen as a failing teacher, but it's emotional for me because I want them to see that I'm not a failing teacher." This was echoed by Di: "There's a constant use of politics to make you feel inadequate. In spite of the fact that you have full evidence that you're not inadequate, you know you're not inadequate...and it does create a climate of fear." And Ellie's fear over lesson observations by the headteacher was similar: "One hour out of eight hundred a year he might come, so that is what he will judge me on ... Why are we making people feel like failures if they don't get 'outstanding'?"

Subordinate theme 1.3: Not having a voice

The participants felt that they were excluded from their school's decision-making process to the extent that their voice went unheard even over issues that affected them directly. As Chloe states, "I tend to tell SLT [Senior Leadership Team] over certain things that I feel are a bit unjustified you know, but you tend to get a bit of a blanket response or, you know, 'this is the decision that's been made' or 'this is what we're doing' and I think, well hang on a minute, that's not very fair." The lack of consultation was frustrating for Ellie: "I was so frustrated because our head had just completely ignored everything we'd been saying and what we'd been doing." Di sums it up by saying, "Nodding's better! They prefer nodding!"

Superordinate theme 2: The focus on outcome measures

Subordinate theme 2.1: Targets/continuous improvement

Since the introduction of school league tables, the increase in the use by secondary schools of target grades and predicted grades has produced a focus on the need to provide evidence of continual improvement. In Di's experience, the focus on improvement has been misused by schools: "I do think in all the schools I've worked in it's kind of misunderstood, misinterpreted and almost used as a bit of a stick for impossible continual improvement for both staff and kids."

The impossibility is reflected by Becky: "Because you can't continue to consistently improve, you know...I think targets and the constant pressure to improve, improve, improve, it's unrealistic." The focus on target grades is something which Ellie finds problematic: "I really object to kids having target grades based on a system that has an error value of plus or minus one, and based on exams they do in one week at the end of Year 6."

Subordinate theme 2.2: The blame culture

Increasingly, the focus on outcome measures has been underscored by a blame culture, particularly represented by what senior managers perceive to be the demands of Ofsted. "We now have what they call learning walks. It's just a disguise for constant lesson observation. Their excuse is that it's 'just in case' Ofsted come in." The critical nature of Ofsted judgements reinforces Ellie's sense of powerlessness: "I have no respect for the Ofsted criteria because I do not believe it assesses anybody, except provides data en masse to say whatever a politician wants it to say. So I have no respect for the Ofsted criteria." The overwhelming focus on Ofsted is a source of pressure for Becky: "You know, they don't seem to ever take a realistic perspective on Ofsted in terms of, this is a bunch of people who don't really know any more than you how to teach. But the importance that's placed on it and the pressure that's put on you to perform, to jump through hoops and to get this 'outstanding'."

Subordinate theme 2.3: Collusion

The participants expressed the notion of collusion, which was inherent in their everyday experience of teaching, particularly over policies they felt were a waste of time. The implication of deception was one which Alison felt angry with: "So we all collude, we all sit there and go, 'Mmm' and you don't say to everyone else do you, 'I'm not blinking doing that.' You just keep your mouth shut and don't do it." Becky also felt anger at being compelled to collude in stressing the importance of exam results: "We all nod our heads and say, 'yes, that's what we're doing.' And yet I know that probably most people recognise it's a nonsense, that it can't happen. There are certain students who will never get a C," For Di, presenting an image that all is well is detrimental to her: ". . . it damages you as a person because you don't feel respected ... The senior management think everything's tickety-boo. They think it's all running well because they're not hearing anything and it all appears nice on the surface."

Superordinate theme 3: The impact in the classroom

Subordinate theme 3.1: Authentic vs. inauthentic emotion

Interestingly, the participants described the suppression of emotion in the classroom as having positive benefits for themselves. For example, Ellie described the effect of suppressing the anger she felt towards pupils: "... first of all you have to suppress your annoyance and do what you know is right rather than what you'll want to do, and then it just becomes habit ... After a while you deal with things in a different way ... instead of me getting annoyed and coming away from the lesson feeling angry, it meant that I felt much calmer." For Becky, this helped forge positive relationships with pupils: "You've got to get them to respect you, and that isn't by being their friend ... It is by setting them an example, but also it's by having a sense of humour, letting them think you like them even if you don't like them ... reinforcing their positives and sort of try and play on that side rather than the negatives of their personality." It also helped reinforce her belief that an important part of teaching is making pupils feel secure and valued: "I think that's kind of part of our job, particularly the more challenging kids who come from challenging backgrounds with, you know, don't feel loved and don't feel wanted in lots of situations, so if we can give them a little bit of security, stability, and a feeling of being appreciated, then they'll value that. You know, they won't always be great but you can usually win them over a bit with that if you've got their respect" [Becky].

Alison described having an expectation of herself to be a good role model: "I have an expectation of myself also to behave in a particular way. It would be inappropriate not to adopt the persona because it can be misconstrued." She felt that this actually helped her: "I don't think it's always appropriate for us to express our authentic feelings ... I think you make better decisions when you're able to be objective." Conversely, the participants felt that the times they were most able to display authentic emotion was also in the classroom. For Alison, this was in the form of acknowledging that like the pupils, she, too, was subjected to following rules: "I think you can acknowledge that at least with the kids, which I think does make for a better relationship. I don't really draw the line completely, but you're able to say, 'I've got to say this so I am saying it." For Chloe, being her authentic self with her pupils was very satisfying: "I think the children who come to my lessons respond to it. And they respond to me and my emotions and I think it works. So in the classroom I don't feel that I've got to be a certain stereotype, I haven't at all." It was an important aspect of the job for Di: "I refuse point-blank to be anybody other than who I am with the children and that's that. I'm not going to change and I think that's the key to my survival at the moment."

Subordinate theme 3.2: Workload issues

For all the participants, workload was an issue, particularly in terms of administrative tasks and how the expectation to prioritise them had an impact in the classroom. Di spoke about this in terms of planning lessons: ". . . it's so ironic because it impacts on the time you get to spend actually preparing lessons in terms of making resources." Ellie took an analytical approach to an extra administrative task required of her: "I worked out that if I did that for every book it would add three hours a year on to my marking time. Now to them that's just three seconds a book, but you've got to cost time out. You can't keep adding up because time doesn't expand." Such tasks prohibited her from focusing on her pupils as individuals: "I find that I end up compartmentalising children into three different groups and writing three different reports because it's the only way you can get through the amount of stuff you've got to do."

Subordinate theme 3.3: "Them and us"

One of the universally accepted truths about school is that the teachers make the rules and the children obey them. The participants' experience here is that the senior management make the rules and the other staff members obey them. For Alison this was evident in meetings: "You're not allowed to say things like that!" This was similar for Becky in the way she conducted herself in the classroom: "You're not allowed to shout, that's not very good for the whole school and you're also not allowed to use sarcasm." Di felt that the focus on administrative tasks to ensure that people were doing their jobs properly was excessive: "... so you've got to say when you're going to do your marking, and your mark book's got to correspond ... you've got to do it in the same colour pens so you can't cheat."

Bringing together the literature and the findings

These findings reflect similar research in this area, in that feelings of personal accomplishment for all five participants were felt to have been eroded by the demands of managing the profound emotion involved in the job of teaching. Overall, there was a sense of the struggle experienced by the participants with the political machine of secondary education. The assertion that teaching is an intensely emotional activity is clear from the literature, and is emphasised by the findings. All five participants acknowledged the importance of emotion in their profession and agreed that there were both advantages and disadvantages to this. The participants experienced differing degrees of emotional labour, but tended to echo Hochschild's (1983) assertion that there was both "surface acting" and "deep acting" involved in their day-to-day experiences of emotional labour. The findings also indicated that, overall, the participants had a degree of "emotional regulation ability" (Brackett et al., 2010) that assisted them in employing strategies to help deal with unwanted or difficult emotions.

The findings appeared to echo Kyriacou's (2001) definition of the stress associated with teaching, that is, "the experience by a teacher of unpleasant negative emotions such as anger, anxiety, tension, frustration or depression, resulting from some aspect of their work as a teacher" (p. 28), in that all participants found many aspects of the emotional work of teaching difficult to deal with. However, determining whether participants were suffering from stress goes beyond the remit of this chapter. For all the participants, the view of teaching as a demanding job was evident, and the findings echoed much of the existing research work in this area. There were three principal themes that emerged from the participants' data, and nine subordinate themes that reflected convergent experiences for all or most participants. In fact, the language, other than the usual terminology associated with the profession, used by each participant was strikingly similar, despite the fact that they did not know each other or work in the same schools. This demonstrates how the participants' themes converge with the existing literature. Yet, there was also evidence of the divergence of some thematic perceptions, thus giving focus to the uniqueness of individual experiencing.

Hargreaves (1998) indicates the importance of creativity for teachers, which suggests that recognising the individuality of teachers has an important role to play. Carlyle and Woods (2002) emphasise the importance for teachers of a strong and well-founded sense of personal identity. Therefore, the increasing expectation upon teachers to conform in myriad new ways had a deep impact on the participants and, thus, became a superordinate theme. In this respect, the erosion of individuality evident in the transcripts carries with it a profound sense of loss. The use of the word "robot" by four of the participants emphasises the expectation on them to conform to an imposed prototype. If, as Carlyle and Woods (2002) suggest, a strong sense of identity heightens teachers' confidence, the consequences of such extensive conformity inevitably have a negative impact on the teacher.

Despite many research articles pointing to the inherently emotional nature of teaching (e.g., Brackett et al., 2010; van Manen, 1985; Woods & Jeffrey, 1996), each of the participants felt that the expectation from their superiors was that they had to behave in an unemotional and prescribed manner. One of the participants, Di, in an attempt to manage the expectation that she should be unemotional, had tried to become robot-like herself as a coping strategy. Hargreaves (1998) goes as far as to say, "It is exceptionally important to honour and acknowledge the emotions of teaching ... and to cultivate their active development" (p. 316). Therefore, it appears that there is a dissonance for the participants as they experience teaching as an emotional activity, yet attempt to conform to the expectation that they will be unemotional. Since one of the effects of excessive or unsatisfying emotional labour can be burn-out (Brackett et al., 2010), it is interesting to note that one of the components of this is depersonalisation (Greenglass et al., 1997; Hochschild, 1983). For Hochschild (1983), depersonalisation relates to the workers' views of their clients and tends to result in negative attitudes towards them. However, here the findings indicate that the participants' emotional labour associated with the erosion of individuality resulted in a sense of depersonalisation for themselves. As Chloe stated, when referring to her senior managers, "they're not seeing you as a person".

The fear of not conforming was strongly evident from each of the five participants, hence it becoming a subordinate theme. There was a sense that a climate of fear pervaded each person's daily life to the extent that they were worried about capability procedures being taken against them. By "toeing the party line" [Alison], the risk of being seen as a failing or inadequate teacher would be reduced. This reflects Hebson and colleagues' (2007) assertion that capability procedures are viewed with "fear and loathing" (p. 692) and need to be managed better if the aim is that teachers are to become more effective. Carlyle and Woods' (2002) research found that some schools actually fostered a culture of fear among staff (p. 27). Kyriacou (2001) makes the case for feedback to teachers on performance being carried out in a supportive manner in order to reduce teacher stress (p. 33).

As a person-centred counsellor, the importance of "having a voice" is something which is significant for me, thus the subordinate theme which concerns the participants' feeling of being silenced particularly resonated. Since so much of teaching is fundamentally to do with communication, it is interesting that the teachers here feel that they are silenced. The participants described experiences of being ignored, not listened to, and being excluded from decision-making in emotive terms. This ties in with Jeffrey and Woods' (1996) findings that describe the effect of inarticulateness as a contributor to feelings of being deprofessionalised. They refer to the "burning need" to express oneself (p. 325). Kyriacou (2001) and Klassen (2010) describe effective communication between managers and staff, and between staff, as a means of avoiding stress and increasing job satisfaction.

Another resonant theme that emerged from the transcripts was the huge focus on outcome measures and how it affected the daily lives of the participants. Schools' adoption of a national curriculum, league tables, and target-setting has had an enormous impact on teachers, and Duffield and colleagues (2000) describe this "standards agenda" as an "obsession", as does Fielding (2001). Schools' use of data on pupil performance as an indicator of success has meant that, for the participants here, the pressure to deliver is so intense that it is overwhelming. For them, the emotional labour involved in making pupils focus on the importance of levels and grades is a source of intense frustration and anger. This is clear in Ellie's plaintive response to the excessive focus on data, "yes, but this is a *person*!" In addition, the requirement for continuous improvement, as evidence of meeting these targets, was also a source of negative emotional labour, as it was viewed by the participants as unrealistic. Yet, the expectation was that it would be implemented without question. Research demonstrates that there is a link between student underachievement and teacher burn-out (Pas et al., 2012). If targets set by schools are unrealistic, it is logical to assume that there will be a vast array of pupils failing to reach their predicted grade or level, thereby reinforcing the idea that teachers are ineffective.

Linked to the subordinate theme of "targets and continuous improvement" is that of providing evidence for achievement, and the blame culture which exists if the targets to improve are not reached. The spectre of Ofsted was raised for the participants in discussing how evidence for performance was gathered. Since there were no direct questions regarding this in the interviews, it was telling that the participants viewed it as a highly emotional aspect of their work. The effect of Ofsted inspections on teachers is illustrated in an article by Jeffrey and Woods (1996), who describe devastating feelings such as "mortification" and "dehumanisation" as part and parcel of the "loss of self" inherent in the process. Ofsted's own vagueness, with statements such as, "How frequently a school is inspected depends on how well it did at its last inspection" (Ofsted, 2014), does nothing to eliminate the anxiety described by Jeffrey and Woods (1996) or to mitigate the sense of deprofessionalisation. The participants here even went as far as using Ofsted's own terminology: "inadequate" [Di], "outstanding" [Ellie], "weak" [Chloe], so embedded is the notion of being "Ofsted-standardly brilliant" [Di] in teachers' day-to-day work.

The blame culture which surrounds perceptions of Ofsted is reinforced by the fact that an inspection is deemed to be something which has to be passed (Perryman, 2007), thus likening it to a test or exam. Therefore, the participants' feeling of being threatened by the process ties in with the research on this topic. Perryman goes as far as describing inspections as "aversive and noxious" (p. 174). The fact that there is no sense of collaboration leaves teachers feeling disciplined and controlled (Perryman, 2007). Since the consequences of "failing" an inspection can include increased monitoring, with schools being put into "special measures" or even closing, and staff losing their jobs, the result is that a blame culture thrives. Perryman's (2007) research focuses on a secondary school as it prepares for an inspection, and she describes the sense of being permanently under a controlled regime.

This was echoed by the participants, who feel under pressure to deliver outstanding lessons all of the time, particularly since schools may be made to undergo further, more frequent and/or impromptu inspections if they fail (Perryman, 2007). This environment of "relentless surveillance" (Perryman, 2007, p. 174) is a feature of the daily lives of teachers, as Chloe stated, "'just in case' Ofsted come in". The emotional labour involved in this type of regime is high, particularly as staff members who are already under pressure are expected to be in "performance mode" (Perryman, 2007), delivering outstanding lessons and talking in positive terms about the school. It is this "surface acting" aspect of emotional labour which has the most adverse effect on employees (Hochschild, 1983; Morris & Feldman, 1996). What is also striking about the findings here is the "mixed messages" about Ofsted that the participants appear to be receiving from their senior managers. It is possible that senior managers, who are not exempt from criticism themselves by Ofsted, use the threat of inspection as a means of controlling teachers. This view is reinforced by Jeffrey and Woods (1996) and Perryman (2007).

Closely aligned with the notion of a blame culture is the third subordinate theme in this section, which deals with the concept of collusion. For the participants, there appeared to be some acceptance of a degree of collusion in teaching, particularly when it involved maintaining classroom discipline and good relationships with pupils. Although playing a role, participants felt that this was an important part of their work. Even though they did not agree with certain school policies, for example, the strictness of the school uniform, they would nevertheless accept that this was part of the general expectation surrounding their role as teacher. This ties in with research in this area, which shows that this type of emotional labour is positive and can actually result in job satisfaction (Brackett et al., 2010).

Where collusion became problematic was when participants felt under pressure to enforce what Perryman (2007) describes as "performative" (p. 173) policies which they saw as potentially damaging to children, or which could not be realistically achieved. Nias (1996) also points to an over-politicised environment that reflects the problematic nature of the experience of collusion in the participants here. There was a strong sense from the data that education was a political football, and teachers and pupils were the means used by school managers and policy-makers in order to achieve political gain. For the participants, having to engage in this type of emotional labour resulted in feelings of exasperation and anger.

Many researchers acknowledge the caring role of teaching, for example, Fried (1995), Forrester (2005), Isenbarger and Zembylas (2006), and Hebson and colleagues (2007). This was something that was strongly reflected in the data in this study and emphasises both the positive and negative aspects of emotional labour (Hochschild, 1983). Hargreaves (1998) describes the emotional labour of teaching as a "labor of love" (p. 840). The real passion the participants felt for the actual job of teaching and their personal investment in the pupils was evident, hence the third superordinate theme of the impact of emotional labour in the classroom.

It was evident that the participants were passionate about several aspects of their job, particularly in the emotional connections they made with pupils, thus echoing Fried (1995) and Hargreaves (1998). In this respect, the emotional labour involved in interactions with pupils had largely positive effects. The subordinate theme of "authentic *vs.* inauthentic emotion" is significant because interactions with pupils, both in and out of the classroom, appeared to be the area where the participants experienced the least stressful aspects of their job. Two participants (Becky and Ellie) discussed the challenges of dealing with difficult pupils and described how they modified their emotions in order to deal effectively with these incidences. Their engagement in "deep acting" (Hochschild, 1983) resulted in a productive classroom environment and contributed to their sense of forging positive relationships with pupils. The other participants felt that they were "real" when they were in the classroom, and that this led them to form meaningful and satisfying authentic relationships with pupils. However, it is possible that these participants were so practised in maintaining a positive classroom environment that they were unaware, on a conscious level, of the strategies they employed in order to achieve this.

The second subordinate theme of workload was a source of frustration for participants. Greenglass and colleagues (1997), Kyriacou (2001), and Chan (2006) describe this as a source of negative emotion for teachers that can lead to stress. Interestingly, the frustration felt by the participants here did not relate to the usual workload tasks associated with teaching, such as marking and preparation, but to what were viewed as "pointless" tasks [Becky]. For the participants, this type of task was usually associated with time-consuming and excessively bureaucratic exercises used for monitoring staff. This type of rigid control not only led to feelings that staff were not to be trusted, something which is echoed by Troman (2000), but, more significantly, impinged on the time available which could be used for lesson preparation, thus having an impact on what teachers were trying to achieve in the classroom. Time for preparation of resources was something that several participants felt was being eroded and this proved difficult, particularly for Di, who prided herself on producing quality resources for her pupils. This is similar to the "industry speed-up", described by Hochschild (1983, p. 121), whereby employees are given less time to accomplish the same number of tasks. For teachers, it manifests itself as the increased number of tasks being accumulated without the old ones being superseded. Thus, Chan's (2006) assertion that a high level of workload does not necessarily lead to burnout appears to bear out the findings here, which demonstrate that the type of workload task is significant in teachers' feeling of being overburdened.

Travers and Cooper (1996) indicate the loss of autonomy as a major source of pressure for teachers, particularly since traditionally the teaching role has involved a large degree of self-governance (p. 58). The third subordinate theme in this section is termed "them and us" because it twists the accepted notion of this as applying to the traditional roles of teachers and pupils. The language used by the participants in this study is interesting, particularly the use of phrases such as, "you're not allowed" [Becky, Alison] and "you get told off" [Ellie, Chloe] because it sounded as though the teachers were being treated like pupils. This suggests a power imbalance and an authoritarian climate, something which Natiello (2001) cautions against. She argues that collaborative power is the most effective means by which workplaces need to operate in order to be most effective (p. 84). Fielding (2001) uses the term "reciprocal responsibility" (p. 696) to describe a more fitting model of shared decision-making.

Thus, the climate in schools appears to be one of a "them and us" culture, with managers and policy-makers on one side, and teachers on the other. Control and discipline, two of the most important features of an effective classroom teacher, appear to be being used as a punitive mechanism against teachers themselves. The feeling of powerlessness experienced by the participants is reflected by

Perryman (2007) in her description of a regime of control that underpins many of the aspects of teaching which were once under the aegis of ordinary classroom teachers.

Conclusion

Since this research was small-scale in nature and participation was through self-selection, it did not represent a cross-section of the population. The participants were all female and from the same ethnicity (i.e., white, British). As it was qualitative rather than quantitative, it focused on the day-to-day experiencing of the participants, and, therefore, there are no generalisations to be made. However, it does record an empirical picture of some teachers' experiences which might very well represent a wider body of experiencing.

Conducting this research has highlighted the fact that very little support exists for teachers, either formal or informal. While there has been a significant focus in recent years on the need for school counselling services to exist for pupils (Department for Children, Education, Lifelong Learning and Skill, 2008), no such intervention exists for teachers. As Lawrence (1999) states, "it is time now to accept that teachers also have needs" (p. xi). For counsellors of teachers, an understanding of the emotional demands and pressures faced by educators today would be of benefit in devising strategies to support such clients.

References

Bakker, A. B., & Demerouti, E. (2007). The job demands–resources model: state of the art. *Journal of Managerial Psychology, 22*(3): 309–328.

Bolton, S. C., & Boyd, C. (2003). Trolley dolly or skilled emotion manager? Moving on from Hochschild's Managed Heart. *Work, Employment and Society, 17*(2): 289–308.

Brackett, M. A., Palomera, R., Mojsa-Kaja, J., Reyes, M. R., & Salovey, P. (2010). Emotion-regulation ability, burnout, and job satisfaction among British secondary-school teachers. *Psychology in the Schools, 47*(4): 406–417.

Brown, E. L. (2011). Emotion matters: exploring the emotional labor of teaching. Unpublished PhD Dissertation, University of Pittsburgh.

Burke, R. J., & Greenglass, E. (1995). A longitudinal study of psychological burnout in teachers. *Human Relations, 48*(2): 187–202.

Carlyle, D., & Woods, P. (2002). *The Emotions of Teacher Stress*. Stoke on Trent: Trentham Books.

Chan, D. W. (2006). Emotional intelligence and components of burnout among Chinese secondary school teachers in Hong Kong. *Teaching and Teacher Education, 22*: 1042–1054.

Chan, D. W., & Hui, E. K. P. (1995). Burnout and coping among Chinese secondary school teachers in Hong Kong. *British Journal of Educational Psychology, 65*: 15–25.

Colley, H. (2006). Learning to labour with feeling: class, gender, emotion in childcare education and training. *Contemporary Issues in Early Childhood, 7*(1): 15–29.

Collinson, V., Killeavy, M., & Stephenson, H. (1999). Exemplary teachers: practising an ethic of care in England, Ireland, and the United States. *Journal for a Just and Caring Education, 5*: 349–366.

Connor, K. E. (2008). You choose to care: teachers, emotions and professional identity. *Teaching and Teacher Education, 24*(1): 117–126.

Demetriou, H., Wilson, E., & Winterbottom, M. (2009). The role of emotion in teaching: are there differences between male and female newly qualified teachers' approaches to teaching? *Educational Studies, 35*(4): 449–473.

Department for Children, Education, Lifelong Learning and Skills (2008). *School-Based Counselling Services in Wales: A National Strategy*. Cardiff: Welsh Assembly Government.

Department for Education (2014). *Schoolteachers' Pay and Conditions Document and Guidance on Schoolteachers' Pay and Conditions*. Accessed at: www.gov.uk/government/uploads/system/uploads/attachment_data/file/341951/School_teachers__pay_and_conditions_2014.pdf.

Department for Education and Skills (2001). *Green Paper on Schools: Building on Success*. London: HMSO. Accessed at: www.gov.uk/government/uploads/system/uploads/attachment_data/file/250873/5050.pdf.

Diefendorff, J. M., Croyle, M. H., & Gosserand, R. H. (2005). The dimensionality and antecedents of emotional labor strategies. *Journal of Vocational Behavior, 66*: 339–357.

Duffield, J., Allan, J., Turner, E., & Morris, B. (2000). Pupils' voices on achievement: an alternative to the standards agenda. *Cambridge Journal of Education, 30*(2): 263–274.

Eisner, E. (1986). The primacy of experience and the politics of method. *Educational Researcher, 17*(5): 15–20.

Erikson, E. (1968). *Childhood and Society.* London: Hogarth Press.
Fielding, M. (2001). Ofsted, inspection and the betrayal of democracy. *Journal of Philosophy of Education,* 35(4): 695–709.
Forrester, G. (2005). All in a day's work: primary teachers 'performing' and 'caring'. *Gender and Education,* 17(3): 271–287.
Fried, R. (1995). *The Passionate Teacher.* Boston, MA: Beacon Press.
Geving, A. M. (2007). Identifying the types of student and teacher behaviors associated with teacher stress. *Teaching and Teacher Education: An International Journal of Research and Studies,* 23(5): 624–640.
Goldberg, L., & Grandey, A. (2007). Display rules versus display autonomy: emotion regulation, emotional exhaustion, and task performance in a call center simulation. *Journal of Occupational Health Psychology,* 12(3): 301–318.
Grandey, A. A. (2000). Emotion regulation in the workplace: a new way to conceptualize emotional labor. *Journal of Occupational Health Psychology,* 5(1): 95–110.
Grayson, J. L., & Alvarez, H. K. (2008). School climate factors relating to teacher burnout: a mediator model. *Teaching and Teacher Education,* 24(5): 1349–1363.
Greenglass, E., Burke, R., & Konarski, R. (1997). The impact of social support on the development of burnout in teachers: examination of a model. *Work and Stress,* 11: 267–278.
Gross, J. J. (1998). The emerging field of emotion regulation: an integrative review. *Review of General Psychology,* 2(3): 271–299.
Hakanen, J. J., Bakker, A. B., & Schaufeli, W. B. (2006). Burnout and work engagement among teachers. *Journal of School Psychology,* 43(6): 495–513.
Hall, G. S. (1904). *Adolescence: Its Psychology and its Relations to Physiology, Anthropology, Sociology, Sex, Crime, Religion and Education.* London: Appleton.
Hargreaves, A. (1998). The emotional practice of teaching. *Teaching and Teacher Education,* 14(8): 835–854.
Heath, D. H. (1994). *Schools of Hope.* San Francisco, CA: Jossey-Bass.
Hebson, G., Earnshaw, J., & Marchington, L. (2007). Too emotional to be capable? The changing nature of emotion work in definitions of 'capable teaching'. *Journal of Education Policy,* 22(6): 675–694.
Hochschild, A. R. (1983). *The Managed Heart.* Berkeley, CA: University of California Press.
Isenbarger, L., & Zembylas, M. (2006). The emotional labour of caring in teaching. *Teaching and Teacher Education,* 22: 120–134.

Jacobs, M. (1986). *The Presenting Past*. Buckingham: Open University Press.

Jeffrey, B., & Woods, P. (1996). Feeling deprofessionalised: the social construction of emotions during an Ofsted inspection. *Cambridge Journal of Education, 26*(3): 325–343.

Jennings, P. A., & Greenberg, M. T. (2009). The prosocial classroom: teacher social and emotional competence in relation to student and classroom outcomes. *Review of Educational Research, 79*(1): 491–525.

Johnson, S., Cooper, C. L., Cartwright, S., Donald, I., Taylor, P., & Millet, C. (2005). The experience of work-related stress across occupations. *Journal of Managerial Psychology, 20*: 179–187.

Kinman, G., Wray, S., & Strange, C. (2011). Emotional labour, burnout and job satisfaction in UK teachers: the role of workplace social support. *Educational Psychology: An International Journal of Experimental Educational Psychology, 31*(7): 843–856.

Klassen, R. M. (2010). Teacher stress: the mediating role of collective efficacy beliefs. *Journal of Educational Research, 103*(5): 342–350.

Kruml, S. M., & Geddes, D. (2000). Catching fire without burning out: is there an ideal way to perform emotional labor? In: N. M. Ashkanasy, C. E. J. Härtel, & W. J. Zerbe (Eds.), *Emotions in the Workplace: Research, Theory, and Practice* (pp. 177–188). Westport, CT: Quorum Books.

Kyriacou, C. (1987). Teacher stress and burnout: an international review. *Educational Research, 29*(2): 146–152.

Kyriacou, C. (2001). Teacher stress: directions for future research. *Educational Review, 53*(1): 27–35.

Kyriacou, C., & Sutcliffe, J. (1977). Teacher stress: A review. *Educational Review, 29*: 299–306.

Lawrence, D. (1999). *Teaching with Confidence*. London: SAGE.

Leckie, G., & Goldstein, H. (2009). The limitations of using school league tables to inform school choice. *Journal of the Royal Statistical Society A, 172*(4): 835–851.

McLaren, P. L. (1986). *School as a Ritual Performance*. London: Routledge and Kegan Paul.

Merazzi, C. (1983). Apprendre à vivre les conflits: une tâche de la formation des enseignants. *European Journal of Teacher Education, 6*(2): 101–106.

Morris, J. A., & Feldman, D. C. (1996). The dimensions, antecedents, and consequences of emotional labor. *Academy of Management Review, 21*(4): 986–1010.

Natiello, P. (2001). *The Person-Centred Approach: A Passionate Presence*. Ross-on-Wye: PCCS Books.

National Union of Teachers (2013). *Teacher Stress: NUT Guidance to Divisions and Associations*. Accessed at: www.teachers.org.uk/files/TACKLING-STRESS-0713.doc.

Naylor, C. (2001). *Teacher Workload and Stress: An International Perspective on Human Costs and Systemic Failure*. BCTF Research Report. Accessed at: www.bctf.ca.

Nias, J. (1989). *Primary Teachers Talking: A Study of Teaching as Work*. London: Routledge.

Nias, J. (1996). Thinking about feeling: the emotions in teaching. *Cambridge Journal of Education*, 26(3): 293–306.

Noddings, N. (1992). *The Challenge to Care in Schools*. New York: Teachers College Press.

Ofsted (2014). *School Inspection Handbook*. Accessed at: www.ofsted.gov.uk/sites/default/files/documents/inspection—forms-and-guides/s/School%20inspection%20handbook.pdf.

Pas, E. T., Bradshaw, C. P., & Herschfeldt, P. A. (2012). Teacher- and school-level predictors of teacher efficacy and burnout: identifying potential areas for support. *Journal of School Psychology*, 50(1): 129–145.

Perryman, J. (2007). Inspection and emotion. *Cambridge Journal of Education*, 37(2): 173–190.

Perryman, J., Ball, S., Maguire, M., & Braun, A. (2011). Life in the pressure cooker – school league tables and English and Mathematics teachers' responses to accountability in a results-driven era. *British Journal of Educational Studies*, 59(2): 179–195.

PricewaterhouseCoopers (2001). *Teacher Workload Study: Final Report*. London: PwC.

Rafaeli, A., & Sutton, R. I. (1987). Expression of emotion as part of the work role. *Academy of Management Review*, 12: 23–37.

Rea, J., & Weiner, G. (1997). Cultures of blame and redemption when empowerment becomes control: practitioners' views of the effective schools movement. Paper presented to the British Educational Research Association Annual Conference, September 11–14, University of York.

Richardson, H. (2012). Ofsted chief Sir Michael Wilshaw: teachers not stressed. *BBC News*. Accessed at: www.bbc.co.uk/news/education-18025202.

Roger, D., & Hudson, C. (1995). The role of emotion control and emotional rumination in stress management training. *International Journal of Stress Management*, 2: 119–132.

Rogers, C. R. (1980). *A Way of Being*. Boston, MA: Houghton Mifflin.

Rothi, D., Leavey, G., & Loewenthal, K. (2010). Teachers' mental health: a study exploring the experiences of teachers with work-related stress and mental health problems. *NASUWT Document*, Birmingham: NASUWT.

Sugarman, L. (2001). *Life-Span Development: Frameworks, Accounts and Strategies*. Hove: Psychology Press.

Sutton, R. E. (2004). Emotional regulation goals and strategies of teachers. *School Psychology of Education*, 7(4): 379–398.

Thrupp, M. (2001). School-level education policy under New Labour and New Zealand Labour: a comparative update. *British Journal of Educational Studies*, 49(2): 187–212.

Titsworth, S., Quinlan, M. M., & Mazer, J. P. (2010). Emotion in teaching and learning: development and validation of the classroom emotions scale. *Communication Education*, 59(4): 431–452.

Travers, C. J., & Cooper, C. L. (1993). Mental health, job satisfaction and occupational stress among UK teachers. *Work and Stress*, 7: 203–219.

Travers, C. J., & Cooper, C. L. (1996). *Teachers under Pressure*. London: Routledge.

Troman, G. (2000). Teacher stress in the low-trust society. *British Journal of Sociology of Education*, 21(3): 331–353.

Turk, D. C., Meeks, S., & Turk, L. M. (1982). Factors contributing to teacher stress. Implications for research, prevention, and remediation. *Behavioral Counseling Quarterly*, 2: 1–26.

Van Dick, R., & Wagner, U. (2001). Stress and strain in teaching: a structural equation approach. *British Journal of Educational Psychology*, 71: 243–259.

Van Manen, M. (1985). *The Tact of Teaching*. Ontario, Canada: Althouse Press.

Warr, P., Cook, J., & Wall, T. (1979). Scales for the measurement of some work attitudes and aspects of psychological well-being. *Journal of Occupational Psychology*, 52: 129–148.

Wharton, A. S., & Erickson, R. J. (1993). Managing emotions on the job and at home: understanding the consequences of multiple emotional roles. *Academy of Management Review*, 18(3): 457–486.

Woods, P., & Jeffrey, B. (1996). *Teachable Moments: The Art of Creative Teaching in Primary School*. Buckingham: Open University Press.

Zhang, Q., & Zhu, W. (2008). Exploring emotion in teaching: emotional labor, burnout, and satisfaction in Chinese higher education. *Communication Education*, 57(1): 105–122.

CHAPTER SIX

The impact of inappropriately referred clients on the counselling trainee in placement

Mair Elinor Sides

Introduction

Grafanaki (2010) reports that research investigating the impact of counselling training and the experiences that trainees encounter during the formative years has frequently relied on quantitative methods to study the acquisition of counselling skills and qualities, often correlating training with therapy outcomes, and often at the exclusion of the trainee's internal perspective. Ronnestad and Ladany (2006) argue that research in this area needs to move towards providing a closer understanding of the training process, the factors that are relevant and meaningful to trainees, and their resultant impact on overall development.

This chapter, therefore, aims to provide a qualitative account of trainees' experiences, with particular interest in the seminal phase of counselling training that involves the important task of working with clients. Indeed, Orlinsky and Ronnestad (2005) documented that direct clinical work with clients is consistently endorsed as the most influential factor in therapist development. They argue that case selection for trainees "should ensure the best possible match between the student's skill level and the clinical challenges that clients present"

(p. 182), and advise avoiding the entrustment to students of clients who might be too difficult. It is also a requirement by many counselling trainers that placement providers ensure that trainees receive referrals that are appropriate with regard to their level of experience, and trainees themselves are obliged to adhere to the British Association of Counselling and Psychotherapy's (BACP's) Ethical Framework (2013), which lays out ethical principles and guidelines around limitations of competence. Despite such requirements, trainees and qualified counsellors become exposed to client referrals that can be deemed inappropriate, and the inspiration for this research arose from my formative training experiences during placement in confronting what I perceived to be inappropriately referred clients whose presenting issues were incompatible with my level of counselling ability. I became aware of the significant impact of such experiences on various aspects of my professional development, including a fluctuating influence on my levels of confidence, self-esteem, and emerging therapist identity. In the context of research by Howard and colleagues (2006), I identified these experiences as significant learning moments, or what they call "critical incidents" (p. 88), that made a telling impact on my professional growth and that had a lasting influence on my perception of being a counsellor.

Therefore, my decision was to investigate this scarcely researched topic and conduct a small-scale qualitative study to explore the experiences of other trainees who had worked with similar clients in their placement settings. It aimed to give voice to the facets of training that are relevant and meaningful to them, and to uncover the ways in which working with such inappropriate referrals made an impact on their professional development as counsellors. This study was conducted with a view to raising greater awareness among clinical educators, trainers, supervisors, and placement providers of the learning needs of trainee counsellors when gaining clinical experience in placement settings. I also hope to highlight the problems involving referrals to trainees, so that improved referral procedures in placement settings can be implemented. I further contend the need for greater integration of the trainee into agency teams, both to improve collaboration and to promote greater understanding between professionals to engender realistic expectations about what trainee counsellors can offer, in order to provide safe and ethical contact with clients.

The key research questions asked were, "What is the impact of managing inappropriate referrals from clinical placement on the trainee counsellor's professional development?" and "Did the experiences enhance and/or impede development?"

What the literature says

A preliminary review of the literature revealed a dearth of research that focused specifically on the experiences of trainees working with clients who were deemed to be incompatible with their level of training. Therefore, the ensuing account of the literature attempts to connect areas of enquiry that are more widely implicated by the research questions.

Several writers have produced comprehensive models (e.g., Ronnestad & Skovholt, 2003; Stoltenberg & Delworth, 1987) that illuminate the gradual process of trainee growth across developmental stages. Ronnestad and Skovholt's (2003) work refers to the "beginning student phase" (p. 11) where several aspects of counsellor training combine to have an impact on, and occasionally overwhelm, the trainee. Of the many challenges faced by trainees at this stage, the ability to bridge the gap between theory and practice in work with real clients is a crucial task to be accomplished. Students normatively question their suitability and capacity to do the work, and the authors report that inexperienced therapists often feel that client sessions are highly challenging.

Complementing developmental theories is empirical research that has positioned itself within the formative experiences of counsellor training in an attempt to identify positive or negative aspects that affect the trainee (Grafanaki, 2010). Hill and colleagues (2007b) assign great importance to such research since "initial training experiences likely provide the foundation for subsequent learning" (p. 434), and there are studies that highlight some of the important difficulties that trainees raise when describing their seminal experiences. For example, Theriault and colleagues (2009) report that feelings of incompetence are a central feature in the novice's professional identity and result from subjective evaluations of their performance as practitioners. Skovholt and Ronnestad (2003) draw on empirical and conceptual literature and identify the ambiguity of professional work to be one major catalyst for novice stress. The complex interaction between cognitive and affective elements related to clinical performance raises difficulties for trainees in regulating and processing their experiences with clients. However, other findings (e.g., Pica, 1998) show that such experiences help foster the development of critical thinking skills and confidence in clinical decision making.

Other research in this area has adopted a critical incident approach to identify experiences that trainees perceive as significant learning moments or turning points as influences on their development (Cormier, 1988; Furr & Carroll, 2003; Howard et al., 2006; Morrissette, 1996). These studies reveal many categories, some of which pertain to trainees wrestling with self-efficacy based issues and identifying with their professional role, while others relate to a critical awareness of the clinical context, the value of supervision, and the highly significant task of client contact.

For Dryden and colleagues (1995), client work is the "sine qua non" (p. 107) of professional counsellor training, and Ronnestad and Skovholt (2003) report that meeting clients for the first time can be a critical incident for the student, and one which symbolises a "major crucible for the development of the practitioner's clinical identity" (Duryee et al., 1996, p. 666). It is the clinical placement that provides opportunities for trainees to practise their skills with real clients (Min, 2012), and trainees are ready to embark on placement when they have developed a working knowledge of the core theoretical model that will underpin their practice (Dryden et al., 1995). As well as being able to offer clients a minimum level of "facilitative functioning" (Carkhuff, 1969, cited in Dryden et al., 1995, p. 108), Ramsey (1962) argues that the counsellor is expected to have developed sufficient skills to enable a preliminary appraisal of the client's issue and recognise signs that might be indicative of an onward referral. This decision involves an evaluation of "professional training, experience, skills, knowledge, areas of specialisation, and command of services" (p. 444) in order to meet the needs of the client. However, the aptitude of the inexperienced novice to make such judgements remains unclear. Kahr (2011) endorses the significance of the clinical placement in forming the cornerstone of professional counsellor training and argues that when trainees are well supported, the placement becomes "the vital vertebral spine of the training experience" (p. 246). The support that he alludes to becomes imperative for the trainee who is highly motivated, but, concurrently, somewhat green and inexperienced in client work, and Duryee and colleagues (1996) advocate that such conditions can leave the trainee feeling inept and insecure about being adequate, or competent, in uncertain situations.

Dryden and colleagues (1995) agree that a well-managed placement is vital for support and can be "instrumental to the development of the student's confidence as a counsellor and their emerging professional identity" (p. 112). They write that the success of a training placement depends in part on the quality of the three-way agreement made between the course, the student, and the placement agency relating to many issues, including the type of clients which the student should, or should not, work with. They point out that unless this agreement has clarity, "there is a danger that unspoken expectations will not be met" creating a "breeding ground for dissatisfaction and resentment" (p. 110).

Wary of the shortcomings inherent in some placements, Pitts (1992) contends a combination of two sources of problems in creating challenges for trainees. Cited by Min (2012, p. 2015), "Type 1" problems relate to individual failures to perform as reasonably expected and might be attributed to lack of information, lack of resources, or unresolved personal issues, and "Type 2" problems might result from a failure of some aspect of the system. Another challenge to the integrity of the placement experience is written by Herrick (2007), who underscores the culture of increasing numbers of students pursuing sparse placements under the tyranny of getting their hours. Coupled with this, Tribe (2005) reported that trainees feel lucky to have been given a placement, and believes that this further complicates circumstances for the trainee when faced with difficulties. Since placements are in considerable demand, Coate (2010) understands that trainees are tempted to forego checking the placement's appropriateness to their circumstances, and points out how this can "undermine the effectiveness and enjoyment" of the placement experience and, for some, the placement can become an "unsafe experience for both trainees and clients" (p. 1).

Carroll (1993) acknowledges that trainees must start somewhere and urges careful monitoring of early client experiences to avoid harming the client and leaving the trainee demoralised. Based on the premise that gradual exposure to complex difficulties complements the trainee's systematic movement through developmental stages

(Ronnestad & Skovholt, 2003), and given the trainee's propensity for "stressful involvement" to which Orlinsky and Ronnestad (2005, p. 182) allude, Carroll's view is that initially trainees should only see carefully selected clients who reflect the experience of the trainee. Also, since client issues range in levels of difficulty, it seems conspicuous that some issues will require different levels of counsellor experience to manage them ethically and effectively. Coate (2010) augments this view within guiding ethical principles (BACP, 2013) that govern the safety of both clients and trainees in clinical work, and desires a pre-assessment process to select suitable clients to work with trainees. Furthermore, Herrick's (2007) guidelines deem it inappropriate for students to be placed where there is no qualified counsellor, or equivalent person, to assess and filter possible referrals.

From a supervisory stance, Dunkley (2007) declares how trainees have to "hit the ground running" (p. 41) when beginning placement, and she advocates a traffic light coding system which communicates levels of client difficulty to provide a graded experience that supports the trainees' need to gradually acquire their competence. This type of pacing limits the number of clients they see, and, through assessment or allocation meetings, the client referral is matched to the trainee's level of competence. The implementation of such referral criteria helps protect therapists from being over-burdened with referrals that are inappropriate (Haworth & Gallagher, 2005). If these views are to be taken seriously, then there is no reason for the trainee to be placed in a situation where she is trying to work with clients who are beyond her capabilities.

Yet, contrary to this notion of providing early protection, there are some who argue "that it does no harm to beginners to 'throw them in the deep end' and allow them to see whatever clients 'come through the door'" (Carroll, 1993, p. 57). However, in light of preceding arguments and strategies that advocate careful screening of trainee referrals, this approach potentially leaves the novice in a precarious position when encountering issues that are best dealt with by more experienced or specialist therapists. Indeed, research by Tribe (2005) found that a number of trainees reported inappropriate referrals as an issue important to their professional and ethical practice and, among the themes uncovered, trainees cited being asked to work at the edge of their professional competence as well as working with complex client issues. Furthermore, Izzard (2001) interviewed supervisors who spoke of placements providing inappropriate clients to trainees, where the client group was "very disordered" or "extremely disturbed" and were not even deemed suitable for an experienced counsellor (p. 88).

Given the reality of the potential for inappropriate referrals in the trainee's practical work, Dryden and colleagues (1995) argue that trainees should invest more in supervision to provide the extra support needed when work with clients proves too challenging. Bernard and Goodyear (2009) argue that supervision should enable a discussion of self-efficacy in such instances, since an important goal of professional training is developing one's confidence with clients. Supervisors can help normalise feelings of incompetence and assist the trainee in attempting to tolerate the many ambiguities in the world of counselling training. Furthermore, Duryee and colleagues (1996) believe that good supervision helps the trainee to locate the courage and wherewithal to approach challenges on their own terms.

However, Izzard (2001) found that the complexity of such concerns raises tensions for the supervisor when faced with trainees who find themselves out of their depth and stretched beyond their level of competence. The supervisors whom she interviewed reported clinical placements as the most troublesome area in their work with trainees, finding that placements were regarded as inappropriate and described as having loose boundaries. Herrick (2007) adds her concern that placements might not be offering their trainees the necessary support, making unfair demands on them, or not understanding their needs.

Furthermore, for supervisors to be able to help trainees with their dilemmas about working with complex clients and help promote their competence, trainees must disclose their difficulties within supervision (Mehr et al., 2010). Duryee and colleagues (1996) wrote that revealing self-doubts to the supervisor can be problematic for trainees, as the supervisor's status ostensibly denotes superiority and this can heighten "the potential for the trainee's shame and self-doubt" (p. 665). However, other research indicates that the supervisory relationship has a facilitative influence on trainee disclosure of clinical issues, particularly when the relationship is bonded by rapport (e.g., Webb & Wheeler, 1998).

Given that actual work with clients is central to the trainee's developmental process and cited as the main driver for change (Folkes-Skinner et al., 2010), De Stefano et al. (2012) report that trainees will inevitably find themselves working with difficult, or challenging, clients who test the limits of their knowledge and competence. Whether or not such clients are deemed to have been referred inappropriately will depend on the perception that the trainee holds of their client's presenting, or emerging, case material. Indeed, Min (2009, 2012) usefully reminds us that trainee perceptions are significant psychological features in the development that they experience, pointing out that trainees are unique and that perception is very subjective. Therefore, the experiences they portray would be different from one to another. This might help to explain the absence of a definition of an inappropriate counselling referral among the scholastic resources appraised for this study, but the notion of trainee's encountering inappropriately referred clients seems to appear as a prominent concern in the aforementioned literature (e.g., Haworth & Gallagher, 2005; Izzard, 2001; Tribe, 2005).

Given the deficiency of research that looks at the specific impact of inappropriate referrals on the trainee, the remaining studies here centre on the impact of early client experiences on the novice, and were selected as the milieu to help understand how trainees who encounter perceived inappropriate referrals are influenced. For example, Hill and colleagues (2007b) noticed that all the trainees in their study felt quite anxious about beginning to see clients and worried about knowing what to do in sessions. They also noted self-criticism directed at therapeutic abilities and clinical skills, and found feelings of incompetence and impatience. Trainees also expressed dismay when their client's behaviour did not conform to their expectations, and they felt anxious when met with a psychologically sophisticated client. More pertinently, they reported that trainees experienced difficulties when clients seemed very disturbed, or fragile, and needed more than the trainee could offer. This latter finding seems to point towards encounters with inappropriately referred clients, and although Hill and colleagues' article does not describe the nature of the difficulties experienced, they do report the trainee's need for control and predictability and their wish to be assigned "easy" or "safe" clients (p. 444).

Folkes-Skinner and colleagues (2010) also report the stressful nature of counsellor training and found significant shifts in identity, self-knowledge, and confidence in their participants that were attributed to working with real clients. They reasoned that work with easier clients provides positive initial experiences of client work, giving trainees a chance to develop the confidence and professional identity that could facilitate them later when clients become more challenging. This claim supports the notion that early positive experiences can enhance professional growth, but does not consider the impact of early work with more difficult clients on the trainee's identity and confidence.

Research focusing on confidence as a central feature of professional development (e.g., Bischoff, 1997; Bischoff & Barton, 2002; Bischoff et al., 2002; De Stefano et al., 2007; Skovholt & Ronnestad, 1992a,b) found that experiences with clients result in the most volatility in confidence and fluctuating levels of self-esteem and the early growth in confidence to which Folkes-Skinner and colleagues (2010) allude can quickly evaporate when faced with a difficult client. This seems to indicate the fragility of confidence in client work that becomes particularly vulnerable when the trainee meets clients who are too challenging for them. Bischoff and colleagues (2002) explain that this could be due to the newness of providing therapy and because trainees lack the internalised experiences on which to evaluate new ones, arguing that ongoing clinical experience can broaden the trainee's limited reservoir of knowledge and promote the process of internalisation to help to stabilise vacillations in confidence. Although these studies do not describe the nature of the complexity of client work, their findings seem to suggest that trainee confidence is in a delicate state when encountering clients in the early stages of training and, while they propose that confidence requires development through consequent experience, they do not specify the type of client experiences that help to strengthen a healthy sense of clinical confidence. However, in their discussion, they do suggest that trainers have the ability to "at least indirectly control the type of clinical contact received by beginning clinicians" (p. 380), which seems to confirm the importance of client features in influencing the development of trainee confidence.

Related to the study of self-confidence is the concept of trainee self-efficacy (TSE) (Lent et al., 2009), which refers to the trainees' beliefs about their ability to perform the tasks inherent in the counselling role, including the negotiation of challenging client scenarios. Larson (1998) implicates TSE beliefs in the trainee's clinical functioning when in session with clients, and Lent and colleagues (2009) found them to interact with affective, cognitive, and behavioural responses. They observed feelings of nervousness and worry, perceptions about the session process, and ease, or difficulty, of the work, and a critical appraisal of behavioural and cognitive strategies in the trainee's performance. In another study, Min (2012) revealed stories that indicate that the strategies that are adopted by trainees contributed to their efficacy; these involved acceptance of tasks and roles, being open to new experiences, and holding realistic perceptions of the goals and limitations experienced in their environment. It was conceded that the "struggles, challenging experiences, and unhappy feelings are part of the experience during learning towards becoming a counsellor" (p. 2019), but also that these processes are part of a meaningful journey to make sense of, and believe in, one's own ability.

One study that is directly related to this topic is one that has examined the experiences of trainee counsellors working with a specific type of challenging clientele (De Stefano et al., 2012). They interviewed trainees working with clients presenting with non-suicidal self-injury to highlight "issues that are potentially inherent to beginners who are working with challenging cases" in the more general practice of counselling (p. 300). Their analysis reported the multiple efforts that their trainees engaged with to deal with the personal struggles and tasks involved in working with this particular client group. Tasks such as managing their emotional reactivity, resolving ethical issues, and deciding on clinical strategies heightened their feelings of uncertainty and stirred up feelings of incompetence, but also focused their intentions in their work and led to significant learning. However, despite their experiences of imparting new clinical lessons, the authors reported an overall uncertainty and many unanswered questions pertaining to the trainee's sense of themselves as clinicians. Yet, where incompetence was openly acknowledged, it was complemented by vigilance, self-monitoring, and a reflexivity that the authors regard as hallmarks of good practice. Although not referring to inappropriate referrals as such, De Stefano and colleagues (2012) claim that any of a number of difficult issues, or client populations, could have produced a very similar pattern of findings.

The general sense imparted by the literature has stressed the importance of gradual exposure to more complex clients as a form of good practice, and which contributes to trainee's confidence and sense of self-efficacy. However, there is a paucity of information regarding how the trainee is affected when this posture is not adopted, and the resultant impact of working with perceived inappropriately referred clients during placement on the trainee's development has, thereby, remained unquestioned.

Participants

A homogenous sample of four participants was obtained by the purposive (non-probability) sampling method. Counsellor trainees in associated placement settings were carefully selected using inclusion criteria based on their training status, clinical experience, and their encounters with perceived inappropriate referrals.

The four participants were white and female; ages ranged from thirty-one to over sixty-one, and all were trained in the person-centred modality of therapy. All had accumulated over sixty hours of clinical practice and had worked with over fifteen clients. Allied placement settings were located within the National Health Service (NHS), a further and higher education establishment, and a rehabilitation facility for problematic drug and alcohol use.

Data collection

The flexible data collection method of semi-structured interviewing was used that was consistent with the aims and focus of qualitative enquiry. Data was collected through audio-taping and, later, transcribing participants' verbal responses to the following questions.

- Please could you start off by telling me about the nature of your placement setting and the process by which clients are referred to you as a trainee counsellor?
- You have indicated that you have worked with at least one client that you have regarded as inappropriately matched to your level of training and experience. Could you outline the circumstances of that referral and the features of it that led you to feel that it was not suitable for you to work with?
- Can you describe how you felt about this situation at the time?
- How did this affect your counselling interaction with this client?

- If you consulted with others about the referral, what were the particular concerns that you raised?
- How has this experience influenced:
  (a) your decision to accept future referrals;
  (b) clinical judgements made about ongoing work with clients?
- In what ways do you feel that your experience has:
  (a) had a positive effect on your learning and development as a therapist?
  (b) had a negative effect on your learning and development as a therapist?
- If there's one thing that you have learnt that you could pass on to other trainees starting placement, what would it be?

What was discovered

Table 6.1 represents the occurrence of three overarching superordinate themes across the data, and includes subordinate themes that aim to encapsulate the potency of the experiences described by the sample of participants. The pattern of themes is presented to reflect the developmental process by which participants have moved through their experiences and which seem to have been influenced by the presence

Table 6.1. Emerging themes.

Superordinate themes	The impact of early experiences on the inner world of the trainee	The impact on practice	The emerging professional self
Subordinate themes	Stirring feelings of disquiet	Grappling with the model	The trainee in process—becoming
	Enduring an inimical residue	Seeking help—the quest for balance and resolve	Positioning the self as a therapist
	Confronting the self		Disenchantment with the agency
	The humble posture of the trainee		

of a perceived inappropriate referral in their initial work with clients. Ensuing participant responses have been anonymised by pseudonym and edited for clarity.

Superordinate theme 1: The impact of early experiences on the inner world of the trainee

When asked to describe how they felt about working with a client whom they perceived to be inappropriately referred, all participants experienced an acute phase of self-awareness, a preoccupation with one's inner state that ignited a journey of self-questioning and discovery about what it means to be a counsellor training in a placement setting.

Subordinate theme 1.1: Stirring feelings of disquiet

All participants were alerted to the notion that perhaps the client had not been appropriately referred to them; however, their perceptions of inappropriateness differed. For example, Liz viewed the client as inappropriate in terms of complexity: "I'm out of my depth with this person and I think actually she needs probably more support and help than some short-term intervention with a trainee counsellor." Two others perceived inappropriateness by regarding their clients as unwilling or unable to engage in counselling: "There was very little willingness to sort of go into his feelings at all . . . My feelings now are that perhaps he shouldn't have come on to my [or] anybody's books really" [Gill]. ". . . it became apparent as you were working with this client that possibly because of the medication they were on, I would never really have been able to engage at a deep level . . ." [Mel]. Abi perceived inappropriateness in terms of lack of referral structure and how her referrers viewed the trainee counsellor's role: ". . . because at times it can kind of feel like you're being used as a free pastoral mentor; it's not always necessarily going to be counselling work that's coming through." Being moved by incongruous feelings about the client's suitability, all participants experienced unsettling sensations in-session. For three participants, these feelings of unease escalated with the emerging complexity of the client's issues, for example: ". . . and the first few sessions were fine, but what started to come out was more complex . . . I became more aware of how I was feeling which were little bells were ringing thinking, ooo gosh she's coming out with some stuff that I'm not really sure about . . ." [Liz]. For another, a tone of risk was perceived which culminated in a strong sense of caution and desire to make something happen: "I guess there is serious potential in what she's talking about; and right big risks involved in the stuff that she was presenting with and the way she was . . . I suppose [it] just sort of made me a bit . . . panicky [is] maybe the right word; almost like there was a sense of urgency in the room like, oh you need to do something" [Abi]. Other immediate feelings were experienced as more personal, as Liz described feeling beleaguered by a difficult client: ". . . and it was quite hurtful, some of it, I think she was wanting to be quite destructive. So I felt some of what she was saying to me was almost like a personal attack, not quite that, but there was definitely I'm having a pop at you."

Subordinate theme 1.2: Enduring an inimical residue

Following their initial encounters with clients, all participants were left with difficult lingering feelings of inadequacy that affected their self-confidence: "I do recall it really sort of affecting my sort of confidence at that point . . . and that's what was really left with me, a sense of why is it that I'm not able to really get a sense of what's going on for this client?" [Mel]. For Abi, this sense of uncertainty trickled into other areas of her life: ". . . it didn't just stick with training to be a counsellor or me being at work, it was like everything, I just feel like I lost all confidence . . ." [Abi].

My sense at this point of analysis was that the participants felt hindered by their disturbance, and Mel became aware of her threshold for working with her client: "There was a limit to the amount of work I could be doing. So I found that quite difficult." Gill felt purposely tested: "And there were times when I thought do they deliberately do this so that you either sink or you swim . . ." Others were left perplexed by a paradoxical sense of knowing, but not really knowing, for example: "I guess I learnt quite a lot from just having sort of not done anything wildly wrong, but not necessarily knowing how. I think it was just knowing how much I needed, how much I could do and how much I couldn't do" [Gill]. An acute sense of responsibility for the confusion left Abi feeling indebted to her client: "I felt like I owed her something almost, like I needed to kind of stick with it as if

I could do something for her or make something happen . . ." For Liz, the experience left an indelible impression that initiated a real fervour to take action: ". . . the client didn't stay with me so much, but the experiences of what I felt was an inappropriate referral did. And that's what sort of motivated me to go and do things about that."

Subordinate theme 1.3: Confronting the self

During the unfolding analysis, I noticed that all participants' attention became inwardly focused, some finding themselves feeling culpable and all of them occupying an acute phase of intensive self-questioning. Frustrations and feelings of confusion and deficiency were described by these participants: ". . . the effect on me is that I just found it completely confusing; and [it] made me really question myself and question my training, and question why I wasn't able to do it" [Abi]. . . . there was a lot of questioning, me questioning myself about what's going on, what am I doing, am I working within my limits?" [Liz]. Further self-questioning appeared to source inadequacy with the self: "I felt that I wasn't doing a good enough job. I felt that there was something about me that wasn't connecting with her adequately . . ." [Mel]. "I kept on thinking well, is it me that's not doing what I need to do?" [Gill]. For Abi, the intensive self-questioning became overwhelming and bore a global impact on her work and sense of self: ". . . but just not [question] to that extent where it's sort of crippling your work almost . . . the questioning got too much and it really started seeping out into everything, and that eats away at your confidence in yourself generally."

Subordinate theme 1.4: The humble posture of the trainee

All participants made reference to their trainee status as an influence on their placement experience. Liz assigned great importance to the value of early trainee experiences and went on to highlight the trainee's tenuous position by questioning how referrers perceive the trainee's capabilities: "I don't think at the beginning I really thought about the importance of the quality of the experiences that we get as trainees with our first clients, or what a profound effect that might have. . . . two thoughts came up for me; one is did the psychiatrist know [when referring] that a trainee was going to be counselling this patient? But also the line manager, what part of her thought that a trainee was capable?" [Liz]. The credulous state of the trainee is illustrated by Mel, who ascribed superiority to her agency to make appropriate referrals, and Liz also admits being trusting of perceived expertise: "... from my perspective [I] quite naïvely assumed that they would know what sort of clients to refer to me. I [thought] well, they're qualified so they know everything and I don't know very much ... particularly very early on when I first went out into placement" [Mel]. "... with trusting the manager totally, [I felt] they're going to match me up with somebody whose presentation is going to match my level of experience and knowledge" [Liz]. The trainee rank was also accompanied by feelings of inferiority for Mel, who felt unable to challenge the perceived authority of her agency: "I think I did feel intimidated ... [I was] quite quick to doubt myself rather than doubting the person who I saw in authority ..." At least two of the participants described the challenges involved in getting a placement, and the sense of relief that was felt left Mel feeling compromised: "I was so grateful to have a placement; I really wanted to work in that field. So I think I compromised quite an awful lot really, looking back ..."

Superordinate theme 2: The impact on practice

At this stage of the analysis, I recognised a deep integrity and commitment of all participants to their counselling endeavour: to deliver ethically sound practice and take action to regain a sense of stability. During this process, three participants reflected on the challenges entailed in doing, and being among, the person-centred approach.

Subordinate theme 2.1: Grappling with the model

Liz described her struggle to implement the core conditions of the model with her difficult client: "My challenges were around trying to be, wanting to be accepting of all that she was, but that's incredibly hard to do when you've got somebody who is, it felt like really judging me." Other participants seem to resist the process of person-centred therapy and their comments indicate a movement away from the model in their practice: "... it's trying to make sense of it in your head as to what this experience is that the client has had. Maybe I don't need to understand it. I need to work with it, which I kind of understand now . . ." [Gill]. "I need to do something to kind of make it OK for her to be here and to engage and somehow sort of speed that process up . . ." [Abi]. For Gill, it took time to inhabit the model: "I'd come in and say [to the supervisor], what he really needs is this, this and this you know . . . so that took me six months to work through." However, it seems that Gill settled into the model and ultimately felt the power of encounter: "I worked where she was really and that's what you do isn't it . . . And she actually ended up going back to work . . . I'm blown away by that." Abi also became more trusting of the model: ". . . in the later stages actually being able to see why it might work and how it can be of value . . . I guess it's about [the connection] and that being the transformative factor."

Subordinate theme 2.2: Seeking help—the quest for balance and resolve

All the participants in the sample sought refuge and acted on a desire to find answers. Liz, in particular, felt compelled to find fairness for trainees: "I went and did something about it. I didn't just accept that this should happen... I feel quite passionate about speaking up for those who maybe wouldn't say anything." Abi sought advice that was not easily forthcoming: "I can't really remember getting any kind of advice or anything like that on what to do with it or where it goes or . . . but I remember feeling quite cross . . . it felt like I wasn't being taken very seriously." All participants recognised supervisory consultation as imperative and my analysis indicated it serving various functions. For Mel, the supervisor was a facilitator in the scrutiny of her practice: "Just to have that place to go to use as a sounding board to really look at your practice very carefully about what it is you're doing, to maintain the best interests for your client." For Abi, the supervisor helped to activate direction and reconcile ethical tensions: "I remember going to my supervisor a lot at that point and [saying] I don't know what to do . . . I don't know where we're kind of going with this, and I don't know whether it does need to go further." Gill felt that supervision was the main instigator of change and growth through helping her to confront issues with herself: "I would've said in the first fifty hours my confidence really did soar because I was kind of confronted. And I always put that down to my supervisor. It isn't about saying you're doing fine, it's making you confront your own stuff."

Superordinate theme 3: The emerging professional self

Towards the end of the interview, participants were asked about the positive impact of their experiences, and their comments allude to both personal and professional growth.

Subordinate theme 3.1: The trainee in process—becoming

Becoming more confident, able to challenge and more self-trusting: "I've had referrals since; I didn't know at the time they were inappropriate but quickly became aware that they were. And I'm certainly a lot more confident now about saying well, actually, I'm not really sure . . . and [the experience] has helped [me] to trust myself more; to not question myself quite so much" [Mel]. Two participants became more accountable for their own experiences: "I [got] to the point where I was actually filtering through the clients myself . . . I just thought, I've got to sort this out haven't I . . . what I think is going to give me the best sort of experience" [Gill]. "I'm more choosy about who I'm going to take on as a trainee" [Liz]. For Gill, working with difficult client issues has enabled her to become more open about topics such as suicide and death: "I had to somehow get to grips with somebody who was talking about suicide on a regular basis. At first I was in a bit of a panic . . . It was useful for me because I began to realise that . . . you could talk about these things without going freaking out about them." Abi was able to reap the benefits of self-questioning through becoming more objective and self-valuing in her work: "I suppose like now I'm kind of able to remove myself from it a bit more and see that it's not about me . . . now I think it's helping me [to] really value what it is that I can bring to the relationship."

Subordinate theme 3.2: Positioning the self as a therapist

While accumulating clinical experience, all participants relayed a sense of feeling more self-assured in their therapist role, as Gill comments, "[It's] less [about] what you're doing isn't it, and more about who you are really." Assertiveness was also a significant area of growth: "I would be far less accommodating and probably would question a lot more now" [Mel]. Furthermore, Abi has modified her practice by doing more checking out with her clients: "Whereas now

I think I do kind of keep that [initial session] a bit tighter and do know that I need to find out a little bit more . . ."

Subordinate theme 3.3: Disenchantment with the agency

All participants expressed a sense of disillusionment with their placement agency for a number of reasons. For example, Gill perceived that referrers had unrealistic views about client needs and what counselling can offer: "I'm often quite appalled at the level of understanding that seems to be the people who refer the [clients] to us." Mel felt unsupported and belittled, and this resulted in anxiety for her: "Not feeling supported by the managers at the placement particularly, feeling as though I was being almost told off if you like for questioning their referring skills . . . I felt that my concerns were kind of dismissed . . . As a trainee I didn't feel as though I could rock the boat almost." Most participants reported feeling unprepared for their placement encounters: "I didn't have an induction at all . . . I just like felt as though I'd been parachuted in [to] just sort it out" [Gill]. "Basically I'd get a phone call, can you see this [client], yes or no, and that was it. So I didn't even know about the fact that there was a kind of process in the background at the time" [Abi]. Gill felt that she was not getting value from her placement and became disenchanted with the counselling profession: "I didn't really get any experiences . . . and I didn't feel that there was enough support either . . . My experience really has been that the whole of the counselling thing is a bit shambolic in patches." All participants expressed concern about referral processes and these final quotes leave a sense of concern for new trainees entering the field: "I was quite shocked actually that there was a lack of, what feels like a lack of commitment to really screening the referrals" [Liz]. "It just felt like somebody did need to keep a kind of check on all that and especially when you're using so many students on placement . . ." [Abi].

The experiences described by this sample of counsellor trainees allude to significant internal shifts on both a personal and professional level that appear to be inextricably linked to the presence of perceived inappropriate referrals in their work. Their narratives highlight the taxing strains that encircle client contact, but also demonstrate the dedication to process their grievances and dig deep to locate the personal resources that would enable them to endure their training phase.

Bringing together the literature and the findings

This study can be considered to have adopted a critical incident approach (e.g., Howard et al., 2006), whereby participants told their story of specific positive or negative moments during training (i.e., working with a perceived inappropriate referral) that made a difference to the trajectory of their novice journey. Overall, their narratives reveal similar categories to those found in other critical incident research (e.g., Howard et al., 2006) that pertain to wrestling with competency based issues and the trainee's sense of self-efficacy, critical awareness of the clinical context, and the value of supervision—all of which are associated with the appointment of client contact.

Ronnestad and Skovholt (2003) agree that meeting clients for the first time is a critical incident and the most important task faced at this phase, and this was echoed by Liz, who placed great value on the quality of the first client experience, and its potential to generate a profound impact on the trainee; other participant narratives describe their early client work as providing the basis for subsequent learning (Hill et al., 2007a) by instigating a huge "learning curve" [Gill, Mel].

Issues relating to the task of client contact were the most prevalent features of this study, and its outcomes support Tribe's (2005) findings that work with clients who are perceived to be inappropriately referred is an important issue for counsellor trainees in that it is highly influential in their ethical practice and professional development. Tribe's (2005) theme of uncovered trainees being asked to work at the edge of their professional competence was also felt by Liz, who sometimes felt out of her depth. Her narrative also illuminated another of Tribe's (2005) themes in recognising complex client issues, as she reported feeling manipulated and challenged by the complexity of her client's material and behaviour. Other narratives further support comments made by Izzard's (2001) supervisors, who spoke of placements providing inappropriate clients to trainees and as operating with loose boundaries.

Ronnestad and Skovholt (2003) suggest that issues of suitability normatively arise during the "beginning student phase" (p. 11), and this holds true for the participants in this study, who all queried the appropriateness of their referrals: for example, Gill elucidates, "my assessment [was] that in fact they [clients] weren't [appropriate]". Due to the absence of an established definition, what was of interest was the different ways in which referrals were regarded as inappropriate by the participants. For example, Abi's experience of receiving referrals that required an intervention other than counselling resonates with Herrick (2007), who expressed concern that placements might not understand a trainee's requirements. In contrast, Mel's experience of feeling mismatched to her clients alludes to the incompatibility between the client's issue and the trainee's skill level that Carroll (1993) and Orlinsky and Ronnestad (2005) argue that case selection should avoid. The diversity of ideas here is espoused by Min's (2009, 2012) reminder that trainee perceptions are significant features in the way in which they experience phenomena and their very subjectivity would naturally give rise to differing views on such a complex issue.

Despite the difficulties in isolating a definition of an inappropriate referral, their occurrence in the narratives of the trainees in this sample concurs with De Stefano and colleagues' (2012) view that it is inevitable that trainees will find themselves working with difficult, or challenging, clients who test their levels of knowledge and competence. Given the preordained nature of such incidents, it would seem a coherent strategy to implement an assessment process (Coate, 2010) or referral criteria (Dunkley, 2007) to protect trainees from the burden of referrals that are inappropriate (Haworth & Gallagher, 2005), and lessen the trainee's propensity for "stressful involvement" with clients (Orlinsky & Ronnestad, 2005, p. 182). However, for the participants in this study, consistent systems of referring, and associated safeguarding, were seemingly lacking.

The need for a gradual introduction of the trainees to more difficult aspects of their work that Carroll (1993) proposes, and that reflects the developmental pathways set out by Stoltenberg and Delworth (1987) and Ronnestad & Skovholt (2003), is also not borne out by the experiences of this sample of trainees. In some cases, neither does there seem to be the presence of careful monitoring (Carroll, 1993) and filtering (Herrick, 2007) of possible referrals by an appropriately qualified gatekeeper; as Abi explains, "nobody recognises the fact that they've [referrers] got no kind of counselling experience, they're not looking at how the referrals are being made . . ." The upshot of situations like this was that the participants felt compelled to screen clients for suitability themselves, and this need for control and predictability is echoed by Hill and colleagues (2007b) trainees, who expressed their wish to be assigned "easy" or "safe" clients (p. 444).

However, the associated impact of a lack of such structure also arose within the third superordinate theme, where a sense of dissatisfaction (Dryden et al., 1995) with the placement agency became evident in participants' accounts. Although writers such as Kahr (2011) and Dryden and colleagues (1995) advocate that a well-managed and supportive placement can be pivotal in the development of self-confidence, all participants spoke of the ineptness and insecurity that Duryee and colleagues (1996) allude to when trainees are in situations where they do not know how to proceed. Comments made by Gill: "I didn't have an induction at all" and Mel: "it was a bit of a whistle-stop tour" refer to the lack of information that forms the "Type 1" problem that Pitts (1992) found in placements and that contribute to a failure to perform as reasonably expected. In addition, the perceived "graft to get a placement" [Liz] and "the need to get 100 hours in" [Abi] supports Herrick's (2007) observation that adds to trainees feeling "grateful to have a placement" [Mel]. Consequently, these feelings coplicate circumstances for the trainee when faced with perceived difficulties (Tribe, 2005) and left at least one participant reporting feeling substantially compromised. The overall sense from the participants' narratives corresponds to Coate's (2010) comment that inappropriate placements can be undermining and feel unsafe for trainees and clients: "I certainly didn't feel very safe at the beginning, and I didn't feel the people around me were necessarily as safe as they might be" [Gill].

The difficulties experienced by the participants led them all to invest more in supervision. Ronnestad and Skovholt (2003) point out that supervisors can exert a major influence on the beginning student and both Gill and Mel's proclivity towards the experience of their supervisors concurs with Skovholt and Ronnestad (2003), who state that many novices plausibly seek the support and guidance of those professional elders who "know the ropes" (p. 55). All of the participants felt able to disclose their difficulties within supervision (Mehr et al., 2010), and although Gill was initially "nervous about asking for help", she was enabled to have the discussions about self-efficacy that Bernard and Goodyear (2009) argue are important in developing self-confidence.

The initiative demonstrated by these, and other, participants in managing their clinical work shows a process of becoming accustomed to the challenges of training as a counsellor, and the third superordinate theme encapsulates the growth in confidence and assertiveness in challenging the suitability of referral processes. However, some of the narratives that are reflected by the first superordinate theme highlight the delicate posture of the trainee that made it initially very difficult to challenge perceived figures of authority, and Liz expressed her concern for new trainees entering the field who might not feel able to challenge referrers. Because of the volatility in confidence that necessarily comes with being a trainee (Bischoff & Barton, 2002), any early growth in confidence can quickly diminish when faced with challenging circumstances, and Mel's narrative revealed that her confidence was certainly affected by her experience. These are findings akin to those of Folkes-Skinner and colleagues (2010), and De Stefano and colleagues (2007) explain that this could be due to trainees lacking the internalised experiences on which to evaluate new ones. However, Mel's journey shows how ongoing clinical experience can help promote the process of internalisation to stabilise such vacillations in confidence: "the latter inappropriate referrals that I've had in my training have helped me with my confidence". Related to confidence are the beliefs that pertain to the trainee's ability to negotiate challenging client scenarios, and the sources of change in trainee self-efficacy found by Lent and colleagues (2009) were also experienced by this sample to be located "in-session" with clients. All participants experienced negative affective states; for Gill "[it] threw me into a bit of a panic", and Liz described feeling "put through the mincer". These states seemed to interact with bewildering cognitive responses that contribute to what Skovholt and Ronnestad (2003) describe as the "anxiety of self-consciousness" (p. 47), and which are fused by the subordinate theme "confronting the self". Skovholt and Ronnestad (2003) argue that focusing on oneself detracts attention away from the task at hand, and becomes directed towards stabilising the internal state, as this participant articulated: "I became a bit wary of watching my brain" [Liz], and Abi: "in those very early stages, it's really difficult to kind of think." These sensations gave rise to the kind of self-criticism that resonates with Hill and colleagues (2007b) and Theriault and colleagues' (2009) trainees who felt incompetent and deficient: "I felt as though there was something lacking in me" [Mel]. Further findings help illustrate Hill and colleagues' (2007b) observation that trainees expressed dismay when clients did not conform to expectations: "I felt very sort of ill-prepared as to what I would expect from a client" [Gill], or felt anxious when faced with a psychologically sophisticated client: "the client told me that she'd also done a counselling course. So there was a lady sitting in front of me who knew a bit about theory [and] terminology, and so I had the experiences of someone saying 'oh nice bit of paraphrasing going on there'" [Liz]. Skovholt and Ronnestad (2003) explain that trainees lack the professional experience that helps to buffer the impact of such anxiety when difficulties are faced. However, as Ronnestad and Skovholt (2003) point out, such experiences are aligned with the typical characteristics of the "beginning student phase" (p. 11), where encompassing features of counsellor training such as theories, clients, and professional elders all combine to force some kind of impact on the trainee.

Ronnestad and Skovholt (2003) further explain that beginning students customarily question their ability to "bridge the felt chasm between theory and practice" (p. 12), but suggest that they might experience a sense of calm when they start using their well-studied frameworks. However, the narratives that form part of the second superordinate theme suggest that, for three participants, there were initial struggles in the execution and occupancy of their practice model. Skovholt and Ronnestad (2003) offer a style of reacting to this dissonance and explain that "premature closure" (p. 49) occurs when trainees feel overwhelmed by their challenge, and its expression can be found in the difficulty of entering or staying in the experiential world of the client. As Liz comments, "feeling like I was stepping back really, rather than just being with and sensing and staying with this client."

Further narratives illuminate the legacy of this dissonance in the intensity with which participants wrestled with self-questioning: "I just found it completely confusing; and [it] made me really question myself and question my training" [Abi]. Skovholt and Ronnestad (2003) offer "insufficient closure" (p. 49) to explain how the participants dealt with the emotional and cognitive overload that they experienced when faced with their perceived inappropriately referred clients, and this helps to explain why the participants continually felt the disturbing reactions produced by the challenge and became preoccupied with processing related thoughts. More examples of this type of reaction are condensed by the first superordinate theme and are illustrated by the narratives that make up how participants were required to *endure an inimical residue*, and the intense self-questioning that forms the subordinate theme "confronting the self". The feelings of culpability experienced by some participants are validated by Skovholt and Ronnestad (2003) who report that the novice often points the finger of blame towards the self, and this is illustrated by Mel—"there's something about me"—and Gill—"is it me . . ."—who both made dispositional attributions to try to understand their experiences. With an accompanying loss of confidence, Abi described becoming full of self-doubt, and Skovholt and Ronnestad (2003) describe the trainee who is having to make decisions while feeling confused as encountering the "white water experience" (Zeigler et al., 1984, cited in Skovholt and Ronnestad, 2003, p. 51), where the conceptual maps acquired through learning seem irrelevant and inadequate for the specific challenges faced in practice. They advocate that "until experience gives one the internal cognitive map, the novice experiences the elevated stress of inexperience" (p. 52).

Similar to those trainees who are working with the challenges of clients with non-suicidal self-injury (De Stefano et al., 2012), the trainees in this sample also experienced feelings of uncertainty and incompetence in their work with the clients whom they perceived to be inappropriately referred. Likewise, where difficulties were acknowledged and answers sought by these participants, the vigilance and reflexivity that they practised appeared to lead to significant learning. The narratives that make up the growth aspects of the third superordinate theme support Min's (2012) findings, which show that the strategies that they developed to manage their client work, contributed to the development of their self-efficacy and enabled them to learn to position themselves more comfortably as therapists. They moved towards accepting the reality of the tasks and roles involved in client work, and adjusted their perceptions of the limitations that they found in their clinical environment. In addition, the importance of an attitude to openness to new learning is vital in facilitating growth and professional development (Ronnestad & Skovholt, 2003), and this is keenly illustrated by Gill, who wrestled with particularly difficult clients issues: "I've grown from where I was to letting these things in."

The overall findings of this study accord with much of the research literature that reports the stressful nature of client work in counsellor training. Although the initial turbulence of working with perceived inappropriate referrals was principally experienced negatively by the participants, it seems that such a critical incident prompted the type of "vigorous internal construction work" (Skovholt & Ronnestad, 2003, p. 50) in the trainee's confidence and self-efficacy that boosted their levels of competence, and that might not have necessarily been experienced in work with "easier" clients. Those who argue that "it does no harm to beginners to 'throw them in the deep end'" (Carroll, 1993, p. 57) might have a point, since the trainees in this sample were not necessarily disadvantaged by their early negative experiences. However, I would regard this statement tentatively, as it is only by the virtue of the courage and wherewithal of the personal efforts of this sample of participants to build the resilience to withstand their difficulties that this could possibly hold some truth.

Conclusion

One limitation of the study is that it worked within a limited time frame and with a restrictive sample that was small in size, selected by criteria, and all female and does not,, therefore permit me to reduce, predict, or extrapolate findings to the wider population of counsellor trainees in other placements. Furthermore, trainees who perceived their experiences to be unusual, or particularly negative, might have felt compelled to participate, and so their views might not fully reflect, or represent, the experiences of a typical novice. In addition, the reporting of experiences described by the participants might be limited because the use of the interview schedule could have impeded the emergence of other important matters. It is also possible that, despite being reassured of anonymity by informed consent procedures, the trainees might have deliberately withheld reporting some experiences if they feared that disclosure might lead to negative consequences. The lack of conceptual homogeneity in defining inappropriate referrals adds a further complication and signifies the need to negotiate meanings derived from the data.

However, this study has endeavoured to contribute to a sparse area of enquiry, and its findings have characterised some of the important tasks involved in the early stages of the trainee's professional development. It is also considered timely, since the burgeoning demand for counselling services in society has led to an expansion in the number of training courses available and applications from trainees wishing to become part of the counselling community. With the inevitability of inappropriate referrals being assigned to trainees, the tentative insights arising from this study can help those involved in training students to be more aware of the referral mechanisms involved when gaining clinical experience in placement settings, and perhaps approach the clinical management of inappropriately referred clients as an important training goal (Hill & Lent, 2006; Hill et al., 2007a; Spruill et al., 2004). Such a position might help to engender healthy professional development (Bischoff et al., 2002), provide a good start to the therapist's training (Todd, 1997), and arrest the "negative avenues of professional development such as incompetence, impairment and disillusionment" (Ronnestad & Skovholt, 2003, p. 7) experienced by this sample of participants. Indeed, Dryden and colleagues (1995) firmly believe that the training course has some responsibility to ensure that the placement context offers the trainee appropriate practice experience, and Koocher and Keith-Spiegel (1998) further allude to the responsibilities of placement providers to monitor and consider such instances coherently. My desire for additional enquiry concurs with De Stefano and colleagues (2012), who propose that further research should help to find an appropriate level of experience for the trainee to enable them to hold a "steady state of creative tension that neither overwhelms nor erodes their fragile sense of competence" (p. 303).

References

Bernard, J. M., & Goodyear, R. K. (2009). *Fundamentals of Clinical Supervision* (4th edn). Boston, MA: Pearson Education.
Bischoff, R. J. (1997). Themes in therapist development during the first three months of clinical experience. *Contemporary Family Therapy, 19*(4): 563–580.
Bischoff, R. J., & Barton, M. (2002). The pathway toward clinical self confidence. *American Journal of Family Therapy, 30*: 231–242.
Bischoff, R. J., Barton, M., Thober, J., & Hawley, R. (2002). Events and experiences impacting the development of clinical self-confidence: a study of the first year of client contact. *Journal of Marital and Family Therapy, 28*(3): 371–382.
British Association for Counselling and Psychotherapy (BACP) (2013). *The Ethical Framework for Good Practice.* Lutterworth: BACP.

Carkhuff, R. R. (1969). *Helping and Human Relations: A Primer for Lay and Professional Helpers, Vols 1 and 2.* New York: Holt, Rinehart & Winston.

Carroll, M. (1993). Trainee counsellors' clients. In: W. Dryden (Ed.), *Questions and Answers on Counselling in Action* (pp. 57–61). London: Sage.

Coate, M. A. (2010). *Guidance for Trainee Placements. T3 Information Sheet.* Lutterworth: BACP.

Cormier, L. S. (1988). Critical incidents in counselor development: themes and patterns. *Journal of Counseling and Development, 67*: 131–132.

De Stefano, J., Atkins, S., Nelson Noble, R., & Heath, N. (2012). Am I competent enough to be doing this? A qualitative study of trainees' experiences working with clients who self-injure. *Counselling Psychology Quarterly, 25*(3): 289–305.

De Stefano, J., D'iuso, N., Blake, E., Fitzpatrick, M., Drapeau, M., & Chamodraka, M. (2007). Trainees' experiences of impasses in counselling and the impact of group supervision on their resolution: a pilot study. *Counselling and Psychotherapy Research, 7*(1): 42–47.

Dryden, W., Horton, I., & Mearns, D. (1995). *Issues in Professional Counsellor Training.* London: Cassell.

Dunkley, C. (2007). Pacing the learning. *Therapy Today, 18*(9): 41–43.

Duryee, J., Brymer, M., & Gold, K. (1996). The supervisory needs of neophyte psychotherapy trainees. *Journal of Clinical Psychology, 52*(6): 663–671.

Folkes-Skinner, J., Elliott, R., & Wheeler, S. (2010). 'A baptism of fire': a qualitative investigation of a trainee counsellor's experience at the start of training. *Counselling and Psychotherapy Research, 10*(2): 83–92.

Furr, S. R., & Carroll, J. J. (2003). Critical incidents in student counselor development. *Journal of Counseling and Development, 81*: 483–489.

Grafanaki, S. (2010). 'Counsellors in the making': research on counselling training and formative experiences of trainee counsellors. *Counselling and Psychotherapy Research, 10*(2): 81–82.

Haworth, R., & Gallagher, T. (2005). Referrals: clinical considerations and responsibilities. In: R. Tribe & J. Morrissey (Eds.), *Handbook of Professional and Ethical Practice for Psychologists, Counsellors and Psychotherapists* (pp. 119–130). New York: Brunner-Routledge.

Herrick, J. (2007). Placements: support or confusion? *Therapy Today, 18*(1): 42–44.

Hill, C. E., & Lent, R. W. (2006). Training novice therapists: skills plus. *Psychotherapy Bulletin, 41*: 11–16.

Hill, C. E., Stahl, J., & Roffman, M. (2007a). Training novice psychotherapists: helping skills and beyond. *Psychotherapy: Theory, Research, Practice, Training, 44*: 364–370.

Hill, C. E., Sullivan, C., Knox, S., & Schlosser, L. Z. (2007b). Becoming psychotherapists: experiences of novice trainees in a beginning graduate class. *Psychotherapy: Theory, Research, Practice, Training*, 44(4): 434–449.

Howard, E. E., Inman, A. G., & Altman, A.N. (2006). Critical incidents among novice counselor trainees. *Counselor Education and Supervision*, 46(32): 88–102.

Izzard, S. (2001). The responsibility of the supervisor supervising trainees. In: S. Wheeler & D. King (Eds.), *Supervising Counsellors. Issues of Responsibility* (pp. 75–92). London: Sage.

Kahr, B. (2011). The clinical placement in mental health training. In: R. Bor & M. Watts (Eds.), *The Trainee Handbook. A Guide for Counselling and Psychotherapy Trainees* (3rd edn) (pp. 241–246). London: Sage.

Koocher, G. P., & Keith-Speigel, P. (1998). *Ethics in Psychology*. OxfordK: Oxford University Press.

Larson, L. (1998). The social cognitive model of counselor training. *Counseling Psychologist*, 26: 219–273.

Lent, R. W., Cinamon, R. G., Bryan, N. A., Jezzi, M. M., Martin, H. M., & Lim, R. (2009). Perceived sources of change in trainees' self-efficacy beliefs. *Psychotherapy Theory, Research, Practice, Training*, 46(3): 317–327.

Mehr, K. E., Ladany, N., & Caskie, G. I. L. (2010). Trainee nondisclosure in supervision: what are they not telling you? *Counselling and Psychotherapy Research*, 10(2): 103–113.

Min, R. M. (2009). Learning experience: development of counsellor trainees while performing counselling practicum at Malaysian schools. *International Journal of Learning*, 16(10): 441–456.

Min, R. M. (2012). Self-efficacy whilst performing counselling practicum promotes counsellor trainees development. *Procedia—Social and Behavioural Sciences*, 69: 2014–2021.

Morrissette, P. J. (1996). Recurring critical issues of student counsellors. *Canadian Journal of Counselling*, 31(1): 31–41.

Orlinsky, D. E., & Ronnestad, M. H. (2005). *How Psychotherapists Develop: A Study of Therapeutic Work and Professional Growth*. Washington, DC: American Psychological Association.

Pica, M. (1998). The ambiguous nature of clinical training and its impact on the development of student clinicians. *Psychotherapy*, 35(3): 361–365.

Pitts, J. H. (1992). PIPS: a problem-solving model for practicum and internship. *Counselor Education and Supervision*, 32(2): 142–151.

Ramsey, G. V. (1962). The referral task in counseling. *Personnel and Guidance Journal*, 40(5): 443–447.

Ronnestad, M. H., & Ladany, N. (2006). The impact of psychotherapy training: introduction to the special section. *Psychotherapy Research*, 16(3): 261–267.

Ronnestad, M. H., & Skovholt, T. M. (2003). The journey of the counselor and therapist: research findings and perspectives on professional development. *Journal of Career Development*, 30(1): 5–44.

Skovholt, T. M., & Ronnestad, M. H. (1992a). *The Evolving Professional Self: Stages and Themes in Therapist and Counselor Development*. New York: John Wiley & Sons.

Skovholt, T. M., & Ronnestad, M. H. (1992b). Themes in therapist and counselor development. *Journal of Counseling and Development*, 70: 505–515.

Skovholt, T. M., & Ronnestad, M. H. (2003). Struggles of the novice counselor and therapist. *Journal of Career Development*, 30(1): 45–58.

Spruill, J., Rozensky, R. H., Stigall, T. T., Vasquez, M., Bingham, R. P., & Olvey, C. D. (2004). Becoming a competent clinician: basic competencies in intervention. *Journal of Clinical Psychology*, 60: 741–754.

Stoltenberg, C. D., & Delworth, U. (1987). *Supervising Counselors and Therapists: A Developmental Approach*. San Francisco, CA: Jossey-Bass.

Theriault, A., Gazzola, N., & Richardson, B. (2009). Feelings of incompetence in novice therapists: consequences, coping, and correctives. *Canadian Journal of Counselling*, 43(2): 105–119.

Todd, T. C. (1997). Self supervision as a universal supervisory goal. In: T. C. Todd & C. L. Storm (Eds.), *The Complete Systematic Supervisor* (pp. 17–25). Boston: MA: Allyn and Bacon.

Tribe, R. (2005). Trainee perspectives on professional and ethical practice. In: R. Tribe & J. Morrissey (Eds.), *Handbook of Professional and Ethical Practice for Psychologists, Counsellors and Psychotherapists* (pp. 317–331). New York: Brunner-Routledge.

Webb, A., & Wheeler, S. (1998). How honest do counsellors dare to be in the supervisory relationships? An exploratory study. *British Journal of Guidance and Counselling*, 26: 509–524.

Zeigler, J. N., Kanas, N., Strull, W. M., & Bennet, N. E. (1984). A stress discussion group for medical interns. *Journal of Medical Education*, 59: 205–207.

CHAPTER SEVEN

Is talking enough? School-based counselling in Wales

Gary Tebble

Introduction

Over the last decade, there seems to have been a major revitalisation in school-based counselling (SBC) services in the UK, with well over 71% of schools providing "individual psychotherapy" (Hamilton-Roberts, 2012). As this chapter specifically investigates SBC in Wales, it is important to note that the Welsh Government (2011) has composed a strategy to fund all secondary school counselling services. As the futures of these SBC services are planned over the next few years, it felt imperative to organise a piece of research that could enhance the awareness and helpful nature of creative and symbolic methods (CSMs) offered in Wales. When consulting the pre-existing literature on SBC, "being able to talk to someone" was rated a significant factor by most young people, who consequently reported feeling better when given the opportunity to "talk through" their difficulties (Cooper, 2009). Although this suggests that talking and a non-directive approach is indeed "enough" in SBC, other literature would disagree with this. This was highlighted when young people also recalled "more active strategies" as being the most considerable element to their therapeutic development, signifying that they needed something more from psychotherapy (Griffiths, 2013). In support of this, key research has also been conducted highlighting that alternative creative interventions need to be in place for those young people who find talking difficult or insufficient (Armstrong, 2013).

The rationale for this research is, therefore, twofold; first, to address the requirement and need for more qualitative research. As SBC is a non-prescriptive intervention, the perspectives and voices of the therapist are significant but appear to have been forgotten in the literature (Fox & Butler, 2009). The second element to the overall rationale for the investigation is centred on the future ideas for research formerly proposed by Cooper (2013). He suggested that more literature is needed around the choice of interventions given in SBC, in order to match the young person's preferences and needs.

While working as an SBC practitioner in Wales for the past two years, I have found the process of therapeutic development with young people has always been an inspiring and humbling journey. This work has often challenged both my personal and professional development, leading me to question whether I was doing "enough" in the therapy room. This persistent feeling from my therapy sessions that some young people needed more than purely talking directed my professional work into the area of CSMs. After implementing a more creative approach, I have been struck by the power of different creative media. Alongside the deepening of some therapeutic relationships, I also noticed that some young people flourished when using CSMs, showing a higher level of interest and engagement in the counselling. It was a combination of therapeutic experience and professional inquisitiveness, which instigated this research.

The overall aim of this chapter is consequently to investigate the therapeutic helpfulness of CSMs, and whether a "talking only" paradigm was enough for the relationship to flourish in SBC. The formulated research question was therefore set as: *Is talking alone enough in the twenty-first century, or is the use of CSMs considered helpful, when developing a therapeutic relationship in SBC (Wales)?* When striving to answer this fully, two main objectives were further included: (i) to explore the experiences of current counselling practitioners in Wales who work in SBC in order to examine their individualistic approach; and (ii) to explore their use of CSMs and the potential outcome and usefulness that this might have had on the therapeutic relationship.

What the literature says

A preliminary review of the literature revealed four interconnecting areas that portrayed a critical picture of the SBC profession (Silverman, 2013). These were: a critical analysis of the SBC field; an intrinsic "young-person-centred approach" to SBC; CSMs in SBC; societal views/perceptions in modern society.

A critical analysis of the school-based counselling field

Although counselling services have been present in schools since the 1960s, the past decade has observed a significant revival. SBC is one of the major providers of psychological therapy for young people, widely delivering it across the whole of the UK. This provision is deemed easily accessible and is a valuable service for young people who are struggling with mental health difficulties, helping to improve their emotional wellbeing. This developing field is believed to be highly respected by the young service users, and has seen a recent increase in positive outcome research (Cooper, 2013). Throughout the literature search, it has become apparent that SBC is highly valued for its young person-centred nature, where the service has been found to commonly adopt a humanistic approach. This approach seems to place person-centred values and the exploration of emotion in high regard (Hamilton-Roberts, 2012). This echoes a pre-existing study conducted by Cooper (2009), who asked the young people to gauge the helpfulness of the counselling that they received, along with the contributing factors. The young service users reflected that the most significant factor of the therapeutic intervention was "being able to talk to someone who would listen", closely followed by the relief of "getting things off your chest". Young people also identified that an "active counsellor who offered challenge" was also helpful. When asked to explore any dissatisfaction with the service, they offered a few insights that included "a need for the counsellor to be more active and do more than just listen". As an overall conclusion, most young people were likely to report feeling better after having a chance to "talk through" their issues (Cooper, 2009, p. 145).

When investigating SBC further, Griffiths (2013) explored different aspects of the service, and again reflected that the helpful elements seem to be practised with a predominantly person-centred approach.

In this study, the young people seem to appreciate hugely the non-directivity of the counselling, where it was felt that a self-directed process was offered. It is interesting that even though the counselling practitioner had a humanistic orientation, the young clients acknowledged that significance was placed on the use of "more active strategies" within the therapeutic intervention. These findings seem to parallel the notion from Cooper (2013) when proposing that SBC might be most helpful for young people when a humanistic framework is adopted, while, at the same time, implementing flexibility and pluralism. It was highlighted that this could enable the young person's individual needs to be therapeutically met more effectively, integrating different strategies when required.

An intrinsic "young-person-centred approach' to school-based counselling

After extensively researching the SBC literature, it became evident that it is essentially humanistic or person-centred in its approach (Cooper, 2009). It is felt that SBC places a great importance on listening to young people and being responsive to their needs, which is often considered an intrinsically young-person-centred approach (Cooper, 2013). This was evidenced when examining the therapeutic orientation of school-based practitioners from Wales, which resulted in 80% of them identifying with a person-centred/humanistic or integrative approach. It was considered that these approaches were all chiefly relational in form, facilitating a helpful, understanding, and trusting relationship. It is hoped that this environment can enable the young person to tackle certain difficulties and improve their overall mental health and emotional welfare. When investigating this further, Smyth (2013) suggests that young-person-centred therapy involves putting the child and his needs first. With the child being the central focus, it is proposed that the counselling practitioner should adopt a sense of adaptability and inventiveness in order to successfully meet the individual needs. The principle objectives of SBC are to provide a supportive place where young people are empowered, giving them the capacity and resources to resolve or explore their difficulties. This support gives a young person the opportunity to talk, when perhaps there is no one else in her life (Griffiths, 2013).

When exploring the notion of a "young-person-centred approach", it seems as though it is an embryonic and developing field, echoing the professional advancement in SBC. This approach to therapeutic intervention seems to be heavily influenced by Carl Rogers, and has person-centred principles at its core (Keys & Walshaw, 2008). Smyth (2013) echoes this and suggests that it is the application of person-centred values, adapted specifically in a child-centred, friendly way. Prever (2010) is also in agreement when stating that the counselling practitioner should place great emphasis on the relationships that he or she builds, focusing individually on the young person and what his therapeutic need might be. In line with the traditional person-centred approach, SBC has a fundamental belief in the counselling relationship, endeavouring to create a therapeutic climate through the six psychological attitudes (Bryant-Jeffries, 2004). These therapeutic conditions, which are deemed necessary and sufficient, echo the original theory proposed by Rogers (1957), emphasising congruence, unconditional positive regard and empathic understanding. It is believed by the person-centred practitioner that if these psychological conditions are present and felt, then therapeutic change can transpire. The notion of therapeutic presence is also important in the literature, where Rogers (1986) proposed it to be a process that is simply healing, releasing, and helpful.

When developing a more child-friendly approach, Smyth (2013) suggested that congruence should be linked inherently to equality and the need to address the obvious power imbalance in the relationship. Bomber and Hughes (2013) also describe this element of empowerment as very significant when working with young people and addressing that power imbalance. Alongside this, it is also proposed that at the heart of being child-centred is the creation of a safe space, through attitudes of genuineness, realness and unconditionality. This involves replacing supposition or judgement with a positive, accepting attitude (Smyth, 2013). Prever (2010) touches on another key element to a young-person-centred approach, which involves endeavouring empathically to understand, and attentively listen to, the young person, allowing them to be more in touch with their inner emotions (Smyth, 2013). Previous research into adolescent counselling undertaken by Bryant-Jeffries (2004) is echoed by the more recent work conducted by Cooper (2013), highlighting the therapeutic climate as being fundamental to therapeutic change. The young people in the study specifically alluded to the therapeutic triad of empathy, genuineness, and respect, allowing them to become more open, when describing helpful aspects of therapy. When further exploring the more effective aspects, Luxmore (2014) and Ruszczynski (2007) suggest that containment is vital to efficacy in therapy. Clients can begin to develop a psychological self, which begins an exploratory process around thoughts, feelings, and experiences. More recent research also suggests that something more might be needed when adopting a young-person-centred approach in order to meet the individual needs of *all* young people (Cooper, 2013). This idea was also documented by Bryant-Jeffries (2004) years before, when he described future practitioners as possibly needing to adjust with a more active sense of enthusiasm and eagerness in order to sit alongside a young person psychologically. He also ponders whether other non-directive activities should be used to help the young person gain what she requires from the therapeutic encounter. Luxmore (2014) also adds to this conversation when feeling that a strict application of the young-person-centred approach to counselling does not work with all young people. He particularly suggests that, when rigorously applied with young people who might feel uncomfortable, introverted, and apprehensive, there could be a passive ineffectiveness. He concluded that some young people need something more interactive, a real relationship where the counsellor is interested and responding to them, their individuality, and their needs.

Creative and symbolic methods in school-based counselling

CSMs in SBC are commonly regarded as a practitioner adopting a creative approach, implementing various creative interventions throughout their therapeutic work (Meekums, 2014). Although non-humanistic approaches can be implemented, humanistic approaches to CSMs have a much stronger evidence base, permitting the young person to tell his narratives at a more manageable speed (Bratton et al., 2005). This is also the view of Hickmore (2000), who believes that this process has particular effectiveness when the young person feels that it is her agenda. These methods are usually non-directive, derived from expressive arts or play therapy, and may take various forms, typically around elements of play: sensorimotor, art, metaphors, fantasy, or games (Meekums, 2014). There is also a tentative suggestion that the use of CSMs can be helpful when working with young people who have special/additional educational needs. However, the Welsh Government (2011) highlights a stark gap in knowledge when stating that there is little evidence regarding the young service users who exhibit additional educational needs in SBC. Even so, it appears that CSMs can be very useful for this group of adolescents, where a clear special/additional need could be required within the therapeutic intervention. The literature tentatively suggests this, where experiences might often be too difficult to put into words for the young person. This could be due to it being too frightening, unawareness, or sometimes when speech is insufficient (Armstrong, 2013). West (1996) echoes this notion when proposing that some young people find talking and verbal communication too direct or intense when in the presence of another person. When applying this notion in a counselling room, the young person might feel overwhelmed, which could hinder their emotional expression and engagement. To combat this, it is proposed that a helpful element of CSMs is an increased depth of psychological contact. This would allow the young person to uncover painful experiences in a controlled way through the use of metaphor (Meekums, 1999). CSMs can also give the young person a chance to become aware and express his thoughts, helping to increase emotional development and literacy (Armstrong, 2013). The use of CSMs in therapy has also been found to decrease psychological distress with young people (McLaughlin et al., 2013).

The counselling practitioner must use her judgement, and reflect on how, and when, to implement a creative intervention. However, there are two key factors for consideration in SBC: first, when a young person is struggling to communicate her emotions through talking alone, and second, when there is a feeling of therapeutic stuckness, or a lack of therapeutic development (Meekums, 2014). As young people are very different to adults in the way that they record, contact, and express emotion, a counselling practitioner must fundamentally tune into each unique client, assessing how best he can tell his story (Geldard & Geldard, 2010).

Throughout the research process there appears to be two main therapeutic processes occurring when CSMs are implemented, helping to describe their effectiveness with young people. The first is centred on the facilitation of emotional expression (McArthur et al., 2012). They found that "expressing emotion" was among the most important of supportive aspects in SBC. When investigating the way that young people express emotion, verbal communication is sometimes difficult or unnatural. This is especially the case when working with young people presenting with language delays or learning disabilities. It is, therefore, vital that the counselling practitioner has creative tools to open up that line of communication at whatever level the young person is (Tait & Wosu, 2013). If a young person has these added difficulties, and struggles to communicate directly, then it is suggested that it often requires a considerable level of trust before she feels comfortable enough to share. It has also been evidenced that some young people express themselves more visibly through a less direct source, projecting through the use of art materials, toys, play, and many other formats. This process can operate as a medium for communication and emotional expression for talking (West, 1996). The therapeutic process should, therefore, be shaped around the discovery of finding alternative ways that young people can express their emotions, which is undoubtedly linked to eventual therapeutic efficacy (Smyth, 2013). Without striving for this, there is implausibility in the notion that SBC can be fully effective with *all* young people.

The second therapeutic process that promotes the use of CSMs with some young people, is the perception of "meaning making" in a therapeutic intervention. This process precedes emotional expression. When a young person is reflecting in a counselling space, it is believed to involve understanding, view, and insight, which, when combined, equals meaning or making sense of something (Meekums, 2008). Hickmore (2000) adds to this idea when describing expression through CSMs, enabling deeper understanding, particularly when in stuck or bewildering situations, helping the young persons to gain some new perspective. Angus and Greenberg (2011) further suggest that the therapeutic process should involve the creation of new understanding, a new story, a fresh way of viewing themselves and their lives, thus making a new meaning and developing emotional awareness.

When gaining a deeper examination of the research field in SBC, it seems logical and significant to revisit the original person-centred theory, which seems to have creativity as its nucleus. Rogers and Dymond (1954) remarked how there was a societal requirement for the creative process to stir, which he believed could be instigated with the psychological conditions. As a conclusion, he proposed two linked elements that would encourage constructive creativity, the first being psychological safety, which is constructed through the six conditions. The second element involves the creation of a positive environment in which psychological freedom can thrive (Rogers & Dymond, 1954). After developing this work, Natalie Rogers (1993) later added a third vital element that involved offering, motivating, and challenging experience. She named this "the creative connection" (p. 27), which encourages individuals also to experiment with art, movement, play, sound, and drama while in the therapy room. It is believed that this self-expression can allow the individual to let go of emotion, gain deeper understanding, and move toward positive development.

Societal views/perceptions in modern society

When further unpicking the research question, there appears to be an emerging theme around the perceptions and views of young people in modern society. Even in today's culture, there seems to be a negative undercurrent that is described by YoungMinds (2014). They acknowledge that children and young people are often demonised and silenced by society, causing an increase in unhappy and negative feelings. When further examining this, it is revealed that there is also a causal link from societal misperception to the development of mental illness, self-harm, and even suicide among the child population. Byron (2009) seems to echo this awareness when suggesting that society appears to stigmatise, discriminate against, and take power away from young people in these modern times. At a time when young people need to be encouraged to thrive and develop, identifying their strengths and needs have to be understood, respected, and listened to. When further investigating this idea, there seems to be an argument that young people progressively have become more accepted in society as individuals with rights (Department for Education and Skills, 2003). Although this highlights some progression, the literature for projecting the voices and opinions of young people is still inadequate (Greene & Hogan, 2005). This paints an interesting picture, as Manion and Nixon (2012) describe how some adults define and understand children today through the lens of negative historical views. This idea is echoed by Rock and colleagues (2012), who explored social constructs of young people being defined as childlike or malevolent, nurtured or contaminated. Adults usually hold the view of young people as vulnerable and confined, or parented and immature, rather than respected individuals who have uniqueness and choice (Manion & Nixon, 2012). There is also a suggestion that our society still holds a paternalistic culture, where adults know best for young people, thus not fully embracing their capability or potential. This view seems to uphold prejudice, and marginalises the young people, deeming them voiceless, devalued, and undermined. Even when a young person is listened to, it is too often the case that she is left feeling misunderstood and without choice. This literature evidence is particularly strong when a trained professional is involved, and when the young person is looked after or linked to children's services (Calvert et al., 2002; Jobe & Gorin, 2013; Manion & Nixon, 2012).

Even though the voices of young people seem to be reported in various research fields, there still appears to be paucity. With this said, there is an increased development of research that is being generated by Children's Services which is purely young-person-centred, publishing and centralising their views. Buckley and colleagues (2010) asked young people what they valued about child-centred professionals, to which the number one reply was a person that heard, valued, and respected their views. Research also published by Cossar and colleagues (2011) echoes this when asking children from a child protection or looked-after background. Again, the most popular answer centralised a need to be involved in decision making and wanting to be fully heard.

Participants

It was essential, for the current research, to recruit participants who were specific to my specialist subject area. This was achieved by using purposive sampling that gave the freedom to choose subjects who had a particular experience. A homogenous group was obtained where all of the participants were comparable. The research question was ever present throughout the project, heightening the chances of any new insights (Flick, 2009). The selection criteria ensured that my selected participants were: grounded in person-centred philosophy, suitably qualified, had a heightened level of personal development, and that they had relevant experiences associated with the research question set. The search for participants began through placing an advertisement notice boards of the British Association of Counselling and Psychotherapy and *Therapy Today*. In partnership with this, phone calls were then made to SBC services across Wales. After making contact with various services, I was then able to email and publicise my research poster to prospective participants. The five selected participants formed a variable and divergent sample group, which incorporated both genders, from a wide age range, who worked in different counties in Wales, and who worked in different educational settings. This encouraged the exploration of different perspectives, insights, and varied experiences with young people (McLeod, 2011). Each of the participants was then assigned a pseudonym colour to protect their identity (Table 7.1).

Table 7.1. Participants.

Participant	Approach	Setting	Age/gender	Experience
Ruby Red	Person-centred therapist	Secondary school (North Wales)	53/Female	10 years
Sunflower Yellow	Integrative counselling practitioner (person-centred/ Egan)	Secondary school (mid Wales)	49/Female	8 years
Sky Blue	Integrative counselling practitioner (person-centred/ CBT/Gestalt)	Secondary school (South Wales)	47/Male	5 years
Lavender Purple	Integrative counselling practitioner (person-centred)	Secondary school (mid Wales)	49/Female	1 year
Apple Green	Person-centred and psycho-analytical counselling practitioner	Secondary school (South (Wales)	41/Female	4 years

Data collection

The implementation of a semi-structured interview technique ensured effectiveness and added continued consistency to the focus of qualitative enquiry. This research design choice ensured that the participants were able to express themselves in-depth, fully exploring their SBC experiences (Smith et al., 2009). The interviews lasted for approximately sixty minutes, which effectively gave the participant enough time to explore the breadth of their experience. These interviews were conducted across five counties in Wales at the various therapeutic service buildings. The research data was collected through digital audio recording, and later transcribed and analysed. An interview schedule was also loosely implemented which acted as a flexible agenda. Participants responded to the following questions.

- Is talking enough in the twenty-first century or does the use of creative intervention enhance the therapeutic relationship with young person?
- Could you please describe briefly the setting where you work and whether this was an area that you specifically chose to be in?
- What approach do you use when engaging the young person in SBC?
- How do you find working with young people in this setting?
- When reflecting on the therapeutic work over your career, have you experienced any changes in the clinical presentations of the young people coming for therapy?
- In your experience, have there been any changes within this young client group when reflecting on their ability to express their feelings/emotions though talking alone/verbal communication?
- Why do you believe this to be the case?
- Do you believe that talking is enough in the modern-day therapy room when working in today's society or do therapists need more to engage the client?
- Do you use creative intervention in your therapy work?
- How come you do not use creative intervention in your therapy work with young people? Are there any reasons for this?
- What techniques/interventions/approach do you implement?
- In your experience, how effective is using creative intervention when engaging young people in therapy?

- In your experience, how effective is using PCT (purely talking therapy) when engaging young people in therapy?
- When thinking back over your experience, have there been any young people who have not engaged in therapy and what may have been the reasons for this?
- When reflecting on your experience, what makes an effective therapeutic relationship with the young person?
- In your experience, can the therapeutic relationship and engagement of the young client be built on talking alone?
- Do you believe that creative interventions in therapy have the potential to enhance the therapeutic relationship with the young person?
- Is there anything you would like to add?

What was discovered

The answers to the questions revealed three superordinate themes, the first two having three subordinate themes and the third having two subordinate themes (Table 7.2).

Table 7.2. Superordinate and subordinate themes.

Superordinate themes	Adopting a young-person-centred approach	From the "silenced youth" to the "expressive person"	The usefulness of CSMs
Subordinate themes	Building an effective therapeutic relationship	Young people seem powerless in a world where the adult knows best	A non-directive offering
	A core belief that the therapeutic relationship is fundamental	Talking is important in SBC and often can be "enough"	The creative process/ connection
	Understanding, assessing, and responding to the young person's therapeutic needs	Creative interventions for those that find talking difficult	

Superordinate theme 1: Adopting a "young-person-centred approach"

The overall theme seems to suggest that SBC adopts an inherent young-person-centred approach to therapy, where participants appear to assume an underlying belief in the necessity of the therapeutic relationship. The therapeutic connection appears to be the primary driving force and foundation for therapeutic movement. It also seems as though participants adopt an individual attitude towards their young clients, holding strong phenomenological values. A concurrent process that has also emerged is the need for a therapeutic assessment and judgement. These then appear to inform the counselling and allow it to cater specifically to the individual's needs. When examining an effective therapeutic relationship, the participants also appear to highlight various elements from the six psychological conditions.

Subordinate theme 1.1: Understanding, assessing, and responding to the young person's therapeutic needs

The participants acknowledged that each individual was unique in his experience, personality, and therapeutic need. There appears to be a core belief that each young person has her own sense of reality and individuality: "There are lots of different personalities, aren't there" [Lavender Purple]. This idea was also echoed by Sunflower Yellow, who highlights this phenomenological principle: "What I'm saying is, you've got to be really, really alert all of the time to the fact that every single one of them that walks through the door is different." With this underlying phenomenological view, there was also a sense that each practitioner would then use their therapeutic judgement in an initial assessment process. This process seemed to involve an evaluation of what the young person needed: "I'm watching, I'm looking, I'm hearing and I'm thinking, well, are you a talker, are you gonna talk? Or are you gonna need a little help to talk?" [Ruby Red]. Sky Blue also shared this notion: "I can quite quickly assess what is needed. Not that I know what the problem is or the stories but I can make a quick assessment of the possible nature of their need."

Subordinate theme 1.2: A core belief that the therapeutic relationship is fundamental

Participants discussed and examined their beliefs around the therapeutic relationship and the significance of this when working in SBC.

The participants appear to hold an elementary person-centred belief that the therapeutic alliance is central: "I have always been trained to think the relationship is everything, but it is everything. The therapeutic relationship is everything" [Lavender Purple]. In addition to this core principle, there was an implication that the therapeutic relationship acted as a basis of stability and needed to be a constant factor: "The relationship definitely needs to be there" [Apple Green]. "That connection . . . It's all about that ongoing connection" [Lavender Purple]. Ruby Red also insinuated that the therapeutic relationship was foundational, which then paves the way for therapeutic progression: "I guess I feel a person-centred approach. It's really important for building up that relationship with that young person. I feel if you get the relationship right other things then follow into place" [Ruby Red]. The concept of the relationship being central to therapeutic movement is also reflected upon by Sky Blue: "My aim is to work on building a relationship with them quite quickly, because that's key. If I don't make contact with that person psychologically, then it's not gonna go anywhere."

Another emerging perception that centres on the therapeutic relationship being primary involves the felt insignificance of having an ideal counselling environment. There is a sense that the therapeutic space becomes a secondary influence: "Sometimes when sitting in a space when I work with someone the walls disappear, like nobody sees the boxes, nobody sees some of the stuff that's there . . . So we could be anywhere . . . but we're together" [Apple Green]. Lavender Purple also reflected how the therapeutic space was insignificant when exploring the relationship later on in the text: "But do you know what, it doesn't matter. Because actually when we're together none of that matters." Further into the text, "Sky Blue" went on to highlight this initial individual assessment: "Some people will respond better to art and those kinds of things I think. But some people respond better to straightforward talking." Sunflower Yellow also reflected upon this initial therapeutic assessment process, questioning what the young person might need: "I'm thinking now, how can I, how can we get somewhere with this, you know, what are they wanting?" During this process, it is also noticeable that the participants describe themselves as responding to the young person's needs, which ultimately involves how best to develop an effective relationship: "I need to get to know the person and know what their limitations are . . . and who they are"

[Apple Green]. This was highlighted again by Sky Blue: "What are the needs of this young person and then working on how I make a relationship with this person?"

Subordinate theme 1.3: Building an effective therapeutic relationship

When exploring the concept of an effective therapeutic relationship in SBC, all participants seemed to be in harmony when highlighting several facets of the six psychological conditions proposed in the person-centred approach: "Core conditions. Without a doubt . . . But in any effective healthy relationship, if those conditions are in place you get that therapeutic contact" [Apple Green]. Ruby Red also described her intimate perception of therapeutic contact: "Almost like I synapse with them, nerves come together. And there's a flow between you." The importance of perceived empathic understanding was also advocated by participants: "And I think working empathically. That empathic understanding and letting them hear you reflecting back, that actually I can hear what you're saying" [Ruby Red]. "That you care about them. That they feel that you care about them. That even if you don't fully understand what it is they're trying to tell you . . . that you're willing to try and understand" [Sky Blue]. Sunflower Yellow also felt that empathic understanding was vital when promoting empowerment: "I think if you can get them to understand that it really is their session . . . You really are mainly interested in trying to understand what it's like to be them."

In line with empathic understanding, there was also an interweaving element when being fully attentive and listening to the young person: "I'm there to be interested and listening. Really listening to whatever it is they're trying to say" [Sky Blue]. Ruby Red also seems to echo this idea, appreciating the whole of the young person: "It was worth just that slowly hearing and letting him know that everything was important about him . . . Even the pushbike was important." The participants also believed that an effective relationship was built on the establishment of trust, which, from the data, seems to involve the therapeutic conditions: Lavender Purple felt strongly that therapeutic presence was at times very difficult, but critical: "I was just being there. And it's hard as a therapist to just be there isn't it . . . but it's really important."

There was also a sense that the trust is promoted through creating a space that is contained and secure: "I think that's what's so special about the therapeutic relationship. Because it's contained and it's in a space. Which is quite different from being out in the world" [Ruby Red]. "Well, I think there's privacy. You know, and all of that safety. And I think it's very contained. That can allow a deeper perhaps level of expression" [Lavender Purple].

Superordinate theme 2: From the "silenced youth" to the "expressive person"

This superordinate theme begins with a sense that some young people seem powerless in today's society, and are often not fully heard in an adult-dominated world. This seems evident when highlighting participant's views around society, education, and the care system. There also appears to be something significant about a young person who has been given the chance to talk in the therapeutic room with an adult in today's society. This seems really powerful, and the participants unanimously agree that for most young people it can be enough for the therapeutic development. Participants also jointly agreed that the use of CSMs in their therapeutic work was helpful. This seemed to create a greater potential when meeting the individual needs of someone who found talking difficult in SBC, with particular reference to young people with special/additional educational needs.

Subordinate theme 2.1: Young people seem powerless in a world where the adult knows best

Participants discussed their insights and experiences around the treatment of young people and how they are valued in today's society. There was a sense that young people are often silenced by the adult world: "Do they have a voice as a child? They don't. They're not being listened to" [Apple Green]. To partner this there was also a feeling that young people were often not fully appreciated or respected by society, seeming to imply a lack of understanding from the adult world: "I say to people now, my stock phrase for when people talk about teenagers is that I think they're much maligned. I think they're misunderstood or criticised and people don't really appreciate how difficult it is to be a teenager" [Sky Blue]. "I just know that they're just misunderstood" [Apple Green]. There was also a perception that the adult world would leave young people feeling disempowered, through dismissing or not fully hearing them: "The teacher comes in, right, OK, what's your problem . . . how are we going to deal with it . . . And completely misses the point and then they go. The young person's feeling very frustrated because they haven't felt heard" [Lavender Purple]. This was also perceived by Sky Blue, who appears to suggest that not only did the adult disrespect the young person's wishes, but also opposed them: "Just recently a young person I was seeing...she didn't want anybody to know that she was coming to counselling, she didn't want her foster mother particularly to know. She went to parents evening and the teacher told her."

Further evidence seems to highlight additional powerlessness around them being in a state of stuckness, lacking any real control, power, or choice: "The youngsters that you're working with are stuck in their situation often . . . They've got no control or power over that" [Sunflower Yellow]. This was also illustrated by Sky Blue: "Particularly with people who are in the care system. You know they've told the social worker . . . they've told their carer, they've told their GP they've told their new foster parent. Everyone . . . and nothing's changed . . . nothing's got better." Apple Green also reflects how some adults seem to foist silence on the young person: "The looked after kids are told what to do, told when to do it, they're taken away from their families and they don't want to be taken away. People talk about them when they're there, they talk about them as if they're not there. They don't give them any choices, it's like we know best for you . . . And yet I don't see how that benefits the child" [Apple Green].

These perceptions of the powerlessness in today's society were also echoed when participants were asked about young people who have not engaged in SBC. There seemed to be a general awareness that this was often linked to the young person being *sent* by an adult: "The young people sometimes I feel are a bit forced into coming. Because the teachers are directing them into the room" [Ruby Red]. Again there seems to be a notion around the adults knowing best for the young person, directing them to SBC: "Almost without exception it's because they've been sent and they didn't want to come" [Sunflower Yellow].

Subordinate theme 2.2: Talking is important in school-based counselling and often can be "enough"

There seems to be an agreement from all participants that, generally, talking therapy in SBC seems to work with the majority young people: "I feel competent as a talker. I feel that good work can be done just through talking" [Apple Green]. Apple Green also later reflected that talking therapy could be completely effective: "Fully. If it's done well with the right person." There was also a sense that most young people want a chance to be heard, almost expecting that talking will be the main focus of the therapeutic work. "I would say by and large they're more interested in talking than anything else" [Sunflower Yellow]. Sunflower Yellow also echoed this later on in more detail: "There are definitely youngsters who come in and talking is enough but that's what they're expecting to do and that's want they want to do. So it can, talking can be enough in some therapeutic relationships." "I think they like to talk. They don't get a voice but they do when they're in the room" [Apple Green]. This is again reflected by Sky Blue when he reveals the significance of facilitating the young person's voice: "I still maintain that for most young people, I think talking is enough. So the skill is about trying to be able to listen to what they're actually saying, be able to connect with them and what they're really saying. So when you talk to them, you're saying something that they really hear ... That's the challenge." There was also a sense that SBC was a unique process for young people, with some favouring more of a purely talking approach and others not, purely dependent on their therapeutic need: "I think some just prefer talking. You know and they're quite okay with that. You really sense that" [Lavender Purple]. Ruby Red also reflected on this uniqueness: "I think for some people it can be. But I think for other young people it can't be. I think it just depends on the individual" [Ruby Red].

Subordinate theme 2.3: Creative and symbolic methods for those that find talking difficult

Although there seemed to be a clear suggestion that talking therapeutic intervention alone seemed to be effective with most young people in SBC, a question is raised when regarding the needs of the young people where talking alone is ineffectual. When asked if CSMs could enhance their therapeutic work, all the participants collectively agreed: "There's a call for it, there's definitely a call for both" [Ruby Red]. "Can it be enhanced with intervention . . . yeah of course, why not?" [Apple Green]. "It would be good to have more tools or armoury" [Sky Blue]. "I do believe they have the potential . . . definitely" [Lavender Purple]. "I honestly don't think you can do young people's work without something beyond talking" [Sunflower Yellow]. This collective response suggests that the participants feel the need to have something beyond talking in order to facilitate effective and meaningful relationships with those young people who require more than words. "And definitely, definitely, definitely that is one of the reasons why I love sand-play so much, because it is definitely a way in with those ones that find talking difficult" [Sunflower Yellow]. It appears that talking alone can also be too intense for some young people, which highlights a need for creative intervention for those that find verbal communication and expression challenging. "It can be quite daunting to come and sit and talk to an adult. . . . You know, those things help to sort of shift that away" [Sky Blue]. He also reflects later, "So that creative stuff I think can be good for that, it can be good as a way of taking the pressure off, or the intensity off."

In relation to this proposal that certain individuals needed more from SBC, there seems to be a perception that creative intervention is vital for young people who have additional educational needs: "Personally I feel a lot of them are suffering with PTSD . . . So with them what I tend to do is listen to a bit of drum and bass . . . one of them might say 'My Mum stabbed me when I was five'. And because . . . it is too much for them to be able to sit in that chair like this . . . because the intensity is so much for them, they can't cope" [Apple Green]. Ruby Red also expressed this perception: "The first time I did buttons was with a young girl who I found had special needs. So again sometimes young people with special needs perhaps need a little bit more help to enter into the therapeutic relationship, into the process" [Ruby Red].

This notion is also echoed by Sky Blue: "I've worked with quite a few Asperger's and autistic young people now. And that, you know, having things to do can be quite good. Making something or playing some game." He then proceeds to explain later in the text: "Yeah. So it's less intense. I mean he was the sort of person who would always have something going on, he would have to be doing something with his hands. Because there's no way you could just sit together and just talk, that would have been too much." To add to the other voices of the participants, Lavender Purple also recognised a creative need for young people with additional cultural needs: "My experience of working in the school is that I'm working with ethnic minorities . . . I think it can be so important for them to have another medium rather than speech. To be able to express themselves."

Superordinate theme 3: The usefulness of creative and symbolic methods

This overall theme seems to suggest that participants are in favour of offering CSMs as a vital tool when meeting the therapeutic need of young individuals. The process of offering also seems to indicate a sense of empowering the young person, where they can crucially take control and direction of the therapy. The use of CSMs was also found to have two helpful elements: the facilitation of talking alongside a more visual and symbolic nature, leading to deeper understanding. Both elements seemed to link back to the enhancement of therapeutic growth and the development of the therapeutic relationship.

Subordinate theme 3.1: A non-directive offering

Being able to offer creative interventions to young people in SBC seemed a major factor when meeting the individual needs of young people: "I would not like to be a talking only therapist for everybody for sure. I think it's really useful having other stuff that you can offer people" [Sunflower Yellow]. Sky Blue also noted: "I have tried different things at different times and sometimes they work with young people and sometimes they don't. I think you have to have a few different things that you can try" [Sky Blue]. Ruby Red noticed that her constant offering was significant when meeting the young person's therapeutic need in SBC: "She'd go straight into that blue box . . . I would have to make sure the blue box was in the room." Lavender Purple also observes how offering promotes a sense of individuality in SBC: "I think I like to keep offering for the right person. And I think that's key isn't it, having a whole load of things that you can just offer and it might appeal." The offered creative interventions also seem to suggest an empowering of the young person, where the choice is theirs, the control is theirs: "I always offer. I always say to the young people, you know you can bring music in if you want" [Lavender Purple].

Subordinate theme 3.2: The creative process

One of the key findings in this research was the participant's reflections regarding the creative process and how this can often enhance the therapeutic connection in SBC. There seems to be a perception that creative intervention can help improve and facilitate emotional expression with some young people, which in turn develops the therapeutic relationship: "I think ideally there's something in the creative stuff that kind of turns on a tap with the talking. There's something about people getting their stuff witnessed, usually verbally, but sometimes it might be through the creative medium. That makes the healing happen" [Sunflower Yellow]. This idea of facilitating a young person's talking is also echoed by Ruby Red: "I think you probably need more to engage these young people . . . I think it's just helping them just to do the talking." In combination with emotional expression, there also seemed to be a key concept around deepening the therapeutic process, enabling the young person to gain some new understanding: "It does create shifts in the relationship" [Apple Green].

Alongside the first component of the creative process, there is a sense that the physical, visual, and symbolic nature can also encourage a deeper sense of understanding, giving the young person a sense of control and acceptance. "Another thing is that often I ask the young person to visualise . . . And then moving out of the mind on to the page somehow there's that almost letting go, or more of an understanding . . . And then beginning to have a relationship with it because I visualise it and then it becomes tangible. And then we'll start to talk about it" [Lavender Purple]. This visual process was also described by Ruby Red: "It's like artwork, it's out there, they can see it. And when they see it they make connections. Giving them something. It's visual, they can then project whatever thoughts through that . . . Then they can talk more, reveal more and it gives them more of a sense of what's actually going on with themselves inside." Sky Blue also illustrates this perception of enhanced control: "We created something there. How did we do that . . . we created some kind of book to record it all in. You word it, what shall we write? So it's kind of giving them ownership over it."

When reflecting on these two creative processes, they both appeared to deepen the therapeutic relationship where Sunflower Yellow alludes to a profound bond: "And it's not that he could not have said that, he probably said that in lots of different ways but I think . . . There's a thing that I remember talking about in training called the 'I–Thou' moments. And it's like that . . . it's a kind of point of deep connection between you and the client. You sometimes get that with a bit of artwork like that. That is just worth its weight in gold I think." Ruby Red also identified a specific deeper moment in her therapeutic experience when the young person was able to gain therapeutic movement: "What I felt I was reflecting back to her, I'm not so sure whether she heard it. So we got the buttons out and I felt that what she did with the buttons was what I felt she was telling me in the room . . . it was amazing . . . very effective." She then went on to reflect that the relationship felt deeper almost: "I think it does enhance the therapeutic relationship . . . We met each other, I guess, in a way that we might not have met normally" [Ruby Red].

Bringing together the literature and the findings

It is evident throughout the literature that SBC in Wales is fundamentally young person centred in its orientation. The research field highlights this, with 80% identifying with this approach (Cooper, 2013), a notion that was echoed by all five participants in the current study. When classifying themselves as inherently young person centred, all participants seem to demonstrate a core belief that the therapeutic relationship was elementary to their work with young people—"The therapeutic relationship is everything . . ." [Lavender Purple]—as it encouraged open and honest communication. This resonates with research conducted by Bryant-Jeffries (2004), who suggests that the SBC practitioner must have a determined and resolute belief in the counselling relationship as a climate of growth. Apple Green again echoes this central person-centred belief when stating that "The relationship definitely needs to be there" as an important underpinning for useful SBC. There was also an aligned perception that a strong and ongoing therapeutic relationship would lead to therapeutic development—"I feel if you get the relationship right, other things then follow into place" [Ruby Red]—alongside it being a constant factor in therapy: "It's all about that ongoing connection" [Lavender Purple]. This underlying belief is also echoed throughout the SBC literature, with a sense that huge significance should be placed upon the counselling relationship, focusing individually on the young person's needs and empowering the way they communicate (Griffiths, 2013; Prever, 2010).

Another emerging awareness that was deemed significant in SBC was the idea that the relationship was primary, with other factors judged to be secondary. This was proposed by a number of the participants when describing their often impractical therapeutic spaces: "But do you know what, it doesn't matter. Because actually when were together none of that matters" [Lavender Purple]. Smyth (2013) seems to echo this notion when highlighting the practitioner's fundamental faith in the relationship, believing it to be the primary factor in their counselling work.

Understanding, assessing, and responding to the young person's individual needs was also recognised as important for all participants in SBC. This fundamental person-centred value previously stated by Rogers (1961) seems to presage current work when suggesting that each young individual was unique in her experiences, reality, and personality, illustrating a need to adopt a phenomenological approach to therapy. This belief was further explained by one participant as follows: "every single one of them that walks through the door is different" [Sunflower Yellow]. It was clear that all participants were in harmony when exploring this concept of individuality. This again seems to echo Keys and Walshaw (2008), who suggest that a clear appreciation of the uniqueness of young people is essential. The participants seemed to value and unify the diverse needs of the young clients that they had experienced. Smyth (2013) illustrates this when stating that the child's needs must be central to the process. This proposal appears to match the participants' experience when evaluating their assessment process: "I can quickly assess what is needed . . . I can make a quick assessment of the possible nature of their need" [Sky Blue]. The participants also felt that therapeutic judgement is needed to promote effective intervention, Ruby Red reflects this: "I'm watching, I'm looking, I'm hearing and I'm thinking, well, are you a talker . . . or are you gonna need a little help to talk?" This idea is also highlighted by Meekums (2014) when suggesting that in SBC the practitioner must use therapeutic judgement, in addition to the consideration of communication and a working knowledge of adolescent development.

The findings of the research also suggest that participants actively respond, and are specifically attentive to the best ways of establishing the working alliance: "What are the needs of this young person and then working on how do I make a relationship?" [Sky Blue]. This goes together with the constant reflexive questioning around how best to do this: "I'm thinking how can we get somewhere with this, you know, what are they wanting?" [Sunflower Yellow]. This sense of adaptability and proactiveness seems to parallel Luxmore (2014), who implies that a crucial part of the therapeutic process is the ability to be interested and responsive to individuality and need. The current study also echoes literature from Geldard and Geldard (2010), who suggest that practitioners must assess how best they can tell their story.

Developing an effective therapeutic relationship with a young client also appears to be a highly valued factor in SBC. It is proposed that this relationship should have a clear underpinning of person-centred values to support the exploration of emotion (Hamilton-Roberts, 2012). According to the current findings, all participants seemed to allude to several features of the traditional person-centred theory, with a clear emphasis on facets of the six therapeutic conditions (Rogers & Dymond, 1954). When asked what makes an effective relationship, one participant emphatically stated, "Core conditions . . . Without a doubt. In any effective, healthy relationship, if those conditions are in place, you get that therapeutic contact" [Apple Green]. The current literature seems to directly correspond in its emphasis on the therapeutic climate, the six necessary conditions, and the ideology of therapeutic change transpiring due to relational factors (Bryant-Jeffries, 2004; Rogers, 1957; Smyth, 2013).

When further analysing the data, the most common factor that was perceived as significant when developing an effective relationship appeared to revolve around empathic understanding: "letting them hear you reflecting back, that actually I can hear what you're saying" [Ruby Red]. The findings appear to correlate with the current research in SBC, which deems empathy and listening as helpful features when engaging the young client (Cooper, 2013). The literature also suggests that when a counselling practitioner endeavours to understand and holistically listens, a further development of self-awareness and inner emotional regulation can ensue (Prever, 2010; Smyth, 2013). This was also established in the current study, where all participants at some stage highlighted the significance of "Really listening" [Sky Blue] and embracing the whole person while "Slowly hearing and letting him know that everything was important about him ... even the pushbike" [Ruby Red]. This empathic process also involved the therapeutic development of empowerment (Bomber & Hughes, 2013), echoing my findings around the impact of profound empathic understanding: "If you get them to understand that it really is their session ... You are mainly interested in trying to understand what it's like to be them" [Sunflower Yellow]. When describing the empathic process, the participants also expressed the significance of a healing, releasing therapeutic presence throughout their work (Rogers, 1986): "I was just being there. And it's hard as a therapist to just be there ... but it's really important" [Lavender Purple]. In further exploration of the helpful characteristics in SBC, the creation of a safe and contained environment appeared considerable. This again echoed previous research conducted, where the safety and supportive atmosphere was deemed fundamental to therapeutic development (Bryant-Jeffries, 2004; Cooper, 2013). Throughout the interviews, participants gave support to this notion of containment and safety, with Lavender Purple reflecting on it as a space with "Privacy", with "All of that safety", which, when created, can "allow a deeper level of expression", while Ruby Red perceived the therapeutic relationship as "special" due to its "contained" nature, juxtaposing it to "being out in the world". Luxmore (2014) also captures this significance when stating that the therapy commences only when containment is created. Ruszczynski's (2007) research also echoes the current study when suggesting that it is essential for the young client to experience containment, to begin the exploratory process around self and feelings. Apple Green captures this containment concept with an eloquent "guardian–therapist" metaphor, exclaiming how she "patrols the boundary", conveying the important message "you are safe in this room".

Children and young people are often demonised and silenced by the modern society they live in, where negative adult perceptions have caused an increase in levels of emotional difficulties (YoungMinds, 2014). When exploring the impact of society, all participants identified this sense of societal devaluation, where young people are often "not being listened to" [Apple Green]. This is also echoed in the literature, where Greene and Hogan (2005) suggest that young people might be more accepted in society; however, in opposition, there is still a clear lack of research that truly captures their voices and opinions. An interesting notion reflected by one participant illustrated this idea in her rhetorical question: "Do they have a voice as a child? They don't" [Apple Green].

The current study seems to contrast with other previous research, which found that young people have become more acknowledged in society as individuals with rights (Department for Education and Skills, 2003). This dissimilarity is highlighted where participants also perceived society's view of young people as "Misunderstood" [Apple Green] and "Much maligned" [Sky Blue]. This seems to correspond with Manion and Nixon's (2012) investigation, since they infer that young people are often left feeling misconstrued and without choice in a marginalised world. The notion of a paternalistic culture proposed by Calvert and colleagues (2002) is also prominent within the current study, with a sense that the adult world knows what is best for the young person, consciously overlooking his or her uniqueness. This was echoed by participants through their experience of SBC, where, at times, key professional adults left the young person frustrated at "not being heard" [Lavender Purple], as well as disrespected when a teacher disregarded the child's rights to confidentiality [Sky Blue]. These key insights seem to support an adult prejudicial culture where young people are deemed voiceless and undermined by factions of society and perceived "child-centred" professionals (Jobe & Gorin, 2013). This notion of paternalism was again duplicated as participants described the major rationale for disengagement from SBC. A popular motive appeared to be due to feelings of being "forced into coming" [Ruby Red] or when sensing that they've been "sent" to counselling [Sunflower Yellow] by an adult. This concept seems to also fit a social construct supposition proposed by Rock and colleagues (2012), who found that adults tended to hold historical views of young people, frequently referring to them as infantile, naïve, and malevolent, and not respecting their individualism (Manion & Nixon, 2012). The current study also further illustrates this concept of young people feeling powerless, often reporting feelings of being "stuck in their situation" and having "no control or power" over their life [Sunflower Yellow].

When exploring this perception further, it is evident that both the literature and the current study appear to exemplify a heightened sense of powerlessness, particularly when the young person is looked after or linked with children's services (Jobe & Gorin, 2013). This sense of little control was particularly strong when participants reflected how "Nothing's changed" or "got better" for the young person, regardless of who or how many professionals they've "told" or confided in [Sky Blue]. Cossar and colleagues (2011) also share this sense when concluding that looked after young people reported strong opinions around inadequate listening and insufficient control in their care, expressing a need to be fully heard and fully involved in life decisions. After highlighting the negative perceptions and silencing of young people in today's society, it feels as if there is a significant connection with the notion that talking alone is an important component in SBC. This overall perception follows previous research by Cooper (2009), where young service users rated the most considerable factor as "being able to talk". This was also demonstrated in the current study, where all participants agreed that for the majority of young people, talking independently can be "enough" and "fully" effective [Apple Green]. When exploring the rationale behind the power of talking, it seems that having a chance to "talk through" various issues with a professional encourages a young person to feel listened to, thus increasing emotional wellbeing (Cooper, 2013). The research findings again correspond with this idea where most young people are "expecting", "preferring", and "wanting" to talk in SBC [Sunflower Yellow]. It was also proposed that "they don't often get a voice, but they do when they're in the room" [Apple Green]. For most young people, it seems as though being able to communicate through the vehicle of talking is enough to develop the working alliance and then to promote therapeutic development. Again, this idea is extrapolated when referring to the core principles of SBC, with key concepts around a supportive, facilitative environment where the young people feel empowered and fully heard, enabling them to verbally explore and resolve their difficulties (Griffiths, 2013). These principles are also reflected through the participants' insights, where "for most young people talking is enough", with the key skills tending to focus around "being able to connect with them and what they're really saying" [Sky Blue]. All of these perceptions are focused on giving the young person an opportunity express themselves with another adult, thus potentially reducing their level of psychological distress (Griffiths, 2013).

When effectively meeting the needs of *all* young people, questions are raised around a talking only therapy approach and whether this is enough for therapeutic development in SBC. All participants commonly agreed that CSMs could, in fact, enhance their therapeutic work giving them "more tools or armoury", opening up lines of communication [Sky Blue]. Although SBC seems to focus around a predominately person-centred approach, Cooper (2013) parallels the findings shown when suggesting that something more might be needed in therapy to successfully meet the individual needs of more young people. This is also implied by Luxmore (2014) in contending that some young people need something more interactive and real, where the counselling practitioner is interested and responding to their individuality. A collective response by participants emphasised this notion, where it was clear that, in order to facilitate effective, meaningful, and communicative relationships, "something beyond talking" [Sunflower Yellow] was needed with those that required more than words in SBC.

It also appears that participants concur that talking alone can at times be insufficient in SBC, where they collaboratively agree that CSMs can reach those young people who struggle to communicate verbally: "I love sand-play so much because it's definitely a way in with those ones that find talking difficult" [Sunflower Yellow]. It also appears that, for some young people, talking alone can feel too direct or can evoke further anxiety, where participants all explore a sense of heightened intensity. Sky Blue explored this added intensity for some young people in SBC when suggesting that "it can be quite daunting to come and sit and talk to an adult". Key research by Luxmore (2014) also seems to observe that some young people could feel uncomfortable and overwhelmed when faced with a practitioner who is strictly one-dimensional, deeming the work ineffective in meeting their therapeutic needs. In order to combat this deficiency, the current study proposes that the use of CSMs in SBC can help diffuse the potential directness and "Shift that away", helping to take "the pressure off, or the intensity off" [Sky Blue], therefore encouraging further communication. Again, this is inferred when evaluating older research by West (1996), who proposed that CSMs can be important when talking is too direct, as it can offer a medium of communication that lessens the feeling of directness.

An additional perception gained from all participants also appeared to consider the use of CSMs as fundamental when working specifically with young people who have special/additional educational needs. As eloquently stated by Ruby Red, "Young people with special needs perhaps need a little bit more help to enter into the therapeutic relationship" [Ruby Red]. There seems to be a dearth of literature in this area, which is highlighted by the Welsh Government (2011), which suggests that little is found regarding young people in SBC who require additional needs in therapy. However, Tait and Wosu (2013) do suggest tentatively that CSMs are especially important when working with young people who have language delays or learning disabilities, as communication via talking can often feel too difficult. Although this gap in knowledge still appears to be present, each participant described a common theme around the young people with additional needs who all found talking too much, thus needing something additional. Armstrong (2013) evaluates this theme and suggests that CSMs are very useful for adolescents who might often find words difficult or when speech is insufficient. This was echoed throughout the current study, where Apple Green reflects an experience of working with traumatised young people, suggesting that direct talking "is too much for them . . . they can't cope" [Apple Green]. With previous research supporting this idea, it suggests that the use of CSMs can encourage deeper psychological contact, often reducing the direct nature of counselling (Meekums, 1999). Again, this process was evaluated by another participant from his experience of working with young people who are autistic. He explained that one client would have to be "doing something with his hands" because sitting together and just talking would have "been too much" [Sky Blue]. It seemed vital for the participant in this example to recognise and appreciate this additional need and, consequently, to implement creative tools to open up that previously daunting line of communication (Tait & Wosu, 2013).

After discussing why CSMs are helpful in SBC, it is, therefore, imperative now to explore the creative processes behind the potential usefulness. When referring back to the core research paper in SBC that was conducted by Cooper (2013), some young people reported "a need for the counsellor to be more active and do more" for a more successful outcome. This was also confirmed in Griffiths' (2013) partner study, which found that "more active strategies" were deemed helpful. This notion was also irrefutably highlighted in the current study, where it is proposed that the creative process can capture this more dynamic therapeutic need, reaching the young people who perhaps need a little help to communicate verbally. During the current study, all participants highlighted the importance of offering CSMs in their SBC work in a non-directive way, to ensure that each individual could access it, develop, and gain something helpful. Again, this is paralleled in the SBC literature, where it was proposed that a more plural way of working can potentially find creative ways to address an individual's additional therapeutic needs (Cooper, 2013). Each participant seemed to find different ways of offering CSMs in their work, but all agreed that it promoted empowerment, self-control, and choice throughout the therapy. With one participant expressing that she would not like to "be a talking only therapist for everybody" because, when offering creative interventions, it can be "really useful having other stuff" [Sunflower Yellow]. Hickmore (2000) also emphasises the significance of individuality when suggesting that a non-directive offering can have further effectiveness, as it is the young person's agenda. This promotion of power was explored further by participants when creating an environment of individual choice: "I always offer ... you can bring music in if you want" [Lavender Purple], alongside the need for Ruby Red to offer and "make sure the blue box was in the room", thus creating further opportunity for personal preference. It is also suggested that the offering process is also linked to participants adopting a more child-friendly approach, in which Smyth (2013) highlights equality and addressing the power imbalance as vital to an effective relationship. Rogers (1993) also echoes this when suggesting that a non-directive creative process can stimulate and inspire empowerment and understanding.

After the initial process of offering CSMs, several therapeutic developments seemed to transpire which centred on deeper communication. These major findings seem to fall in line with existing literature produced by McLaughlin and colleagues (2013), who concluded that the use of CSMs with young people has been found to develop the therapeutic connection, resulting in a reduction of psychological distress. All participants were undivided in their perceptions of the effectiveness of CSMs; however, two key processes seemed to run through the data. The first involved an apparent improvement and facilitation of emotional expression, which appeared to develop the counselling relationship. This is further borne out by McArthur and colleagues (2012), who found that young people placed a high level of importance on the expression of emotion as a supportive element in SBC. One participant highlighted this significance when describing that the implementation of CSMs are "Just helping them to do the talking" [Ruby Red]. It is, therefore, vital that the counselling practitioner has the equipment to open up that line of communication when talking alone is not enough (Tait & Wosu, 2013). The effectiveness of CSM is also paralleled through other SBC research, when the young person is struggling to convey their emotions through verbal communication alone (Meekums, 2014). This is again illustrated by Sunflower Yellow's encapsulation of the process as "the creative stuff kind of turns on a tap with the talking" so that they can then begin to communicate emotion, which "makes the healing happen" [Sunflower Yellow]. The use of CSMs in the current study also illustrated the participants' willingness to encourage young people to express and communicate their feelings through a number of different sources. Again, this seems to coincide with Smyth's (2013) notion of young-person centeredness, when stating that the counselling process should be created through the discovery of finding alternative ways that young people can express themselves.

A second key process that was discovered by participants was centred on the visual and symbolic nature of CSMs, giving the work an additional tangible feel. This was highlighted several times by participants, where Ruby Red reflects that it is "moving out of the mind and on to the page" which encourages the young person to accept and understand further, "visualising it ... then it becomes tangible" [Lavender Purple]. This process seems to echo preceding research where certain young people can express themselves more visibly and deeply in a less direct way, through projection and symbolism (West, 1996). This visual process was again illustrated by another participant when suggesting that "It's out there, they can see it ... they make connections", enabling a deeper sense that "they can talk more, reveal more" [Ruby Red]. This process is again confirmed in the literature when Meekums (2014) offers that this ocular creative process can function as a medium for communication, especially with young people who have added difficulties. Both of these processes have been thought to enhance the therapeutic relationship in SBC, where all participants have reflected a deeper level of understanding and connection in the counselling process. The literature again supports this notion when using CSMs through the promotion of meaning making and evolved understanding, where the young person can make sense of something in a new way (Meekums, 2008). This insightful relationship that appears to be created by using CSMs has been described in many ways in the current study; including an "'I–Thou' moment . . . point of deep connection" [Sunflower Yellow], where another participant also revealed "We met each other, I guess, in a way that we might not have normally" [Ruby Red]. This deeper connection that seems to "create shifts in the relationship" [Apple Green] is essentially linked to offering the young person a chance to express themselves through CSMs, which can facilitate further understanding, helping them gain some new perspective (Hickmore, 2000). Angus and Greenberg (2011) also appear to summarise the participants' experience well when suggesting that SBC should involve being helpful in ways that will create new understanding, enabling new meaning to occur which can ultimately develop therapeutic growth.

The research appears to sit alongside pre-existing literature where a principally young-person-centred approach is adopted in SBC. The forming and developing of an effective therapeutic relationship was also regarded as "highly valued", alongside the need to assess and respond to individual counselling needs. The current research outcomes are also reflected in the contemporary literature where young people were deemed silent within society, which appears to link to the effectiveness of talking in SBC. Finally, the usefulness of CSMs also appeared to echo current literature, with a particular emphasis on helpfulness with young people who exhibit additional educational needs. An extensive summary follows this section, with the principle objective of critically exploring and illustrating key points examining the research question.

Conclusion

There were several limitations to the current study, which need acknowledging. It was a time limited, small-scale study where my participants were all counselling practitioners from Wales. The study was also qualitative in nature, which raised some potential biases; however, an ongoing reflexive process and focus on trustworthiness was paramount. Finally, I must state that, regrettably, I was not able to give the young people a voice, which gave my research a one-dimensional feel.

The main objective for this piece of research was to investigate the concept of whether "talking" alone was enough in SBC, from a therapeutic practitioner perspective, with a secondary linked concept of whether the use of CSMs was considered helpful when developing a therapeutic relationship. It is apparent from the data that SBC is predominately young person centred in its therapeutic values, where the relationship is the primary focus (Cooper, 2013). With this notion at the core, it also appears that counselling practitioners have an underlying phenomenological belief that all young people are unique in personality and communication (Cooper, 2013; Rogers, 1961; Smyth, 2013). This was echoed in both the current study and in previous literature, where practitioners must understand, recognise, and assess their individual needs to ensure that an effective therapeutic encounter takes place (Geldard & Geldard, 2010). The therapeutic relationship was found to be most effective when a safe and contained environment was created through the six psychological conditions.

In order to give the SBC service context, a link to the wider society was also significant to the research question, where it was felt that young people still often felt demonised and deemed powerless by factions of the adult world (Jobe & Gorin, 2013; Manion & Nixon, 2012; YoungMinds, 2014). This seemed pivotal to the effectiveness of SBC, which aimed to give voice to, and empower, the young person, something that perhaps modern society appeared to disregard. This societal notion or viewpoint seems to enhance the power of SBC, where talking was often found to be enough to promote development in the young person. It appears that being able to express emotion with an adult in a safe space was considered as effective, successfully meeting the needs of *most* young people (Cooper, 2013; Griffiths, 2013). However, the current study challenges whether *all* young people have their therapeutic needs met through talking alone, with the current study appearing to deem the use of CSMs helpful in enhancing the therapeutic relationship, predominantly for those young people who found talking "too difficult" (Luxmore, 2014; West, 1996). There was also a sense that the use of CSMs was particularly powerful for young people who have special/additional educational needs, as it appeared to lessen both the directness and intensity (Tait & Wosu, 2013).

Finally, it was essential to explore how the processes of CSMs are helpful in SBC. The use of CSMs was deemed fundamental when fully meeting the therapeutic needs of a variety of young people (Cooper, 2013). A non-directive offering was also illustrated as an important component that seemed to promote empowerment, choice, and control (Hickmore, 2000). The use of CSMs was also found to enhance the therapeutic relationship through two main processes: the first is the facilitation of emotional expression, with the second key element involving a deeper sense of understanding through its visual and symbolic nature (Angus & Greenberg, 2011; Meekums, 2014; West, 1996). When reflecting on the implications for counselling practice and when pondering the question of how it has added to the pre-existing literature, there is a suggestion that it raises the importance of individuality and the need to shape the therapeutic intervention around the young person. It also corroborates previous research, when highlighting the significance of adopting a predominately young-person-centred approach in schools. There is also a notion that the helpfulness of CSMs could be offered and applied more frequently in SBC, potentially increasing interest and effective outcomes.

It is hoped that the current study ignites and paves the way for future research in many areas in SBC, as it is still a developing field and one that needs to increase its literature base. The key areas that are identified could involve future work around the use of CSMs with young people who have special/additional needs and its applied therapeutic efficacy. This was a particularly sparse area for research and needs further attention, again to meet the needs of more young people. Finally, future research must include the young people themselves and their views around the helpfulness and effectiveness of CSMs.

References

Angus, E. L., & Greenberg, L. S. (2011). *Working in Narrative in Emotion Focused Therapy*. Washington, DC: American Psychological Association.

Armstrong, V. (2013). Modelling attuned relationships in art psychotherapy with children who have had poor early experiences. *The Arts in Psychotherapy*, 40: 275–284.

Bomber, L. M., & Hughes, D. A. (2013). *Settling Troubled Pupils to Learn: Why Relationships Matter in School*. London: Worth.

Bratton, S. C., Ray, D., & Rhine, T. (2005). The efficacy of play therapy with children: a meta-analytic review of treatment outcomes. *Professional Psychology*, 36(4): 376–390.

Bryant-Jeffries, R. (2004). *Counselling Young People: Person-centred Dialogues*. Oxford: Radcliffe Medical Press.

Buckley, H., Carr, N., & Whelan, S. (2010). Like walking on eggshells: service users' views and expectations of the child protection system. *Child and Family Social Work*, 16: 101–110.

Byron, J. (2009). The fear of young people damages us all. *Daily Telegraph*, 23 September. Accessed at: www.telegraph.co.uk.

Calvert, M., Zeldin, S., & Weisenbach, A. (2002). *Youth Involvement for Community, Organizational and Youth Development: Directions for Research, Evaluation and Practice*. Madison, WI: University of Wisconsin.

Cooper, M. (2009). Counselling in UK secondary schools: a comprehensive review of audit and evaluation data. *Counselling and Psychotherapy Research*, 9(3): 137–150

Cooper, M. (2013). *School-Based Counselling in UK Secondary Schools: A Review and Critical Evaluation*. Glasgow: University of Strathclyde.

Cossar, J., Brandon, M., & Jordan, P. (2011). *'Don't Make Assumptions': Children's and Young People's Views of the Child Protection System and Messages for Change*. London: Office of the Children's Commissioner and University of East Anglia.

Department for Education and Skills (DfES) (2003). *Every Child Matters: Change for Children* (Green Paper). London: The Stationery Office.

Flick, U. (2009). *An Introduction to Qualitative Research*. London: Sage.

Fox, C. L., & Butler, I. (2009). Evaluating the effectiveness of an SBC service in the UK. *British Journal for Guidance and Counselling*, 37(2): 95–106.

Geldard, K., & Geldard, D. (2010). *Counselling Adolescents: The Proactive Approach for Young People*. London: Sage.

Greene, S., & Hogan, D. (Eds.) (2005). *Researching Children's Experience: Approaches and Methods*. London: Sage.

Griffiths, G. (2013). *Helpful and Unhelpful Factors in School-Based Counselling: Clients' Perspectives*. Lutterworth: BACP.

Hamilton-Roberts, A. (2012). Teacher and counsellor perceptions of a SBC service in South Wales. *British Journal of Guidance & Counselling*, 40(5): 465–483.

Hickmore, H. (2000). Using art and play in assessment and intervention for troubled children. In: N. Barwick (Ed.), *Clinical Counselling in Schools* (pp. 108–123). London: Routledge.

Jobe, A., & Gorin, S. (2013). If kids don't feel safe they don't do anything: young people's views on seeking and receiving help from Children's

Social Care Services in England. *Child Family Social Work, 18*(4): 429–438.
Keys, S., & Walshaw, T. (2008). *Person-Centred Work with Young People: UK Practitioner's Perspective*. Ross-on-Wye: PCCS Books.
Luxmore, N. (2014). *School Counsellors Working with Young People and Staff*. London: Jessica Kingsley.
Manion, K., & Nixon, P. (2012). Listening to experts: children and young people's participation. *Social Work Now: The Practice Journal of Child, Work & Family, 49*: 4930–4939.
McArthur, K., Cooper, M., & Berdondini, L. (2012). School-based humanistic counselling for psychological distress in young people: pilot randomized controlled trial. *Psychotherapy Research, 23*(3): 355–365
McLaughlin, C., Holliday, C., & Clarke, B. (2013). *Research on Counselling and Psychotherapy with Children and Young People: A Systematic Scoping Review of the Evidence of its Effectiveness: 2003–2011*. Lutterworth: BACP.
McLeod, J. (2011). *Qualitative Research in Counselling and Psychotherapy* (2nd edn). London: Sage.
Meekums, B. (1999). A creative model of recovery for child sexual abuse trauma. *The Arts in Psychotherapy, 26*(4): 247–259.
Meekums, B. (2008). Developing emotional literacy through individual dance movement therapy: a pilot study. *Emotional and Behavioural Difficulties, 13*(2): 95–110.
Meekums, B. (2014). *Introducing Creative and Symbolic Methods*. Counselling Mind-ED. www.minded.org.uk.
Prever, M. (2010). *Counselling and Supporting Children and Young People: A Person-Centred Approach*. London: Sage
Rock, L., Karabanow, K., & Manion, K. (2012). Childhood and youth in international context: life course perspectives. In: K. Lyons, T. Hokenstad, M. Pawar, N. Huegler, & N. Hall (Eds.), *Handbook of International Social Work* (pp. 343–357). London: Sage.
Rogers, C. (1959). A theory of therapy, personality and interpersonal relationships as developed in the client-centred framework. In: S. Koch (Ed.), *Psychology: A Study of a Science. Vol. 3: Formulations of the Person and the Social Context* (pp. 185–252). New York: McGraw Hill.
Rogers, C. R. (1957). The necessary and sufficient conditions of therapeutic personality change. *Journal of Consulting Psychology, 21*: 95–103.
Rogers, C. R. (1961). *On Becoming a Person*. Boston, MA: Houghton Mifflin.
Rogers, C. R. (1986). Reflection of feelings. *Person-Centered Review, 1*: 375–377.
Rogers, C. R., & Dymond, R. F. (1954). *Psychotherapy and Personality Change*. Chicago, IL: University of Chicago Press.

Rogers, N. (1993). *The Creative Connection: Expressive Arts as Healing*. Palo Alto, CA: Science and Behavior Books.

Ruszczynski, S. (2007). The problem of psychic realities: aggression and violence as perverse solutions. In: D. Morgan & S. Ruszczynski (Eds.), *Lectures on Violence, Perversity and Delinquency* (pp. 23–42). London: Karnac.

Silverman, D. (2013). *Doing Qualitative Research*. London: Sage.

Smith, J. A., Flowers, P., & Larkin, M. (2009). *Interpretative Phenomenological Analysis: Theory, Method and Research*. London: Sage.

Smyth, D. (2013). *Person-Centred Therapy with Children and Young People*. London: Sage.

Tait, A., & Wosu, H. (2013). *Direct Work with Vulnerable Children*. London: Jessica Kingsley.

Welsh Government Social Research (2011). *Evaluation of the Welsh School-Based Counselling Strategy: Final Report*. Cardiff: Crown Copyright.

West, J. (1996). *Child-Centred Play Therapy*. London: Hodder Arnold.

YoungMinds (2014). The problems in society. Mind. Accessed at: www.youngminds.org.uk.

INDEX

Abaied, J. L., 94
abandonment, 98, 107, 114–115
  expectations of, 102
  experience of, 114
  maternal, 107, 114
  parental, 97
  sense of, 107
  shock of, 114
  survival of, 114
  theme of, 113
  threat of, 98
acceptance, 13, 17–18, 73, 78, 95, 98, 101–102, 107–109, 115–116, 118–119, 148, 166, 208
  calm, 87
  maternal, 95
  other-, 102
  parental, 96–98, 107–108, 113, 115–116, 120
  partner's, 24
  paternal, 94–95
  perceived, 100, 102, 121
  self-, 93, 98–99, 102, 106, 112–113, 118–120
  universal, 27
  warm, 93
Achoui, M., 94–95, 114–115
Adams, E., 2–4, 22, 25–26, 97, 99, 104, 116
Adler, A., 63, 82
Ainsworth, M. D. S., 94, 97, 115–116
Alexander, B. B., 38
Alexy, W., 8, 22–23
Allan, J., 131, 136, 146
Altman, A. N., 158, 160, 176
Alvarez, H. K., 129
American Cancer Society, 9
anger, 23, 44, 47, 53, 82, 96, 141–142, 144, 146, 149
Angus, E. L., 194, 219, 221
Anllo, L. M., 28
Anton, L. H., 37–39, 50
anxiety, x, 4, 8, 22, 36, 48, 95–96, 98, 100, 133, 144, 147, 164, 175, 179–180, 215
Archer, G., 66
Archibald, S., 7, 22

Armes, J., 2–4, 22, 25–26, 97, 99, 104, 116
Armstrong, V., 188, 193, 216
Arnett, J. J., 99, 116
Arntz, A., 36, 50
Arolt, V., 36
assumptions, 35, 49–51, 67, 80
　core, 50
　cultural, 64
　existential, 78
　external, 61–62
　implicit, 51
　negative, 65
　unfair, 77
Atkins, S., 163, 166, 177, 181, 183
attachment, 42, 110, 118
　adult, 100
　behaviour, 99
　bonds, 115
　emotional, 42
　figure, 98–99, 110, 114, 117
　insecure, 78
　intensity of, 49
　poor, 99
　primary, 95, 98, 114
　problematic, 101
　safe, 103
　secure, 78
　style, 100
　warm, 98
Attig, T., 52
autonomy, 103, 150
　inner, 94, 98, 113, 120
　organism, 118
Avis, N. E., 3, 7

Back, K. W., 94
Bacon, J., 37
Badenhorst, W., 36
Baez, E., 36
Bagchi, D., 50
Baker, L., 49
Bakker, A. B., 129
Ball, S., 136
Banks, P. J., 3, 6

Bansen, S. S., 49–50
Barnes, J., 85
Bartholomew, K., 100–101
Barton, M., 165, 179, 183
Baumrind, D., 94
Beaujouan, E., 48
behaviour(al), xii, 98, 114, 116–117, 131, 164, 166, 176 *see also*: attachment
　dependent-type, 96–97, 100
　desirable, 96
　enforced, 96
　harmful, 96
　maternal, 95, 115
　outcomes, 95, 114
　parenting, 121
　paternal, 95
　reaction, 98
　responses, 166
　self-nurturing, 97
　symbolic, 96, 116
　threatening, 101
　unsociable, 64
Bennet, N. E., 181
Benzies, K., 33, 35–36
Berdondini, L., 193, 217
Bernard, J. M., 163, 178
Bertero, C. M., 7, 9, 25
Bhattacharya, S., 35
Bhrolchain, M., 48
Bilardo, C. M., 36
Bingham, R. P., 183
Bischoff, R. J., 165, 179, 183
Black, R., 33, 37–39
Blake, E., 165, 179
blame, 78, 96, 136, 181
　culture, 139, 141, 147–148
　self-, 95, 97, 114
Blehar, M. G., 97, 115–116
Blinkhorn, A., 65
Bloom, J. R., 3, 6
Boelen, P., 104
Bohart, A. C., 101, 119, 121
Bolton, S. C., 133
Bomber, L. M., 191, 212

Bond, T., 105–106
Booth-LaForce, C., 99, 117–118
Borbasi, S., 3–4
Borges, V. F., 6
Bornstein, R. F., 97
Bost, K. K., 95
Botella, L., 2, 9, 26
Bower, J. E., 4, 23
Bowlby, J., 94, 98, 100, 115, 117
Boyd, C., 133
Brackett, M. A., 131, 134, 137, 144–145, 148
Bradshaw, C. P., 147
Brandon, M., 196, 214
Brandt, M., 9
Bratton, S. C., 192
Braun, A., 136
Breast Cancer Care (BCC), 2–3, 7–8, 10, 26–27
Bretherton, I., 94
Brier, N., 33, 36
Briere, J., 103
British Association of Counselling and Psychotherapy (BACP), 105, 158, 162, 197
Brody, G. H., 66
Brown, E. L., 134–135
Brown, G. L., 95
Broyard, A., 10, 21
Bryan, N. A., 165, 179
Bryant-Jeffries, R., 191–192, 209, 211–212
Brymer, M., 160–161, 163, 178
Buber, M., 99, 117–118
Buckley, H., 196
Bulow, C., 36–37
Burgess, K. B., 99, 117–118
Burke, R. J., 132, 135, 145, 149
Burwell, S. R., 3
Bush, F., 37
Butler, I., 188
Butow, P., 3, 7–8
Byers, E., 7, 22
Byron, J., 195

Callahan, S., 51
Calvert, M., 196, 213
cancer, 2–3, 5, 8–9, 12, 15, 20, 24
   see also: American Cancer Society
   breast, xiii, 1–11, 14, 17–21, 23, 26–28
      see also: Breast Cancer Care (BCC)
   post-, 9, 23
   terminal, 10
Cancer Research UK, 3
Cardoso, F., 3, 7
Carkhuff, R. R., 160
Carlyle, D., 135, 145–146
Carr, N., 196
Carroll, J. J., 160
Carroll, M., 161–162, 177, 182
Carroll-Lind, J., 97
Cartwright, S., 132
Case, L. D., 3
case studies
   Abi, 169–171, 173–175, 177–181
   Adam, 68, 71–87
   Alison, 138–139, 141–143, 146, 150
   Apple Green, 197, 201–206, 208–209, 211–214, 216, 219
   Becky, 138–139, 141–143, 149–150
   Ceri, 10, 13–16, 18–27
   Chloe, 138–140, 143, 145, 147–148, 150
   Christine, 69–70, 72, 74, 76–79, 81–82, 84, 87–88
   Colette, 40, 42, 44–48, 51–53
   Di, 138–141, 143, 145, 147, 150
   Ellie, 138, 140–143, 146–147, 149–150
   Gill, 169–171, 173–176, 178–181
   Jessica, 10–13, 15–17, 19–21, 23–25
   Lavender Purple, 197, 200–210, 212–213, 217–218
   Liz, 169–176, 178–180
   Lizzie, 10–25
   Maria, 40, 42–45, 48, 51, 53

Mel, 169–179, 181
Mia, 107–113, 115–120
Rachel, 69–70, 73–74, 77–81, 83–84, 86–87
Richard, 107–112, 114–120
Ruby Red, 197, 200–213, 215–219
Sadie, 10, 12–21, 23–26
Sally, 107–112, 115–120
Sarah, 40, 43–47, 52–53
Sky Blue, 197, 200–202, 204–208, 210–211, 213–216
Sue, 107–112, 114–120
Sunflower Yellow, 197, 200–202, 204–208, 210–215, 217–219
Susanne, 71, 73–79, 81, 83–87
Sylvia, 40, 42, 45–48, 50–53
Tessa, 40, 42, 44–48, 51–53
Zaina, 40, 42–46, 51
Caskie, G. I. L., 163, 178
Casullo, M. M., 94–95, 114–115
Cebeci, F., 7
Chabrol, H., 51
Chaille, C., 98, 120
Chamodraka, M., 165, 179
Chan, D. W., 129, 136, 149–150
Chang, S., 3, 6
chaos, 9, 26, 68, 76
Chapman, J. W., 97
chemotherapy, 7, 11–12, 20, 25
Chen, X., 94
childbirth, xiii, 34–36, 54
childlessness, xiv, 33–34, 36–38, 43, 48–51, 53, 55
 involuntary, xiii, 33–35, 37–39, 49–51, 54–55
Cinamon, R. G., 165, 179
Clarke, B., 193, 217
Claudy, J. G., 64
Coate, M. A., 161–162, 177–178
Coles, P., 66
Colley, H., 137
Collinson, V., 136
Come, S. E., 6
Condon, C., 7, 20

connection, xii, 6, 38, 45, 51, 61, 68, 78, 80, 84, 113, 118, 173, 199, 201, 208, 218
congruent, 116
creative, 195
deep, 209, 219
dis-, 12, 14, 21
emotional, 81, 131, 149
lack of, 71
ongoing, 201, 209
significant, 214
therapeutic, 200, 208, 217
Connor, K. E., 132
conscious(ness), 12, 34, 46, 48, 54, 80, 82, 85, 87, 106, 114, 213
 see also: unconscious
choices, 35, 48, 54
level, 149
management, 134
self-, 22, 179
Cook, J., 133
Cooke, A., 35–36, 48
Cooper, C. L., 131–132, 135, 137, 150
Cooper, K., 3, 6, 21–22, 24
Cooper, M., 103, 187–193, 209, 211–212, 214–217, 220
Cooper, S. L., 37, 39, 50
Cooper-Hilbert, B., 37–38, 50
Corbet-Owen, C., 50–51
Cormier, L. S., 160
Corney, R., 3, 8, 23–26
Cossar, J., 196, 214
Cournoyer, D. E., 96, 104
Coyne, B., 3–4
Crawford, S., 3, 7
creative and symbolic methods (CSM), xiv, 187–189, 192–194, 199, 203, 205, 207, 214–221
Crisp, R., 101, 116–117
Croyle, M. H., 133

Daniluk, J. C., 33, 35, 37, 39, 49–50
Day, J., 39, 44
de Keijser, J., 104

De Stefano, J., 163, 165–166, 177, 179, 181, 183
death, 72–73, 75, 78, 84, 103, 174
  row, 11, 20
Delaloge, S., 3, 7
Delworth, U., 159, 177
Demerouti, E., 129
Demetriou, H., 129
Demir, M., 98–99, 102, 115, 117
Department for Children, Education, Lifelong Learning and Skills, 151
Department for Education, 134
Department for Education and Skills (DfES), 136, 195, 213
depression, 36–37, 66, 109–110, 112, 116, 119, 144
  symptoms, 4, 37
Desmond, K. A., 3
development(al), xi, 69, 83, 94, 98, 102, 106, 113, 120, 159–161, 164–165, 167–168, 178, 181, 220
  active, 145
  adolescent, 210
  child, 63, 94, 114
  emotional, 94–96, 131, 193
  evolution, 102
  of deeper empathy, 52
  of intimacy, 117
  of mental illness, 195
  of positive feelings, 117
  of research, 196
  of self-awareness, 211
  of strategies, 46
  overall, 157
  pathways, 177
  personal, xiv, 79–80, 93–94, 101, 103–104, 106, 188, 196
  positive, 195
  process, 163, 168
  professional, xiv, 158–159, 165, 176, 181–183, 188
  readiness, 94
  social, 63
  stage, 98–100, 130, 134, 159, 161
  theory, 159
  therapeutic, 187–188, 193, 203, 207, 209, 212, 214, 217
  therapist, 157
Dewell, J. A., 97, 99, 104, 116
Diamond, M. O., 34
Dick, E., 36
Diefendorff, J. M., 133
D'iuso, N., 165, 179
Doka, K., 34
Donald, I., 132
Donati, M., 101
D'Onofrio, C., 3, 6
Douglas, B., 68
Downey, G., 98
Dozier, M., 99, 117
Drapeau, M., 165, 179
Dryden, W., 160–161, 163, 178, 183
Duffield, J., 131, 136, 146
Dunkley, C., 162, 177
Dunn, J., 4, 7–8, 65–66, 94
Duryee, J., 160–161, 163, 178
Dwairy, M., 94–95, 114–115
Dwyer, K. M., 99, 117–118
Dymond, R. F., 194–195, 211

Earnshaw, J., 131, 136, 146, 149
Egner, T., 98
Eisner, E., 131
Elliott, R., 163–165, 179
Emerson, D., 66
Emilee, G., 5–7, 22
emotion(al), xiii, 19, 46–47, 72, 76, 119, 129–134, 138, 140, 143–145, 149, 193–195, 198, 218 *see also*: attachment, development
  activity, 130, 144
  aspects, 134, 147
  associated, 38
  attunement, 71
  authentic, 138–139, 142
  awareness, 194
  bonds, 131
  burn-out, 137

commitment, 135
complex, 45
connections, 81, 131, 149
demanding, 129, 134, 138
demands, 129–130, 132–133, 151
dependency, 120
difficulty, xv, 18, 82, 144, 212
display, 133–134
distress, 109
disturbance, 95–96, 114–115
effects, 101
exhaustion, 129, 137
exploration of, 189, 211
expression, 96, 193–194, 208, 217, 220–221
extremes, 42
health, 94
hugely, 1
impact, 23, 34, 50, 106
inauthentic, 142, 149
incongruence of, 103
independence, 97–98, 120
inner, 191
intense, 48–49
labour, xiv, 129–130, 132–137, 144–149
level, 84, 139
life, 67
managing, 134
maturity, 63, 85
negative, 131, 135, 144, 149
overload, 180
over-reliance, 98
pain, 103, 111, 119
positive, 135
profound, 144
reach, 71
reactivity, 166
reality, 137
regulation, 134, 144, 211
relationships, 69
response, 82, 84, 94
rewarding, 131
rollercoaster of, 25
satisfaction, 95

security, 103
shift, 101
stability, 98
support, 66, 130
suppression of, 142
survival, 51
true, 133, 138
turmoil, 52, 54–55, 107
un-, 11, 139, 145
welfare, 190
wellbeing, xiv, 189, 214
work, 136–137, 144
Engelhard, I. M., 36, 50
Erickson, R. J., 133
Erikson, E., 71, 98–100, 103, 130

Falbo, T., 62–64
Fallbjork, U., 3, 6
Feldman, D. C., 132, 134, 148
Fernald, P. S., 96–97, 102, 114, 116, 119–120
fertility, xiii, 8, 11, 18–20, 25, 34–35, 39–40
    challenges, 49
    concerns, 8
    decline, 35
    end of, 49
    in-, 5, 8, 19, 33, 37–39, 52, 54
    issues, 3–4
    loss of, 7–8, 19, 24–25
    preserving, 26
    related-distress, 37, 55
    treatment, 8, 25, 35, 42, 47, 53
Fey, W. F., 102, 118–119
Fielding, M., 132, 134, 146, 150
Fife, B. L., 8, 22–23
Figueras, S., 2, 9, 26
Filus, A., 94–95, 114–115
Fisher, J. R. W., 5, 25–26
Fiske, S., 63
Fitch, M. I., 1, 3, 7–8, 23
Fitzpatrick, M., 165, 179
Flick, U., 196
Flowers, P., xi, 61, 104, 106, 198
Fobair, P. M., 3, 6

INDEX 231

Folkes-Skinner, J., 163–165, 179
Forrester, G., 135, 149
Fourquet, A., 3, 7
Fox, C. L., 188
Fox, P., 51
Franche, R.-L., 36–37
Frank, A. W., 132, 134, 146, 150
Frankl, V., 86
Fraser-Lee, N., 33, 35–36
Fried, R., 135, 149
Friedman, T., 37, 50
Fromm, E., 85
Furr, S. R., 160

Gallagher, T., 162, 164, 177
Gallop, R., 97, 116
Ganz, P. A., 3–4, 7, 23
Garcia, F., 95
Gath, D., 36–37
Gazzola, N., 159, 179
Geddes, D., 137
Gelber, S., 6
Geldard, D., 193, 211, 220
Geldard, K., 193, 211, 220
Geller, P. A., 36
Gentilini, O., 3, 7
Geving, A. M., 131
Gillan, A., 66
Gillon, E., 102–103
Girgis, A., 3, 7–8
Glazer, E. S., 37, 39, 50
Gluhoski, V. L., 2, 8, 22–24
Gold, K., 160–161, 163, 178
Goldberg, L., 137
Goldstein, H., 136
Gonzalez, L., 38–39
Goodman, M., 38
Goodyear, R. K., 163, 178
Gorey, E., 2, 8, 22–24
Gorin, S., 196, 213, 220
Gorman, E., 1
Gosserand, R. H., 133
Gould, J., 1, 3, 7–8, 23
Gracia, E., 95
Grafanaki, S., 159

Grandey, A. A., 137
Grassau, P., 1, 3, 7–8, 23
Gray, R. E., 1, 3, 7–8, 23
Grayling, A. C., 66
Grayson, J. L., 129
Graziottin, A., 3, 7
Greenberg, L. S., 194, 219, 221
Greenberg, M. T., 134
Greenberg, R. P., 97
Greene, S., 195, 212
Greenglass, E., 132, 135, 145, 149
Gregory, J., 97
Greil, A. L., 49
grief, 25, 34, 36–38, 41, 43–55, 99, 104,
  116, 120
Griffiths, G., 188–190, 210, 214, 216,
  220
Gross, J. J., 134

Hakanen, J. J., 129
Hall, G. S., 131
Hamilton, G. N., 96, 114–115
Hamilton-Roberts, A., 187, 189, 211
Han, G., 99
Harbeck, N., 3, 7
Hargreaves, A., 129–131, 135, 145,
  149
Harris, D. L., 38
Hawley, R., 165, 183
Haworth, R., 162, 164, 177
Heath, D. H., 136
Heath, N., 163, 166, 177, 181, 183
Hebson, G., 131, 136, 146, 149
Hefferon, K., 21
Herrero, O., 2, 9, 26
Herrick, J., 161–163, 177–178
Herschfeldt, P. A., 147
Hewlett, S. A., 36
Hickmore, H., 192, 194, 217, 219,
  221
Hill, C. E., 159, 164, 176–177, 179,
  183
Hirsch, J., 98
Hochschild, A. R., 132–133, 135, 137,
  144–145, 148–150

Hogan, D., 195, 212
Hogstrom, L., 33, 53
Holliday, C., 193, 217
Holman, A. R., 97, 99, 104, 116
Holmberg, S. K., 8, 22–23
Hoogstad, J., 98, 116
Horowitz, L. M., 100–101
Horton, I., 160–161, 163, 178, 183
Houghton, D., 34, 37–38, 50, 52
Houghton, P., 34, 37–38, 50, 52
Houston, G., 102–103
Hout, M. A., 36, 50
Howard, E. E., 158, 160, 176
Howard-Anderson, J., 4, 23
Howe, M. G., 64
Hubbard, G., 2–4, 22, 25–26, 97, 99, 104, 116
Hudson, C., 137
Hughes, D. A., 191, 212
Hughes, P., 36
Hui, E. K. P., 129
Hunfeld, J. A. M., 36
Husserl, E., 84
Hutti, M. H., 49
Hyde, J. S., 65

identity, xiv, 1, 5, 12–13, 20–22, 38–39, 49, 62, 70, 76, 87, 100, 158, 164–165, 197
  change, 11, 28
  clinical, 160
  confusion, 100
  feminine, 21, 51
  loss of, 10, 12, 46
  non-, 51
  personal, 145
  professional, 133, 159, 161, 165
  sense of, 20, 24, 145
  shock, 39
Iles, S., 36
Inman, A. G., 158, 160, 176
International Society for Interpersonal Acceptance and Rejection (ISIPAR), 95, 104

interpersonal perceived acceptance–rejection theory (IPARTheory), 100, 104
interpretative phenomenological analysis (IPA), xi–xii, 104
intervention, 93, 100, 151, 177, 188, 198, 206
  creative, 188, 192–193, 198–199, 206–208, 217
  effective, 210
  medical, 37, 52
  non-prescriptive, 188
  short-term, 169
  therapeutic, 117, 189–191, 193–194, 205, 221
  useful, 121
intimacy, 2, 23, 100, 103, 117, 120
  craving for, 100
  desire for, 102
  initial mutual, 94
  need for, 100
  shared, 118
Ireland, M. S., 51
Irving, J. A., 94
Isenbarger, L., 135–137, 149
Izzard, S., 162–164, 176

Jacobs, B. J., 100, 116
Jacobs, M., 130
Jaffe, J., 34
Janoff-Bulman, R., 50
Jeffrey, B., 131, 136, 145–148
Jeffreys, J. S., 103
Jeffries, J., 35
Jennings, P. A., 134
Jezzi, M. M., 165, 179
Ji, G., 64
Jiao, J., 64
Jing, Q., 64
Jobe, A., 196, 213, 220
Johns, H., 101–103, 119–120
Johnson, J., 37
Johnson, S., 132
Jordan, P., 196, 214
Joseph, S., 101
Josselson, R., 102, 120

Kaelin, C., 3
Kahr, B., 160, 178
Kanas, N., 181
Karabanow, K., 195, 213
Karlsson, S., 3, 6
Keefe-Cooperman, K., 36
Keith-Speigel, P., 183
Kennell, J. H., 36
Kereakoglow, S., 6
Kerns, D., 36
Kersting, D. M., 36–37
Keys, S., 191, 210
Khaleque, A., 96–97, 100, 104, 114
Killeavy, M., 136
Kim, A. H., 99, 117–118
Kinman, G., 129, 132, 135
Kirkman, M., 5, 25–26
Kissane, D., 3, 6, 21–22, 24
Kitzinger, S., 25
Klaeson, K., 7, 25
Klassen, R. M., 129, 135, 146
Klaus, M. H., 36
Klier, C. M., 36
Kline, J., 37
Knox, S., 159, 164, 177, 179
Kobak, R., 99, 117
Koert, E., 35
Konarski, R., 132, 145, 149
Koocher, G. P., 183
Korenromp, M. J., 36
Korth, B., 95
Kotti-Kitromilidou, A., 3, 7
Kowal, S., 107
Kreulich, C., 36
Kross, E., 98
Kruml, S. M., 137
Kyriacou, C., 129, 131–132, 135–136, 144, 146, 149

Ladany, N., 157, 163, 178
Lafarge, C., 51
Lalos, A., 33, 53
Larder, M., 7, 22
Larkin, M., xi, 61, 104, 106, 198
Larson, L., 165

Lavender, T., 35–36, 48
Lawrence, D., 151
Leavey, G., 136
Leckie, G., 136
Leff, P. T., 36
Lemieux, S., 7, 22
Lent, R. W., 165, 179, 183
Letherby, G., 39, 53–54
Li, D., 94
Lila, M., 95
Lim, R., 165, 179
Liu, M., 94
Lobil, S., 3, 7
Loewenthal, K., 136
Lok, I. H., 36, 50
Luborsky, M., 38
Luxmore, N., 192, 211–212, 215, 220

MacDonald, J. A. P., 98
MacNeill, L., 35, 48
Madgett, M. E., 64
Maguire, M., 136
Maheshwari, A., 35
Maker, C., 37, 49
Mancillas, A., 65
Manion, K., 195–196, 213, 220
Mann, G. B., 5, 25–26
Mann, J. R., 37
Manthorne, J., 1, 3, 7–8, 23
Manuel, J., 3, 7
Marchington, L., 131, 136, 146, 149
Marotti, L., 3, 7
Martin, H. M., 165, 179
Martincich, L., 3, 7
mastectomy, 6–7, 12–13, 18–20, 22
Matthews, A. M., 39
Matthews, R., 39
Maxwell, G., 97
Mazer, J. P., 129
McAdams, C. R., 97, 99, 104, 116
McArthur, K., 193, 217
McBride, B. A., 95
McCann, L., 2–4, 22, 25–26, 97, 99, 104, 116

McCreight, B. S., 36
McKeown, R. E., 37
McKibben, B., 65
McLanahan, S., 95
McLaren, P. L., 130
McLaughlin, C., 193, 217
McLeod, J., 61, 67, 83, 87–88, 105, 197
McQuillan, J., 49
Mearns, D., 67, 83, 101–103, 119, 160–161, 163, 178, 183
Meeks, S., 135
Meekums, B., 192–194, 210, 216, 218, 221
Mehr, K. E., 163, 178
Meleis, A. I., 36
Melges, F. T., 98
Menning, B. E., 37–38
menopause, 5–7, 40
Merazzi, C., 135
Merton, R. K., 98
metaphor, 47, 52, 118, 120, 192–193, 212
Meyerowitz, B. E., 3, 7
Miller, A., 94, 96–97, 114–115, 118–119, 121
Millet, C., 132
Mills, T. A., 35–36, 48
Min, R. M., 160–161, 164, 166, 177, 181
Mitchell, J., 67
Mitchell, K., 51
Mojsa-Kaja, J., 131, 134, 137, 144–145, 148
Moller, A., 33, 53
Monach, J. H., 34, 37–38
Monti, J. D., 94
Morris, B., 131, 136, 146
Morris, J. A., 132, 134, 148
Morrissette, P. J., 160
mother, 38, 41, 46, 51, 62, 69, 71–73, 76, 94–95, 107, 109, 113–116, 118
  see also: world
  biological, 33–34, 51, 53–54
  –father bond, 95
  -figure, 111, 118
  foster, 204
  grand-, 48
  -hood, 34, 51
  inadequate, 95
  missing, 69, 73
  nurturing, 95, 98
Moulder, C., 36
Mulder, E. J. H., 36
Munn, P., 94
Murphy, D., 96, 104, 116
Murray, J., 65

Nackerud, L., 49
Natamba, E., 35
Natiello, P., 132, 150
National Fatherhood Initiative, 95
National Health Service (NHS), 167
National Union of Teachers (NUT), 129
Naylor, C., 136
Neil, S., 5, 25–26
Neimeyer, R., 2, 9, 26
Nelson Noble, R., 163, 166, 177, 181, 183
Neugebauer, R., 36–37, 50
Newburn-Cook, C., 33, 35–36
Nias, J., 129–130, 148
Nickels, J. B., 98
Nixon, P., 195–196, 213, 220
Noddings, N., 136
Norman, P., 35

objective, 63, 142, 174, 188, 219
  descriptions, 97
  key, 34
  principle, 190, 219
  statement, xi
Ochsner, K., 98
O'Connell, D. C., 107
O'Connor, P., 37
Offermans, J. P. M., 36
Office of National Statistics (ONS), 33, 35

Ofsted, 134, 136, 141, 147–148
Ogden, J., 37, 49
Ohrmann, P., 36
Olvey, C. D., 183
Orlinsky, D. E., 157, 162, 177
Osborne, C., 95
Özen, A., 98–99, 102, 115, 117

Pachecho, M., 2, 9, 26
Pagani, O., 3, 7
Page-Christiaens, G. C. M. L., 36
Palomera, R., 131, 134, 137, 144–145, 148
Panizza, P., 3, 7
Parkes, C. M., 4
Partridge, A. H., 6
Pas, E. T., 147
Peccatori, F., 3, 7
Penaut-Lorca, F., 3, 7
Pendlebury, S., 3, 7–8
Peppers, L. G., 49
perinatal
 Bereavement Grief Scale, 36
 Grief Intensity Scale, 36
 Grief Scale, 36
 loss, 37
Perryman, J., 134, 136, 147–148, 151
Perz, J., 5–7, 22
Petersen, G., 36
Pfeffer, N., 37, 49, 53
Pica, M., 160
Pitkeathley, J., 66
Pitts, J. H., 161, 178
Polit, D., 64
Porter, M., 35
Power, S., 7, 20
pregnancy, 8, 34, 36, 42, 44, 47–49, 51, 54
 ectopic, 40
 loss, xiii, 33–37, 39–41, 43, 45, 47, 49–51, 53–55
 postponing, 34–35, 39, 48
Prever, M., 191, 210–211
PricewaterhouseCoopers, 129, 136

Prouty, G., 101, 117
Puthussery, S., 3, 8, 23–26

Quinlan, M. M., 129

Rafaeli, A., 133
Ramsey, G. V., 160
Rasmussen, B. H., 3, 6
Ravelski, E., 37
Ray, D., 192
Rea, J., 136
rejection, 24, 96, 97–101, 107–108, 115–116, 119–120
 childhood, 99, 114
 cycle of, 100
 experience of, 96, 100, 113, 115, 120
 fear of, 8
 feelings of, 96
 interpersonal, 98, 109, 117
 maternal, 94, 96, 114
 pain of, 8, 97, 107, 113
 parental, xiv, 93–94, 96–97, 99, 101, 104, 106, 108, 113–115, 120
 paternal, 95, 115
 perceived, 95, 97, 101, 106, 121
 self-, 93
 sensitivity, 98, 102
 threat of, 110
 total, 116
 unexpressed, 116
resilience, 52, 78, 86, 102, 182
Reutemann, M., 36
Reyes, M. R., 131, 134, 137, 144–145, 148
Rezvannia, P., 94–95, 114–115
Rhine, T., 192
Richardson, A., 2–4, 22, 25–26, 64, 67, 97, 99, 104, 116
Richardson, B., 159, 179
Richardson, H., 132
Riggs, S. A., 99
Ritsher, J., 36
Robinson, G., 37
Robinson, M., 49

Rock, L., 195, 213
Roder, A., 3, 7
Roffman, M., 176, 183
Roger, D., 137
Rogers, C. R., 62, 79, 87, 94, 96–98, 101–103, 114–119, 132, 191, 194–195, 210–212, 220
Rogers, N., 195, 217
Rohner, E. C., 96, 98, 100, 120
Rohner, R. P., 93–100, 104, 114, 116–117, 120
Ronnestad, M. H., 157, 159–160, 162, 165, 176–183
Roos, S., 99
Rose, C., 62
Rose-Krasnor, L., 99, 117–118
Rosenberg, B., 65
Rosenberg, M., 99, 117
Rosenberg, S. M., 6
Rothi, D., 136
Rowe, D., 67, 85
Rowland, J. H., 3, 7
Rozensky, R. H., 183
Rubenstein, R. L., 38
Rubin, K. H., 99, 117–118
Ruddy, K. J., 6
Rudolph, K. D., 94
Ruszczynski, S., 192, 212

Sachs, O., 87
Salander, P., 3, 6
Salovey, P., 131, 134, 137, 144–145, 148
Sandell, A. K., 7, 25
Sartre, J.-P., 66, 86
Schapira, L., 6
Schaufeli, W. B., 129
Schlosser, L. Z., 159, 164, 177, 179
Schmitt, J. P., 95
Schover, L. R., 7, 9, 20
Schwerdtfeger, K. L., 37, 50
Scott, L. L., 8, 22–23
Scull, L., 33, 37–39
Sejourne, N., 51
Sekaquaptewa, D., 63

self, 9, 21, 41, 50, 52–53, 93, 96, 98–103, 107, 113–120, 135, 168, 171, 174, 179, 181, 212
see also: acceptance, blame, conscious, rejection
-adequacy, 96
-assured, 174
authentic, 103, 143
-awareness, 62, 88, 102, 169
see also: development
-care, 5
-centred, 66
changed, 52
-compassion, 94
-concept, 61, 69–70, 76–78, 115–116
-confidence, 15, 165, 170, 178
-control, 217
-criticism, 164, 179
-defeating, 100
-determination, 78
different, 46
-directed, 190
-disclosure, 102–103, 111, 120
-doubts, 163, 181
-drive, 78
-efficacy, 160, 163, 165–166, 176, 178–179, 181–182
-enhancement, 115
-esteem, 5, 15, 64, 71, 96, 158, 165
exploration of, 101
exposure of, 118
-expression, 195
-fulfilling, 98
-governance, 150
-growth, 93, 118–121
guarded, 110, 117
-harm, 195
-heal, 101, 119
-help, 66
-image, 20
-implemented, 93
-inadequacy, 100
incomplete, 51

-injury, 166, 181
issues of, 50
-knowledge, 62, 164
-like, 112
-loathing, 93
loss of, 45–46, 99, 116, 119, 147
-monitoring, 166
-nurture, 97–98, 116 *see also*: behaviour
organismic, 62
-pity, 86
-protect, 54, 110
psychological, 192
-questioning, 169, 171, 174, 180
real, 137
-regard, 94
-reinforced, 99, 117
-responsibility, 112, 120
-selection, 151
sense of, 10, 21, 77, 82–83, 87, 93, 96, 98, 100, 102, 171
sexual, 5
-soothe, 97, 116
-trusting, 174
-understanding, 106, 112
-valuing, 174
-worth, 21, 39, 99, 118
sexual, 8, 12, 107 *see also*: self
 activity, 4
 attractiveness, 6
 changes, 8
 desire, 25
 difficulties, 7
 experience, 18
 function, 7
 hetero-, 8
 life, 20
 partners, 16
 person, 17
 relationships, 5, 15, 18
 response, 16, 23
 satisfaction, 5
 scripts, 8
 sensation, 5
 undesirable, 8

sexuality, xiii, 1–3, 5–6, 11, 20, 22, 24–26
 impaired, 8
Shah, D., 65
shame, 18, 38–39, 62, 64, 72, 83, 95, 163
Shetty, A., 35
Shin, N., 95
Shreffler, K. M., 37, 49–50
Shrout, P., 37
Siegl, K., 2, 8, 22–24
Silverman, D., 189
Skodol, A., 37
Skovholt, T. M., 159–160, 162, 165, 176–183
Slomkowski, C., 66
Slyter, H., 36
Smith, J. A., xi, 61, 104, 106, 198
Smyth, D., 190–191, 194, 210–211, 217–218, 220
Sorensen, B., 64, 66–67, 82–83
Spinelli, E., 62
Spitz, R. A., 94
Spruill, J., 183
Sroufe, L. A., 99
Stahl, J., 176, 183
Stanton, A. L., 4, 23
Stark, D., 2–4, 22, 25–26, 97, 99, 104, 116
Steginga, S. K., 4, 7–8
Stephenson, H., 136
stereotype, xiv, 61–65, 68–70, 76–77, 82–83, 88–89, 143
Stern, N. C., 5, 25–26
Stevens, H. A., 49–50
Stewart, A. E., 67, 83
Stewart, D., 37
Stewart, S. L., 3, 6
Stigall, T. T., 183
Stirtzinger, R., 37
Stoltenberg, C. D., 159, 177
Strange, C., 129, 132, 135
Strickland, B. R., 98
Strull, W. M., 181
Sugarman, L., 87, 99–100, 117, 130

Sullivan, C., 159, 164, 177, 179
Sümer, N., 98–99, 102, 115, 117
Susser, M., 37
Sutcliffe, J., 132
Sutton, R. E., 133–134, 137
Sutton, R. I., 133
Swanson, K. M., 37, 49
Swinglehurst, J., 3, 8, 23–26
symbol(-ic), 103, 111, 160, 218
 see also: behaviour
 interactionism, xi
 methods, xiv, 187, 192, 205, 207
 nature, 207–208, 218, 221

Tait, A., 194, 216, 218, 220
Takahashi, M., 3
Tallman, K., 101, 119, 121
Tamimi, R. M., 6
Tamlyn, K., 7, 22
Taylor, P., 132
Tekeli, A., 7
Tesch-Romer, C., 2
Theriault, A., 159, 179
Thewes, B., 3, 7–8
Thober, J., 165, 183
Thomas, H. E., 95, 114
Thomas-MacLean, R., 7, 20–21
Thorne, B., 67, 83, 102, 119–120
Thrupp, M., 136
Titsworth, S., 129
Todd, T. C., 183
Tofflemore, K., 33, 35–36
Tomasik, M. J., 2
Tonelli, M., 36
Tough, S., 33, 35–36
Travers, C. J., 131–132, 135, 137, 150
Tribe, R., 161–162, 164, 176, 178
Troman, G., 134, 150
Tromans, N., 35
Tronstad, S.-E., 33, 53
Turk, D. C., 135
Turk, L. M., 135
Turner, E., 131, 136, 146
Turner, L. J., 6

unconscious(ness) 77, 87 *see also*
 conscious
 social schema, 63
Ussher, J. M., 5–7, 22

Valliant, G., 96, 113, 102
Van, P., 36, 51
van den Bout, J., 36
van den Hout, J., 104
van den Hout, M., 104
Van Dick, R., 129
Van Manen, M., 131, 145
Vargas, P., 63
Vasquez, M., 183
Vaughn, B., 95
Veneziano, R. A., 95
Vesselinov, R., 37
Visser, G. H. A., 36
Vitetta, L., 3, 6, 21–22, 24
Vohra, N., 94–95, 114–115
Von Hippel, W., 63

Wagner, B., 36–37
Wagner, U., 129
Wall, S., 97, 115–116
Wall, T., 133
Walshaw, T., 191, 210
Warner, M. S., 101, 117, 121
Warr, P., 133
Waters, E., 97, 115–116
Watson, E., 2–4, 22, 25–26, 97, 99, 104, 116
Watts, M., 101
Webb, A., 163
Weiner, G., 136
Weingarten, K., 99, 116, 119
Weisenbach, A., 196, 213
Weisz, A. E., 98
Welsh Government Social Research, 187, 193, 216
Werner-Wildner, L. A., 2, 9, 26
West, J., 193–194, 215, 218, 220–221
Wharton, A. S., 133
Wheeler, S., 163–165, 179
Whelan, S., 196